The Essential Guide to Werewolf Literature

T0318721

A RAY AND PAT BROWNE BOOK

Series Editors
Ray B. Browne and Pat Browne

The Essential Guide to Werewolf Literature

Brian J. Frost

THE UNIVERSITY OF WISCONSIN PRESS

POPULAR PRESS

The University of Wisconsin Press
1930 Monroe Street
Madison, Wisconsin 53711

www.wisc.edu/wisconsinpress/

3 Henrietta Street
London WC2E 8LU, England

1   3   5   4   2

Printed in the United States of America

Library of Congress Cataloging-in-Publication Data
Frost, Brian J.
The essential guide to werewolf literature / Brian J. Frost.
p.   cm.
"A Ray and Pat Browne book."
Includes bibliographical references and index.
ISBN 0-87972-859-0 (hardcover: alk. paper)
ISBN 0-87972-860-4 (pbk.: alk. paper)
1. Werewolves in literature.
2. Literature, Modern—History and criticism.   I. Title.
PN56.W45 F76 2003
809'.93374—dc21   2003007229

Flee and fear the wolf; for, worst of all,
the wolf may be more than he seems.

Angela Carter

Table of Contents

Preface

The present volume is the first full-scale survey of werewolf literature covering both fiction and nonfiction works, and although primarily intended as a guide for collectors and researchers it should be of interest to all devotees of the horror genre. Chapter 1 identifies the main elements in the werewolf myth and considers some of the intriguing theories that have been advanced to account for the phenomenon of shapeshifting; this is followed by a survey of nonfiction books, ranging from medieval treatises to modern studies. The following chapters trace the history and development of the werewolf tale, and include synopses or excerpts of all the major novels and short stories utilizing the man-into-beast motif—as well as many obscure ones. Also included is an extensive bibliography that lists nonfiction works, novels, short stories, poems, and anthologies.

The werewolf myth is eternal, and like all the world's great myths it draws from the deepest reserves of human psychology and culture, upon ancient fears and desires, symbols and taboos. Even today it continues to influence people's lives; for although modern science has all but eradicated our belief in supernatural monsters, it is still difficult—even for the most skeptical among us—to dismiss the werewolf as nothing more than a figment of the imagination. Psychologists may try to assure us that werewolves are merely monsters spawned in the unconscious and have no real substance, but something deep inside us cannot fully accept this proposition. We may justifiably scoff at the idea of someone being physically transformed into a wolf, but it does not alter the fact that under certain circumstances it is possible for a person to assume the personality of a wolf and imitate its behavior. Evolution may have made humans separate from the other animals on our planet, but there are, nevertheless, bestial instincts lurking beneath our civilized exteriors; and we are occasionally reminded of our brute heritage when the beast lying dormant within us unexpectedly irrupts into conscious life, bringing on bouts of lycanthropic madness. Let us also not forget that the werewolf is the personification of that potential for evil and sin that is so much a part of us all; and we disregard at our peril the seeds of destruction inside us, which are ineradicable.

In fiction, the werewolf has evolved considerably over the years and is now a much more complex creation than it was initially. Looking back to the stories from the early nineteenth century one finds that the shape-changing protagonist invariably bears a strong resemblance to his counterpart in folklore, and is usually depicted as a supernatural monster or someone in the thrall of a sorcerer's spell. It is also customary for stories from this period to have rural settings, involve witchcraft, and slavishly follow the conventions established in legends dating from the Middle Ages or earlier.

In the Victorian era the werewolf was a more ambivalent figure. Writers of horror stories either portrayed him as a divided man, prey to impulses both noble and bestial, or as an outsider who posed a threat to the natural order. It is also recognized today that many Victorian tales about terrifying monsters are charged with hidden meaning and significance and can be interpreted as sexual allegories. Because of false anxieties and awesome taboos surrounding sex, authors from this era were generally unable to deal openly with the subject—especially anything connected with the sadistic side of the sexual instinct—and were obliged to use symbolism to circumvent this constraint. Forbidden desires, therefore, were translated into terms of violence and bloodshed, which led to the werewolf's brutal methods of predation being equated with an aggressive, self-indulgent form of sexual gratification.

Now that these outmoded social and religious taboos no longer have any relevance, the focus of horror in the werewolf story has shifted from the nature of the threat to its physical effects. As a result, contemporary stories tend to be visceral in the extreme, with graphic descriptions of disembowelments almost obligatory. The protagonists are rarely supernatural monsters but are more likely to be homicidal maniacs or sexually deviated psychopaths who perpetrate their bestial acts without the necessity of assuming lupine form. Other significant changes to the werewolf's image have resulted from efforts to make the werewolf a credible phenomenon in the modern world. Some writers have reinterpreted the myth by combining the residual fears that have always haunted the human imagination with the contemporary demons of our cultural neuroses; others have achieved an effect of verisimilitude by concocting pseudoscientific explanations for the existence of these anomalies. A recent development has been the vogue for novels in which colonies of werewolf-like creatures are discovered living among us, having remained undetected for millennia by existing on the fringes of society.

Over the past two decades the werewolf novel has enjoyed an unprecedented peak of popularity, and there is every indication that this is not just a momentary upsurge but will be sustained for some time yet. There is, after all, nothing more effective than the werewolf story for exploring the murky realm of the unconscious and revealing the awful deeds it can inspire. And human nature being what it is, there will always be people who welcome such an expression in literature of their hidden aggressiveness.

Acknowledgments

Writing this book has been a painstaking and at times frustrating labor of love, involving years of hard toil. Fortunately I was able to count on the support of two of the world's greatest authorities on weird fiction, Richard Dalby and Mike Ashley, who not only helped me track down elusive items but also alerted me to stories I might otherwise have overlooked. To them and another old friend, Eric Held, who also gave me valuable assistance, I extend my gratitude.

The Essential Guide to
Werewolf Literature

I

The Werewolf Phenomenon

The Origins of the Myth

From time immemorial the dark domain of the supernatural has been the habitat of a host of nightmarish
monsters, but none are more terrifying or enjoy as
much popular appeal as the werewolf. Traditionally depicted as the embodiment of evil, this strange phenomenon is regarded by occultists as the most terrible of all
Satan's bond-slaves, while in folklore it has ever been the
emblem of treachery, savagery, and bloodthirstiness. It
is, therefore, no exaggeration to claim that of all the
half-human monsters in myth, fiction, and reality, the
werewolf dominates, both in its dreadful lore and in the
depths of loathing its diabolical practices can inspire.

The legends surrounding the werewolf are immea-
surably old and can be traced back to the earliest

records of civilization. In the ancient world it was thought that man and wolves shared a common ancestry, hence the various wolf myths and wolf cults then in existence. In more recent times there has been speculation that werewolves are a hybrid species: a by-product, as it were, of man's transition from the animal kingdom to the higher order of humanity. Another suggestion, put forward by anthropologists, is that belief in these anomalies may have arisen from the survival beyond their time of small groups of modern man's hairy predecessors, who could have lingered on in isolated forests and other desolate places. The most credible theory yet advanced, however, is that the werewolf superstition is based on exaggerated accounts of nocturnal attacks on Stone Age settlements by bands of fur-clad warriors masquerading as wolves.

Primitive man's apparent readiness to accept shape-shifting as a natural phenomenon is explained in Frank Hamel's *Human Animals* (1915):

> The belief that men can change into animals and animals into men is as old as life itself. It originates in the theory that all things are created from one substance, mind or spirit, which according to accident or design takes a distinctive appearance, to mortal eyes, of shape, color, and solidity. Transformation from one form to another then becomes a thinkable proposition, especially if it be admitted that plastic thought in the spirit world takes on changed forms and conditions more readily than in

the world of matter. The belief of primitive races that all created beings have an immortal soul dwelling in a material body applies equally to brute creation and to the human race. "In the beginning of things," says Leland, "men were as animals and animals as men." [Leland, C. G., "Algonquin Legends of New England," 1884.] The savage endows brutes with similar intelligence and emotions to his own. He does not distinguish between the essential nature of man, of various beasts, and even of inanimate objects, except where outward form is concerned; and he senses, even more clearly than his civilized brother, the psychic bonds which unite man and the animals.

The phenomenon of shapeshifting was well documented by classical authors, and in ancient Rome the term commonly used for people who transformed themselves into wolves and other savage animals was *versipellis* (turn-skin). The word "werewolf," which literally means man-wolf, was coined much later and is Anglo-Saxon in origin. Its first recorded usage was in the Ecclesiastical Ordinances of King Canute (1016–1035), where it occurs as a synonym for the Devil. Names used in other European countries for this phenomenon include loup-garou (France), lupo-manaro (Italy), lobombre (Spain), vrykolakas (Greece), and varulf (Sweden). It should also be noted that in countries outside the Northern Hemisphere, where the wolf is not the predominant predator, the transformation is related to animals more familiar to the native population.

The peasants of India, for instance, used to live in fear of were-tigers, while their African counterparts were similarly afraid of were-leopards and were-lions.

Guises and Characteristics of the Werewolf

By definition, a werewolf is a man or woman who, either voluntarily or involuntarily, is supernaturally transformed into the shape of a wolf and endowed with all the physical characteristics of that animal—a shaggy covering of fur, glowing eyes, long canine teeth, and razor-sharp claws. Werewolves also exhibit many of the traits associated with the beasts they resemble, such as cunning craftiness, swiftness of movement, bestial ferocity, and unbridled cruelty. Moreover, they are possessed of a ravenous hunger and are seized periodically by an irresistible desire to feast on the flesh and blood of both the living and the dead.

Werewolves can vary considerably in appearance. Usually when someone is transmogrified they change entirely into a wolf, but sometimes they are a fearful mixture of beast and man, either having a man's body and a wolf's head or a wolf's body with human eyes and hands. The transformation can be temporary or permanent and traditionally occurs under the influence of the full moon. By day the werewolf hides his villainy by resuming human form, so that even members of his family are unaware of his terrible secret. If wounded while in his wolf shape, a corresponding wound is simultaneously inflicted on the human body, and an immediate restoration to human form takes place if the werewolf is killed.

Predestination to become a werewolf is thought to be indicated by certain peculiarities in a person's appearance. Such signs include bushy eyebrows that meet together above the nose; long, curved fingernails; small ears set low on the head; an exceptionally long third finger on each hand; and extreme hairiness, especially on the hands and feet.

The bite of a werewolf is the usual method of transmitting the curse to others, but there are several alternative ways a person can become one of these fearsome monsters. A voluntary metamorphosis is often achieved through a pact with the Devil; an involuntary transformation is usually brought about by demonic possession or is the result of a sorcerous spell. In some cases the curse is hereditary and affects generations of one particular family.

In any voluntary metamorphosis there must initially be the will to do evil and a desire to exert power through fear. A witch or someone who misguidedly dabbles in black magic is the sort of person most likely to wish for this ability, although it is possible that someone might want to become a werewolf from sheer loneliness and dissatisfaction with life. In the latter case a prime candidate is the shunned outcast from society who falls into such a depressed state of mind that it leads to scorn and hatred for his fellow men. If, at the same time, he develops a burning desire for revenge, then bodily transference to animal shape becomes very desirable, especially with the complete disguise and total freedom it provides.

In direct contrast, the world of the involuntary or "innocent" werewolf is one of constant dread and agony. At night he becomes a creature of blind, animal savagery, unable to stop himself from attacking even those he loves the most; but during the daytime, when he is permitted to resume human form, he is driven to utter desperation by contemplating the horror of his position, suffering the tortures of the damned as he recalls the atrocities he has committed. Weighed down by his terrible affliction, the reluctant werewolf becomes increasingly depressed and withdrawn; he longs to be slain and know the bliss of release from a predicament that has totally alienated him from all human standards of decency and morality. His one hope of salvation is that death will eventually come to him at the hands of a loved one, for then his soul may yet be saved.

A word commonly used as a synonym for werewolf is lycanthrope. There is, however, an important difference between the two words, and strictly speaking they are not interchangeable. Lycanthropy—a word derived from the Greek words for wolf *(lykos)* and man *(anthropos)*—is best used to describe an authentic form of insanity in which the afflicted person imagines himself to be transformed into a wolf, whereas a genuine werewolf can actually shift his shape.

Someone suffering from lycanthropy is easily identifiable. Mentally he is in a depressed, misanthropic state of mind, while physically he is weak and debilitated with a gaunt, emaciated body. His legs are covered in scars and ulcerated sores caused by groveling on all fours in a wolflike posture; his face is deathly pale, the eyes dry and hollow yet blazing with a demoniac fury as if mirroring the bestial thoughts within his diseased mind. Although his mouth is parched, the lycanthrope craves only warm blood to quench his thirst and exhibits an uncontrollable hunger for raw meat—often preferring it in a state of putrefaction.

Ways That Shapeshifting May Be Accomplished

Although the legends surrounding the werewolf are almost as old as man himself, much of what we regard as werewolf lore was accumulated during the Middle Ages. This infamous era of ignorance and brutality provided a fertile soil for diabolism and the cultivation of superstitions, and those concerning the werewolf were among the most fanciful. Ways of becoming a werewolf included drinking water out of a wolf's footprint, eating a wolf's brains, sleeping on the ground in an open field on a Friday night when the moon is full, drinking from a lycanthropous stream, and plucking or wearing certain flowers. Resuming human form was an equally strange procedure. Plunging into water or rolling over and over in the dew were both thought to do the trick, while a much slower method was to kneel in one spot for a hundred years. Cures for the affliction included being saluted with the sign of the cross, to be called three times by one's baptismal name, or to be struck three blows on the forehead with a knife. Wolfsbane, a plant rumored to bloom only during the full moon, was also considered to be an effective remedy for this terrible condition.

In the late Middle Ages and throughout the Renaissance, shapeshifting was associated principally with witchcraft, and the Devil was thought to be the prime instigator whenever the phenomenon occurred. Opinion was divided, however, on the way this diabolical transformation was effected. Some theologians were convinced that it was an actual, corporeal change, while others argued that it was merely fantastical. One popular theory was that the Devil wrought a subjective and objective glamour that duped the sorcerer into thinking he had been transformed into a wolf or some other animal, and similarly deluded all who gazed upon him. Another suggestion put forward by theologians was that the Devil put the sorcerer in a trance, then took the form of a wolf and carried out atrocities on behalf of his disciple, who was convinced, on waking, that he had been changed into a ferocious animal. No less far-fetched was the theory that an aerial effigy of a wolf was superimposed upon the human form.

Other alleged methods of transformation included

smearing the body with magical ointments, donning a wolf skin, or wearing a belt or girdle made from a wolf's pelt. These ritualistic methods were generally favored by witches, as the following dramatic passage from Montague Summers's *The Werewolf* (1933) confirms:

> Masqued and clad in the shape of the most dreaded and fiercest denizen of the forest the witch came forth under the cover of darkness, prowling in lonely places, to seek his prey. By the force of his diabolic pact he was enabled, owing to a ritual of horrid ointments and impious spells, to assume so cunningly the swift shaggy brute that save by his demoniac ferocity and superhuman strength none could distinguish him from the natural wolf. The werewolf loved to tear raw human flesh. He lapped the blood of his mangled victims, and with gorged reeking belly he bore the warm offal of their palpitating entrails to the sabbat to present in homage and foul sacrifice to the Monstrous Goat who sat upon the throne of worship and adoration.

The practice of witchcraft became so widespread that the Church felt compelled to use all its powers to stamp it out. The foremost treatise on the subject was Heinrich Kramer and James Sprenger's *Malleus Maleficarum* (1486–1487), which served as the witch-hunters' bible. Largely consisting of intricate arguments about the nature of matter, God, and Satan, it touched upon lycanthropy in the following passage:

> Question X deals with whether or not witches can by glamour change men into beasts, and with the question of Lycanthropy—whether ravening wolves

are true wolves, or wolves possessed by devils. They may be either. But it is argued in another way, it may be an illusion caused by witches. For William of Paris tells of a certain man who thought that he was turned into a wolf, and at certain times went hiding among the caves. For there he went at a certain time, and though he remained there all the time stationary, he believed that he was a wolf which went about devouring children; and though the Devil, having possessed a wolf, was really doing this, he erroneously thought that he was prowling about in his sleep. And he was for so long thus out of his senses that he was at last found in the wood raving. The Devil delights in such things, and caused the illusion of the pagans who believed that men and old women were changed into beasts. From this is seen that such things only happen by the permission of God alone and through the operation of devils, and not through any natural defect; since by no art or strength can such wolves be injured or captured.

In 1597, the future King James I of England published an equally famous treatise on witchcraft and demonology. Aptly titled *Daemonologie,* it included a brief section on "Men-Woolfes" in which the royal author concluded that werewolves were not supernatural creatures but self-deluded, severely depressed people who imitated wolf behavior.

The incidence of alleged werewolf activity reached a peak between 1520 and 1630, and according to historical accounts approached the proportion of an epidemic. This in turn gave rise to a corresponding outbreak of persecution mania, resulting in many hundreds of innocent suspects being burned at the stake. At the notorious witchcraft trials, one of the main accusations leveled against those witches suspected of being werewolves was that they possessed a two-sided skin—human on the outside and furry on the inside—the theory being that they turned their skin inside out to become a wolf, which often resulted in suspects being hacked to pieces by their captors in an effort to find the hairy growth.

It was also believed that spirits of the dead could appear as werewolves. Perhaps the most famous example of the ghost werewolf, as this phenomenon is called, was England's infamous King John (1167–1216), who was said to have risen from his grave in the guise of a wolf as a consequence of his excommunication by the pope. The first reasoned explanation for this phenomenon was given by the sixteenth-century alchemist Paracelsus, who claimed that a man possesses two spirits—human and animal—and that in the afterlife he appears in the shape of whichever spirit he allowed to become dominant. Therefore, if a man has given way to his baser instincts, his earthbound phantasm is likely to appear in the guise of a wolf or some other terrifying animal. A similar hypothesis was advanced by Elliott O'Donnell in *Werwolves* (1912). In the chapter "What Is a Werwolf?" he speculates that werewolves may be

> phantasms of dead human beings—vicious and carnal-minded people, idiots, and imbecile epileptics. It is an old belief that the souls of cataleptic and

epileptic people, during the body's unconsciousness, adjourned temporarily to animals, and it is therefore only in keeping with such a view to suggest that on the deaths of such people their spirits take permanently the form of animals.

My own view is that so complex a creature as man—complex both physically and psychologically—may have a representative spirit for each of his personalities. Hence on man's physical dissolution there may emanate from him a host of phantasms, each with a shape most fitting the personality it represents. And what is more thoroughly representative of cruelty, savageness, and treachery than a wolf, or even something partly lupine.

Despite their supernatural and superhuman powers, werewolves can be killed or destroyed by conventional methods. Shooting will normally suffice, but success is guaranteed only if the gun is loaded with silver bullets. Even then the werewolf's reign of terror may not be over; in some parts of Eastern Europe it is believed that a man who has been a werewolf in his life becomes a vampire after death. A fascinating examination of the close relationship between the werewolf and vampire superstitions was made by Wilhelm Hertz in *Der Werwolf* (1862), in which he claimed that the most striking admixture of the conceptions of werewolf and vampire occurs in the Dantsic legend, which took its name from a town in the German province of West Prussia. In the book it is summarized as follows:

A werewolf must be burned not buried, for he has no rest in earth and will awaken a few days after burial. In his ravenous hunger he then devours the flesh of his own hands and feet, and when he can find nothing in his own body to eat he burrows out of the grave at midnight and attacks the sheep and cattle, or even climbs into houses so as to lie on those asleep and suck the warm heart's blood out of them; after he has sated himself he returns to his grave. The bodies of murdered people are found in their beds the next day with only a small bite on the left side of the breast to show the cause of death.

According to occultists, werewolfism nearly always involves the projection of the astral body; they argue that the werewolf form that wanders abroad at night is a spectral, quasi-material simulacrum of a living person. A memorable allusion to a psychic manifestation of this type was made in Dion Fortune's *Psychic Self Defense* (1930), in which the author related how she accidentally formulated a werewolf when she had been plotting revenge against someone who had wronged her. On drifting into a state of semiconsciousness while resting one afternoon, there came to her mind the thought of going berserk: visions of ancient Nordic myths about werewolves passed before her eyes, and soon she felt a curious "drawing-out" sensation from her solar plexus. To her horror the ectoplasmic form of a huge wolf materialized beside her, tethered to her by a psychic umbilical cord. Eventually, by sheer willpower, the occultist was able to draw the life out of this terrifying manifestation and send it back from whence it came, but at the precise point of absorption she experienced a furious impulse to rend and tear anything and anybody near at hand. Fortunately this experience had no harmful repercussions; it was, nonetheless, a timely warning about the frightening forces trapped within us all.

Eliphas Lévi, the great nineteenth-century magical philosopher, explained the principle behind this particular type of manifestation in *Transcendental Magic: Its Doctrine and Ritual* (1856).

> A werewolf is nothing else but the sidereal body of a man whose savage and sanguinary instincts are typified by the wolf; who, further, whilst his phantom wanders over the country, is sleeping peacefully in his bed and dreams that he is a wolf indeed. What makes the werewolf visible is the almost somnambulistic excitement caused by the fright of those who behold it, or else the tendency, more particularly in simple country persons, to enter into direct communication with the Astral Light, which is the common medium of visions and dreams. The hurts inflicted on the werewolf do actually wound the sleeping person by an odic and sympathetic congestion of the Astral Light, and by correspondence between the immaterial and material body.

A similar view is held by Theosophists, adherents of the Wisdom-Religion founded by Madame Blavatsky (Helena Petrovna 1831–1891). They, however, go a step farther by suggesting that nonhuman agencies may sometimes be involved in the process. For instance, in one of the Theosophical Society's most popular manuals, *The Astral Plane: Its Scenery, Inhabitants, and Phenomena* (1895), C. W. Leadbeater has this to say about werewolves:

> It is always during a man's lifetime that he first manifests under this form. It invariably implies some knowledge of magical arts—sufficient at any rate to be able to project the astral body.
>
> When a perfectly cruel and brutal man does this, there are certain circumstances under which the body may be seized upon by other astral entities and materialized, not into the human form, but into that of some wild animal—usually the wolf; and in that condition it will range the surrounding countryside killing other animals, and even human beings, thus satisfying not only its own craving for blood, but that of the fiends who drive it on.

Another way that werewolves can be created is by the performance of certain black magic rituals. Occultists claim there is a latent power in man that enables him to project thought-forms, and anyone who has developed this hidden faculty could, if he so desires, seize upon the plastic elemental essence of the spirit world and mold it into a wolflike manifestation. If motivated by malice, the magician might then send forth his creation to prey upon or terrorize anyone against whom he had a grudge.

Through Kenneth Grant's fascinating books on magic, *Cults of the Shadow* (1975) and *Nightside of Eden* (1977), it has come to light that sexo-magical rituals of the kind associated with black magic cults sometimes involve a form of lycanthropy. One of the many amazing disclosures made by Grant is that adepts of the Left-Hand Path, in particular those belonging to modern voodoo cults, have devised a magical formula called *Le Mystère Lycanthropique,* which entails the assumption of the form of a wolf on the Astral Plane for the purpose of trafficking with powerful astral forces. For this ritual to succeed, the magician must undergo a form of regression to a primal state of consciousness, which is achieved by a complex technique of mind control and sexual sorcery.

Auto-suggestion undoubtedly plays a major part in producing a belief in the power to change form, and it is highly unlikely that any physical transformation occurs during magical rituals of this kind. What probably happens is that the psychosexual techniques used in sorcery bring about an overstimulation of the adept's senses; and in this hallucinogenic, expanded-consciousness state he is able to awaken and control dormant forces of the subconscious mind. Significantly, this particular magical ritual can also be explained in terms of the need to periodically regain the contents of the subconscious lost or suppressed during man's transition from the animal kingdom to the world of humans.

It would appear, therefore, that what members of contemporary black magic cults are trying to do is tap into that submerged part of the mind known as the collective unconscious, which psychologists describe as a vast, unfathomable reservoir consisting of the accumulated experiences of organic existence on earth. Secretly governing our lives, the collective unconscious expresses itself in symptoms, complexes, images, and symbols that we encounter in myths, visions, and dreams. The most powerful and universal of these primordial forces can sometimes manifest as archetypal images, the most disturbing of which are the terrifying monsters—like the werewolf—that sometimes appear in our nightmares.

Also lurking in the dark miasmal swamp of the mind's hinterland is the Shadow, which consists of a conglomerate of inborn collective predispositions, consciously abhorred and rejected by the ego for ethical and rational reasons. Instinctual, amoral, and savage, the Shadow is none other than the bestial "Mr. Hyde" imprisoned inside all of us—an inescapable nemesis always threatening to block out the conscious principles of the ego. Also known as our "dark twin" or "other self," the Shadow usually manifests itself in dreams, though sometimes it irrupts into consciousness, causing irrational thoughts and insane behavior. All that is needed is a suitable catalyst, and a normally placid, well-balanced person can suddenly become a raging wolf in all but form. It is a well-known fact that people who have committed horrible murders often say afterward: "I don't know why I did it—something came over me." That "something" we might reasonably assume was the unleashed Shadow, which had broken through the inhibiting barrier of the preconscious and temporarily gained control over the conscious ego.

According to Freudians, werewolves are dream images that are either representations or personalizations of abnormal organic sensations, or projections of unconscious and repressed sexual impulses, particularly incestuous wishes and infantile forms of sexuality. This view is supported by the American psychoanalyst Dr. Nandor Fodor, who claims that whenever transformation into a wolf occurs in our dreams it is symbolically a self-denunciation for secret deeds and desires of a sexual or cannibalistic nature.

From a medical viewpoint, lycanthropy is a recognized mental disorder in which the patient suffers from the delusion that he or she has been transformed into a wolf. In most cases the condition takes the form of a syndrome, the main symptoms of which are an altered state of consciousness, acute physiological stress and anxiety, an obsession with diabolism, and an uncontrollable desire to eat raw meat. Eventually most sufferers from this condition become incurably insane and end up hospitalized. It is possible that persistent drug abuse is a major factor in the increase in the number of people with this distressing affliction; and one can only assume that the reason this increase has failed to cause any noticeable public concern is because the term "lycanthrope" has been dropped from modern-day medical reports. Patients with this particular psychological disorder are now diagnosed as suffering from chronic pseudoneurotic schizophrenia coupled with dissociative hysterical neurosis, which is usually shortened to chronic brain syndrome.

Modern research into the human brain has revealed that each of us is really two separate personalities combined into one. Scientists who support the "split brain" theory claim that the two halves of the brain are quite different, with the conscious person, as it were, inhabiting the left side and the person who "lives" in the right side seemingly a stranger. In the brain, the left cerebral hemisphere controls language and ideas, while the right hemisphere is concerned with recognition and intuition. The two halves are joined by a knot of nerve fiber called the *corpus callosum;* if this is severed the patient splits into two distinct personalities. It is possible, therefore, that future research into the way the right side of the brain functions will shed further light on why certain individuals are prone to lycanthropic behavior.

An alternative medical explanation of the werewolf "disease" has been advanced by the British neurologist Lee Illis. In his paper "On Porphyria and the Aetiology of Werewolves," presented on October 2, 1963 to the Royal Society of Medicine, Dr. Illis argues that so-called werewolves actually suffer from a rare form of congenital porphyria. The evidence for this, he says, "lies in the remarkable relation between the symptoms of this rare disease and the many accounts of werewolves that have come down to us." The condition is characterized by a reddish-brown pigmentation of the urine, similar discoloration of the teeth due to the deposition of porphyrins, and a severe photosensitivity to light, as a result of which lesions form on the skin, which tend to ulcerate over a period of years causing severe mutilation of the extremities. From this circumstantial evidence Dr. Illis concludes:

> Such a person, because of photosensitivity and the resultant disfigurement, may choose only to wander about at night. The pale, yellowish, excoriated skin may be explained by the haemolytic anaemia, jaundice, and pruritus. These features, together with hypertrichosis and pigmentation, fit well with the descriptions, in older literature, of werewolves. The unhappy person may be mentally disturbed, and show some type or degree of abnormal behavior. In ancient times this would be accentuated by the physical and social treatment he received from the other villagers, whose instincts would be to explain the apparition in terms of witchcraft or Satanic possession.

While this and some of the other explanations for the werewolf phenomenon previously mentioned are within the bounds of possibility, the physical transformation of a member of one species into an entirely different species does, on the face of it, seem utterly impossible. Despite the fact that metamorphosis into a wolf goes far beyond any scientifically acceptable biology, let us, for the sake of argument, examine what the basic requirements would be for a human being to undergo such a remarkable transformation. To begin with, he or she would have to be the offspring from a union between a human female and a wolf. And even supposing this *were* possible, the resultant hybrid would also need to have been born with two independent sets of genotypes, so that in order to metamorphose into a wolf one genetic set is turned off and the alternate set activated. It sounds incredible, to say the least, and goes against all known scientific principles—but then, strange phenomena always do. Let us not forget that our knowledge of the world we live in is far from complete; every day we are discovering something new, and perhaps some day the piecing together of all this dissociated knowledge will open up terrifying aspects of reality.

Real-life Werewolves

Among the thousands of people accused of being werewolves in the past were some of history's most notorious criminals. They include Gilles Garnier, Peter Stump, and Jean Grenier, all of whom were convicted of the most heinous crimes. Garnier, whose name has become synonymous with lycanthropic savagery, was executed in the French town of Dôle in 1573, having been found guilty of murdering several children and devouring their flesh while allegedly in the shape of a wolf. Peter Stump (or Stubb), who went on trial at Cologne in 1589, had an even longer catalog of atrocities to his credit, including multiple murders, rape, incest, and cannibalism, which he committed over a twenty-five-year period. As a deterrent to others, the authorities ordered him to be cruelly tortured prior to having his head struck off and his body burned to ashes. Jean Grenier, in contrast, received a surprisingly lenient sentence. A young boy of thirteen at the time of his trial in 1603, his story is recounted by Sabine Baring-Gould in *The Book of Were-Wolves* (1865):

> Near the village of S. Antoine de Pizon, a little girl of the name of Marguerite Poirier, thirteen years old, was in the habit of tending her sheep, in company with a lad of the same age, whose name was Jean Grenier. The little girl often complained to her parents of the conduct of the boy: she said that he frightened her with his horrible stories; but her father and mother thought little of the complaints, till one day she returned home before her usual time so thoroughly alarmed that she had deserted her flock. Her parents now took the matter up and investigated it. Her story was as follows:
>
> Jean had often told her that he had sold himself to the Devil, and that he had acquired the power of ranging the country after dusk, and sometimes in broad day, in the form of a wolf. He had assured her that he had killed and devoured many dogs, but that he found their flesh less palatable than the flesh of little girls, which he regarded as a supreme delicacy. He had told her that this had been tasted by him not infrequently, but he had specified only two instances: in one he had eaten as much as he could, and thrown the rest to a wolf, which had come up during the repast. In the other instance he had bitten to death another little girl, had lapped her blood,

and being in a famished condition at the time, had devoured every portion of her, with the exception of the arms and shoulders.

Grenier was subsequently arrested and put on trial. Under examination he claimed he had committed the murders at the command of a mysterious stranger called the Lord of the Forest, who had given him a wolf-skin cape and a magic salve that, used together, transformed him into a wolf. Despite his confession and the severity of his crimes, the court showed the utmost clemency to the mentally disturbed youth, sentencing him to life imprisonment in a local monastery.

Even today, the activities of alleged werewolves still surface in the media from time to time, although many of the reports are of dubious origin and authenticity. The tabloid press, in particular, is fond of such sensational headlines as "Werewolf Killer Strikes Again" or "Wolfman Charged with Girl's Brutal Murder." In many of the cases though, the perpetrator of the atrocities is a serial killer who has earned the tag "werewolf" because of the bestial nature of his crimes. Invariably these modern-day werewolves turn out to be narcissistic psychopaths who bite and rend the flesh of their victims as a substitute for sexual intercourse.

Occasionally a case arises that is genuinely mysterious and has no apparent criminal or sexual connotation. In 1975, for instance, a seventeen-year-old youth from Staffordshire in England committed suicide after he became convinced he was turning into a werewolf.

The subsequent press coverage included the following report in the *London Daily Mail:*

> Apprentice joiner Andrew Prinold plunged a knife into his heart because he feared he was turning into a werewolf. He told of his fears in a desperate phone call to a friend minutes before he killed himself.
>
> His death came after he had started attending seances in a bid to contact his dead father, an inquest at Eccleshall, Staffordshire, was told yesterday.
>
> His weird flirtation with spiritualism started after he saw the film *The Exorcist,* it was said. The first seances were described by 18-year-old workmate Stephen Williams, who told the jury: "Five lads took part. They put a glass on the table with numbers and names round it and started talking to it. Within five to ten minutes Andrew started shaking. He was sweating, moaning and groaning.
>
> "Five or ten minutes later they held another seance. Andrew didn't take part, but within minutes he had started shaking again. Andrew said the devil was inside him. I had to punch his jaw to bring him round and he remembered nothing. Then we went off on our motorcycles and Andrew said he could not see, but later he was all right.
>
> "The Monday before he died he said he saw his father in the mirror."
>
> Stephen then told of the telephone call. He said: "Andrew said his hands and face were changing color and he was turning into a werewolf. He would go quiet and then start growling. I told him to see his brother. He said he had a knife and was going to kill himself."
>
> Pathologist Dr. Frank Pick said Andrew's wound appeared from its angle to be self-inflicted.

Only two explanations seem possible in this case: Either the youth suffered a mental breakdown due to the stress of losing his father, or he was possessed by a malevolent spirit of some sort. Whether he was actually changing into a werewolf, as he claimed, we shall never know, but there can be no doubt that he genuinely believed it was happening.

Another important aspect of the werewolf phenomenon is that metamorphosis into a ferocious animal or simply wearing the skin of an animal that is regarded with fear and loathing is closely linked with the desire to control a group of people by terror. Indeed, this was precisely the reason for the formation of a band of warriors known as the Leopard Men of Africa, who took on the appearance of savage beasts of prey. A more sophisticated form of this idea was the underground paramilitary group called the Werewolf Organization, which was formed by Adolf Hitler and his Nazi cronies in the 1920s. Operating in packs like their mythical counterparts, members of this fanatical gang hunted down their quarry in the dead of night, thereby maximizing the terror felt by their victims. It is also interesting to note that psychoanalysts who have studied Hitler's bloodstained career claim to have discovered a strong lycanthropic streak in his personality. For instance, there can be little doubt that it was of wolves that the Führer was thinking when, speaking about the education of the Hitler Youth, he said: "Youth must be indifferent to pain. There must be no weakness or tenderness in it. I want to see once more in the eyes of a pitiless youth the gleam of pride and independence of a beast of prey, and to eradicate the thousands of years of human domestication." Reading such chilling words is a reminder of how apposite was Winston Churchill's description of Hitler as "the Nazi Beast."

When all these different aspects are taken into consideration, it becomes evident that the essential constituents of the werewolf superstition are not restricted to the most obvious ones like shapeshifting and cannibalism, but include other important elements such as nocturnal wandering (the supposition that a person can be in two places at the same time) and regression to a lower or more primitive state, which may involve a return to an ancestral type or the reappearance of ancestral characteristics. Unconscious archetypal fears and deep-seated racial experiences are also important pieces in the jigsaw puzzle, as is the part played by inner conflict and the concept of the "other self."

Only when viewed from these different perspectives is it possible to gain an appreciation of the complex nature of the werewolf phenomenon and the insidious influence it has had on people's lives. Moreover, in the reality behind this ancient superstition can be discerned the most awful, most secret forces at work. Most frightening of all, perhaps, is the knowledge that we all harbor the werewolf inside us, and that at any time this hidden beast can spring into violent life should we temporarily lose control. With lawlessness showing an alarming increase in today's world, we should all do well to remember that there is a fine dividing line between civilization and barbarism; and unless we can sublimate and restrain the monsters within us a new dark age may descend upon the world, bringing with it untold horrors.

2

A Survey of Reference Works

Primary Sources

Lycanthropy has fascinated scholars and philosophers since the days of ancient Greece and Rome, and has been treated or briefly referred to by many authors throughout the centuries. The first important studies were written in the sixteenth century by leading theologians and senior members of the judiciary, all of whom discussed the subject in the wider context of witchcraft and demonology. The most contentious treatise, and the instigator of a lengthy debate about lycanthropy, was Jean Bodin's *De la Démonomanie des Sorciers,* published in France in 1580. Primarily a study of witchcraft and diabolism, it contained a controversial chapter on werewolfery in which the author maintained that it was possible for people to be materially transformed into wolves, and, indeed, he cited examples from Scripture and history to support his dogmatic viewpoint. However, apart from Joannes Wolfeshusius, whose *De Lycanthropis* (1591) was the first comprehensive examination of the werewolf superstition, there was little support for Bodin's opinions among other European scholars. Opposing or alternative theories were expounded in Johann Weyer's *De Praestigiis Daemonum* (1563), Reginald Scot's *The Discoverie of Witchcraft* (1584), Henri Boguet's *Discours des Sorciers* (1590), Claude Prieur's *Dialogue de la Lycanthropie* (1596), Le Sieur de Beauvoys de Chauvincourt's *Discours de la Lycanthropie* (1599), and Jean de Nynauld's *De la Lycanthropie* (1615). In each of these works the authors quote from the Bible and other ancient authorities to support convoluted arguments about the true nature of werewolves. Opinions vary slightly, but the general consensus is that lycanthropy is a mental illness, and alleged transformations are merely a deception of the Devil's. Key extracts from some of these primary sources have been reproduced in *A Lycanthropy Reader: Werewolves in Western Culture,* edited by Charlotte F. Otten (Dorset Press, 1989).

Modern Studies

Scholarly interest in werewolfery declined during the seventeenth and eighteenth centuries and wasn't rekindled until the middle of the nineteenth century, when

Wilhelm Hertz's *Der Werwolf* (1862) and Sabine Baring-Gould's *The Book of Were-Wolves: Being an Account of a Terrible Superstition* (1865) brought the subject to the public's attention once more. Hertz's volume, a miscellaneous collection of myths, legends, and strange superstitions connected with the werewolf, has been described by Montague Summers as "a careful study which contains much of value." Baring-Gould's book, of which there have been several reprint editions, is less erudite and concentrates on dramatized factual accounts of the lives of notorious real-life werewolves, such as Gilles Garnier, Jean Grenier, and Sergeant Bertrand. Like the more enlightened medieval scholars, Baring-Gould attributes lycanthropy to a species of madness in which the person afflicted by it believes himself to be a wild beast—and acts accordingly.

In another book from the 1860s, Eliphas Lévi's *Mysteries of Magic,* there is a brief but significant reference to lycanthropy when the author digresses from his main discourse to make the following observations:

> We must speak here of lycanthropy, or the nocturnal transformation of men into wolves, histories so well substantiated that skeptical science has had recourse to furious maniacs, and to masquerading as animals for explanations. But such hypotheses are puerile and explain nothing. Let us seek elsewhere the solution of the mystery, and establish—First, that no person has been killed by a wer-wolf except by suffocation, without effusion of blood and without wounds. Second, that wer-wolves, though tracked,

hunted, and even maimed, have never been killed on the spot. Third, that persons suspected of these transformations have always been found at home, after the pursuit of the wer-wolf, more or less wounded, sometimes dying, but invariably in their natural form.

There are many other books from the Victorian era that give some slight reference to werewolfery. Worth singling out are two wide-ranging surveys, *Curiosities of Indo-European Tradition and Folk-lore* (1863) by Walter Kelly, and *Curious Creatures in Zoology* (1890) by John Ashton, both of which include a section on the werewolf. Also of interest is Kirby Flower Smith's monograph "An Historical Study of the Werewolf in Literature," published in 1894.

Among the many reference works about werewolves and shapeshifting produced in the twentieth century, the first to achieve popularity was Elliott O'Donnell's *Werwolves* (1912). The author, a professional ghost-hunter and self-styled scientific psychic researcher, makes it clear from the outset that he regards the existence of werewolves to be an established fact, and he launches into a unique theory to account for their origin. Contrary to what the Bible says—not to mention modern scientific theories—O'Donnell speculates that Earth and its inhabitants were created by many forces, some benevolent, others malevolent. The evil forces, he would have us believe, brought werewolves into existence by bestowing the property of lycanthropy on certain individuals, who passed it on to their descendants. Fortunately, only a small part of the book is given over to these strange ideas; the rest is devoted to "authentic" werewolf tales garnered from different parts of Europe. These are not the usual matter-of-fact accounts but are dramatized to such an extent that they are almost indistinguishable from fiction. One especially interesting story concerns a beautiful, gentle-natured countess who becomes bewitched after drinking from a lycanthropous brook, another tells of a little girl who unwittingly plucks a flower that can turn anyone who wears it into a ferocious wolf.

It was, perhaps, in order to prevent others from suffering a similar fate that O'Donnell supplied the following information about these anomalies of nature:

> Lycanthropous water is said, by those who dwell near to it, to differ from other water in subtle details only—details that would, in all probability, escape the notice of all who were not connoisseurs of the superphysical. A strange, faint odor, comparable with nothing, distinguishes lycanthropous water; there is a lurid sparkle in it, strongly suggestive of some peculiar, individual life; the noise it makes, as it rushes along, so closely resembles the muttering and whispering of human voices as to be often mistaken for them; whilst at night it sometimes utters piercing screams, and howls, and groans, in such a manner as to terrify all who pass near it. Dogs and horses, in particular, are susceptible to its influence, and they exhibit the greatest signs of terror at the mere sound of it.

Lycanthropous flowers, no less than lycanthropous water, possess properties peculiar to themselves; properties which are, probably, only discernible to those who are well acquainted with them. Their scent is described as faint and subtly suggestive of death, whilst their sap is rather offensively white and sticky. In appearance they are much the same as other flowers, and are usually white and yellow.

Following quickly upon the heels of O'Donnell's book came Frank Hamel's *Human Animals* (1915), a broad-based survey dealing with a wide variety of human-to-animal transformations. The many examples are selected from the world's treasury of myths, legends, and folktales, and include stories about werewolves, were-foxes, lion- and tiger-men, bird-women, human serpents, lamias, swan-maidens, and a curious mouse-girl. The book's comprehensive scope does mean, however, that the werewolf superstition gets only limited coverage.

The 1930s saw the publication of two milestone works, the first of which was Ernest Jones's *On the Nightmare* (1931). Written from a psychoanalytical perspective, this enduring classic is based on the premise that nightmares and anxiety dreams have exercised a considerable influence on the formation of the werewolf, vampire, and witchcraft superstitions, which became fused together and, from 1450 to 1750, were responsible for an incalculable amount of suffering. A follower of Freud and a noted analyst in his own right, Jones contends that the elements out of which the werewolf and vampire superstitions were built are projections of unconscious and repressed incestuous wishes and infantile forms of sexuality.

The other major study from the interwar years was Montague Summers's *The Werewolf,* which since its publication in 1933 has been regarded as a work of emi nent scholarship and supreme authority. Unlike Ernest Jones, Summers expresses a strong belief in the existence of werewolves and approaches the subject entirely from a theological and philosophical point of view. Indicative of the meticulous research carried out by the author (who was also a noted authority on vampires) are the quoted passages from scores of different sources. There is also a lengthy discourse on the etymology of the word "werewolf," which is the ultimate in thoroughness. Unfortunately, Summers assumed that everyone was well versed in Greek, Latin, German, and French, and did not think it necessary to provide English translations for any of the extracts from foreign works, making them useless to many readers. The main part of *The Werewolf* brings together an impressive assortment of werewolf stories culled from the rich storehouse of European folklore and also includes case histories of notorious real-life werewolves. There is also a substantial bibliography and a useful survey of werewolf fiction. Despite unfavorable reviews, the book was well received by the public and established Summers as the world's foremost authority on werewolves, a position he retained until his death in 1948.

Another work from the same period, Rollo Ahmed's *The Black Art* (1936), includes a chapter titled "Witchcraft, Vampires and Werewolves in Europe," but it is merely a rehash of what others have written on the subject. More original, and allegedly based on firsthand experience, is William Seabrook's *Witchcraft: Its Power in the World Today* (1940), which devotes a chapter each to two authentic cases of lycanthropy.

In 1950, the distinguished Austrian anthropologist Robert Eisler made some intriguing observations about lycanthropy in a book called *Man into Wolf: An Anthropological Interpretation of Sadism, Masochism, and Lycanthropy*. Based on a lecture he gave to the Royal Society of Medicine, the book elaborates on the theory that there is a prehistorical, evolutionist derivation of all crimes of violence. Eisler claims that man was not always carnivorous or aggressive, but in order to survive the onset of the Ice Age he had to turn to meat as a new source of food. Thereafter men wore animal skins and hunted in packs, changing from peace-loving vegetarians to savage, wolflike killers. According to Eisler, the deep emotional upheaval this caused left indelible scars on man's subconscious, superindividual, ancestral memory and is reflected in the surviving atavistic beliefs surrounding lycanthropy. This book was also the first to suggest that Adolf Hitler may have suffered from bouts of lycanthropic madness; it also caused something of a stir by alleging that women who dress in furs and paint their fingernails red are psychological werewolves. The furs, it is argued, represent the animals the women secretly want to become, and the red fingernails symbolize the blood of victims. Finally, a brief word about the book's unusual format. The lecture itself takes up only a small portion of the text; the rest consists of extensive explanations and annotations, all of which constitute a rich source of information.

In the 1960s, nonfiction books about werewolves and other archetypal monsters began to appear more regularly. Bernhardt J. Hurwood produced a number of commercially successful studies in this category, of which *Vampires, Werewolves and Ghouls* (1968) gives the most coverage to lycanthropy. Like many popular studies from this period it recycles information from earlier works but is, nonetheless, a readable and engaging starting point for juvenile readers. Werewolves and vampires also figure prominently in *The Supernatural* (1965) by Douglas Hill and Pat Williams. A good mix of the scholarly and the popular, this wide-ranging survey was originally touted as "the first objective investigation of psychic phenomena and those who have long practiced occult powers." Less serious in its approach is *Horror!* (1966) by Drake Douglas, which examines the popular image of the werewolf and other figures of terror associated with horror fiction and movies. In contrast, real-life werewolves and vampires are among the gruesome gallery of criminals and psychopaths whose monstrous deeds are chronicled in Raymond Rudorff's *Monsters: Studies in Ferocity* (1968). Two similar compilations are

Scoundrels, Fiends, and Human Monsters (1968) by Cliff Howe, and *Strange Monsters and Madmen* (1969) by Warren Smith. Werewolves also get a brief mention in John Pollard's *Wolves and Werewolves* (1964), which is a comprehensive history of the wolf in folklore.

The 1970s saw the publication of an even greater number of books that were wholly or partly about werewolves and lycanthropy. One of a growing number aimed at a young audience was Bernhardt J. Hurwood's *Vampires, Werewolves, and Other Demons* (1972), which featured authentic historical cases of vampirism and lycanthropy. Other books that targeted readers in the young adult category were *Werewolves* (1973) by Nancy Garden, *Vampires, Zombies, and Monster Men* (1975) by Daniel Farson, *Meet the Werewolf* (1976) by Georgess McHargue, and *Vampires, Werewolves, and Demons* (1979) by Lynn Myring.

One of the most comprehensive popular studies from this decade was Basil Copper's *The Werewolf in Legend, Fact, and Art* (1977), a companion volume to his earlier work, *The Vampire in Legend, Fact, and Art* (1973). The first of the book's three sections includes some useful information about the myths and legends associated with the werewolf and gives dramatized accounts of the crimes of sixteenth-century lycanthropes and their subsequent trials. The second section concentrates on various medical explanations of lycanthropy, with several pages devoted to a detailed analysis of Dr. Lee Illis's theory that a rare form of porphyria was largely responsible for the werewolf legends. There are also two fascinating chapters about wolf-boys, although it could be argued that feral children brought up among wolves have little, if any, connection with werewolves. The third and longest section is concerned with the werewolf's image in weird fiction and its various cinematic manifestations, the highlights of which are the author's detailed summaries of two key novels, G. W. M. Reynolds's *Wagner, the Wehr-Wolf* and Guy Endore's *The Werewolf of Paris,* and his enthusiastic appraisal of werewolf films of the 1940s, especially those starring Lon Chaney Jr. A selected bibliography and filmography are also included.

An even better popular study from this period is Ian Woodward's *The Werewolf Delusion* (1979), which claims to be the first fully documented, thoroughly researched investigation into the world of the werewolf. In the introduction, Woodward boasts that his research took him all over the globe, and he claims to have witnessed black magic rites and communications with the Devil. In an effort to examine every possible explanation for the werewolf phenomenon the author has inquired into spiritualism, theosophy, cannibalism, astral projection, psychiatric medicine, and contemporary newspaper reports. After disentangling the facts from the fantasy, Woodward concludes that the werewolf as a psychic phenomenon could, did, and perhaps still does exist. In describing this book one should add that not only does it make interesting reading but its attractiveness is even more enhanced by the numerous illustrations supporting the text. These range from old engravings and woodcuts to modern movie stills, many of which are accompanied by informative captions.

Werewolves also feature prominently in *Werewolves, Shapeshifters, and Skinwalkers* (1972) by Marika Kriss, and there are chapters on them in *Return from the Dead: The History of Ghosts, Vampires, Werewolves, and Poltergeists* (1970) by Douglas Hill, and *Flesh and Blood* (1973) by Reay Tannahill. There are also many references to lycanthropy in Kenneth Grant's *Cults of the Shadow* (1975) and *Nightside of Eden* (1977), which are veritable grimoires of the Dark Doctrine. Of particular interest are Grant's accounts of the activities of the Chicago-based voodoo coven The Cult of the Black Snake, whose high priest, Michael Bertiaux, is said to perform magical rituals involving lycanthropy. The werewolf element in folklore is examined in two rather stodgy essays, "The Social Biology of Werewolves" by W. M. S. Russell and Claire Russell, and "Shape-changing in the Old Norse Sagas" by H. R. Ellis Davidson, both of which are included in *Animals in Folklore* (1978), edited by J. R. Porter and W. M. S. Russell. Much more fun to read is Elliott O'Donnell's "Vampires, Were-wolves, Fox-women, etc." in *Satanism and Witches* (1974). This irresistible piece, part folklore, part hokum, is notable for some fascinating tidbits about the fox-women of Japan and China. Apparently, it is a common belief in these countries that foxes have shape-changing powers and can attain an age of between eight hundred and a thousand years. It is also alleged that at the age of fifty they can assume the form of a woman, and at one hundred that of a young and lovely girl called "Our Lady."

The final two decades of the twentieth century saw further additions to the list of werewolf-oriented nonfiction books, the most impressive of which was *A Lycanthropy Reader: Werewolves in Western Culture* (1986), edited by Charlotte F. Otten. This comprehensive survey of all aspects of werewolfism and lycanthropy is divided into six sections: (1) Medical Cases, Diagnoses, Descriptions; (2) Trial Records, Historical Accounts, Sightings; (3) Philosophical and Theological Approaches to Metamorphosis; (4) Critical Essays on Lycanthropy (Anthropology, History, and Medicine); (5) Myths and Legends; and (6) Allegory. Each section has an introduction that summarizes and interprets the subject matter.

In the book's introduction, Otten claims that lycanthropy has social, religious, and medical implications. These include the significance of violence and criminality, the role of the demonic in aberrant behavior, and the nature of good and evil. She further asserts that a study of the literature of lycanthropy uncovers basic issues in human life and "helps to clarify the needs, hopes, aspirations, and commitments of a human being and of society." It is also her view that this type of literature "addresses the problems, struggles, conflicts, anxieties, triumphs, and joys of humankind. It looks honestly at the destructive urges that attack and devour the fabric of human life, at the dark moments in the human soul, but it also looks for sources of healing and restoration." To support her views, Otten has drawn on primary sources, presenting relevant passages from medieval and Renaissance treatises (such as Sprenger and Kramer's *Malleus Maleficarum,* Reginald Scot's *The Discoverie of Witchcraft,* and Henri Boguet's *Discours des Sorciers*) and has supplemented these with scientific papers and modern critical essays by psychologists, anthropologists, and medical historians. There is also a choice selection of fictional stories, which include Petronius's werewolf story from the *Satyricon,* Marie de France's "Lay of the Were-Wolf," Count Eric Stenbock's "The Other Side," and Clemence Housman's "The Were-Wolf." This is undoubtedly one of the best books of its kind ever published and should be regarded as a basic core title for any reference collection.

More limited in its scope is Harry A. Senn's *Were-Wolf and Vampire in Romania* (1982). The author, a noted folklorist, claims that werewolves are regarded as a natural phenomenon in Transylvania and, contrary to popular belief, are not in the habit of stalking human prey. For nonacademics a wealth of basic information about werewolves can be found in the well-illustrated "coffee table" book *Mysteries of the Unknown: Transformations,* published by Time-Life Books in 1989. *Mythical and Fabulous Creatures* (1987), edited by Malcolm

South, is another excellent book in which the history of werewolves and other supernatural or mythical creatures is traced in a series of articles. There is also an interesting chapter on werewolves in Raymond McNally's *Dracula Was a Woman* (1983), which includes a fascinating study of the whole vampire/werewolf tradition. In contrast, Jim Haskins's juvenile-oriented *Werewolves* (1981) is somewhat superficial, and a similar lack of depth mars Basil Copper's essay on werewolves and vampires in *The Octopus Encyclopedia of Horror* (1981). Also woefully inadequate is Colin Wilson's werewolf survey in *The Penguin Encyclopedia of Horror and the Supernatural* (1986).

More recently, British author Adam Douglas has reexamined the werewolf myth in *The Beast Within* (1992), which reaches the conclusion that, although the werewolf may not be a real, flesh-and-blood creature, it has, nonetheless, played a significant part in mankind's religious and social development. To support his argument, Douglas traces the myth back to the earliest known beliefs of human societies. He contends that the werewolf legend has its basis in the prehistoric association of a killing frenzy arising from primitive man deliberately taking on the feral attributes of a wolf while hunting and mimicking its methods of predation to gain success in the kill. Having established what he considers to be its origins, the author then traces the development of the werewolf myth throughout history, paying particular attention to its connection with the pagan wolf-cults of antiquity and the later association with the medieval witch-craze. There is, of course, nothing startlingly new about all this, but *The Beast Within* is, nonetheless, a thorough and well-researched history of the werewolf—one that will probably be more acceptable to modern readers than the outdated studies by earlier authorities. The only flaw that limits the book's usefulness is the selective and spotty coverage of werewolf fiction and movies; but this quibble aside, it must be considered a worthwhile acquisition for researchers.

Although it is not obvious from the title, werewolves also feature prominently in Nigel Jackson's *Compleat Vampyre* (1995), which is based on the premise that vampires and werewolves are intimately interrelated and have their origins in the pre-Christian tribal culture of Indo-European warrior societies. The book is of interest mainly for its detailed examination of the vampire-werewolf's role in pagan lore and shamanism, during which the author makes some extravagant claims. Perhaps the wildest of these is that vampires and werewolves inhabit a paradoxical intermediate state of liminal time, which exists mysteriously in-between the ordinary time states we normally experience. Mixed in with this fanciful speculation are some authentic pieces of folklore, although at times it is difficult to differentiate between the two.

An allegedly true account of werewolfery is related in *Werewolf: A True Story of Demonic Possession* (1991) by Ed and Lorraine Warren, and several similar cases of lycanthropy are featured in Richard Noll's *Vampires, Werewolves, and Demons* (1992), which partly comprises authentic reports from modern medical journals. There are also chapters on werewolves in *Moon Madness* (1990) by Paul Katzeff and in *The Oxford Book of the Supernatural* (1996) edited by D. J. Enright.

Where surveys of werewolf fiction are concerned, all have fallen well short of being comprehensive—a deficiency this present volume hopes to remedy. After Montague Summers's pioneering survey in *The Werewolf* (1933) the next one of any significance was compiled by Brian J. Frost for *Book of the Werewolf* in 1973. Much broader in its scope than the one by Summers, this survey covered British and American stories up to 1970 and was the first to include details about werewolf stories in American pulp magazines. In its day it was considered to be quite thorough, but it is now evident that it only scratched the surface.

As was mentioned earlier, Basil Copper's *The Werewolf in Legend, Fact, and Art* (1977) includes a lengthy survey of werewolf fiction, but too much of this is spent on a lengthy discussion of two of the best-known novels in the werewolf canon, while other important examples of the form are either mentioned briefly or overlooked altogether. Shorter and more easily digestible are the capsule histories of the werewolf subgenre in Franz Rottensteiner's *The Fantasy Book* (1978) and Ian Woodward's *The Werewolf Delusion*

(1979), both of which are accompanied by some splendidly lurid illustrations.

The werewolf theme was also analyzed by Stephen King in his first nonfiction book, *Danse Macabre* (1981). In this masterly overview of the entire horror genre, King links lycanthropy with narcissism, claiming that traditional werewolf stories almost always—knowingly or unknowingly—mimic the classic tale of Narcissus. Like other commentators before him, he regards Robert Louis Stevenson's *The Strange Case of Dr. Jekyll and Mr. Hyde* as a werewolf story, suggesting that at its most basic level it represents a pagan conflict between man's Apollonian potential and his base, Dionysian desires. Many other novels, he contends, have a disguised werewolf motif and cites Robert Bloch's *Psycho* as a prime example.

Another all-embracing survey, which might justifiably be described as an academic version of King's blockbuster, is *Dreadful Pleasures* (1985) by James B. Twitchell. In a chapter titled "Dr. Jekyll and Mr. Wolfman" there is a lengthy discussion of werewolf stories and movies with a similar theme, in which the author points out the differences between the werewolf and the wolfman. The werewolf, Twitchell maintains, is not sufficiently anthropocentric to arouse much more than stark terror; but the wolfman, he argues, is more horrifying because he is really "one of us" and can act out clearly human behavior.

A valuable research resource published in Switzerland during the 1980s was *La Bibliographie de Dracula* (1986) by Jacques Finné. Obviously, a good knowledge of French is needed to interpret the survey of vampire and werewolf fiction that constitutes the first part of the book, but the massive bibliography of vampire, werewolf, and ghoul stories that makes up the remainder of the book presents less of a problem since most of the novels and short stories listed are in English. Researchers will also find Everett F. Bleiler's huge reference work *The Guide to Supernatural Fiction* (1983) very useful. This has plot summaries of hundreds of novels and short stories, including an appreciable number with a werewolf motif. Also worth checking out are the chapter "Monsters, Vampires, and Werewolves: The Sympathetic Beasts of Anne Rice and Chelsea Quinn Yarbro" in *Presenting Young Adult Horror Fiction* (1992) by Cosette Kies, and Gina Wisker's essay "At Home All Was Blood and Feathers: The Werewolf in the Kitchen—Angela Carter and Horror," which can be found in *Creepers: British Horror and Fantasy in the Twentieth Century* (1993).

Professor Jack Zipes, who has chosen fairy tales as a focus for his scholarship, provides some interesting insights into the werewolf's role in sixteenth-century "warning-stories" in the introduction to *The Trials and Tribulations of Little Red Riding Hood* (1983). Tracing the origins of this classic folktale in the light of the socio-historical background of the European witch craze, Zipes claims that the story's villain was originally a werewolf but was later changed to a natural wolf when werewolves lost their significance after the decline of the witch hunts.

Finally, an honorable mention must be given to the special "Werewolves" issue of the American magazine *The Scream Factory* (autumn 1994), which contains no fewer than seven articles on werewolf fiction. The most important of these articles from a bibliographical standpoint are Laurence Bush's essay on the werewolf in literature up to 1940, Stefan Dziemianowicz's survey of werewolf stories in the pulp magazines, Scott H. Urban's survey of contemporary short werewolf fiction, and Don D'Ammassa's mammoth guide to lesser-known novels, which provides over ninety capsule synopses. Accompanying the text are numerous line drawings and halftone reproductions of paperback book covers, all suitably garish. This is undoubtedly a landmark publication and should be a high priority acquisition for all werewolf buffs.

3

The Werewolf Enters Fiction

Ensorcelled Werewolves: Classical and Medieval Stories

The earliest werewolf stories were in the form of poems and trace their origins back to the myths and legends of antiquity, in which metamorphosis into animal form is a frequent—almost natural—phenomenon. The theme's first significant expression in literature was in Virgil's eighth Eclogue (39 B.C.), which tells of a warlock named Moeris who effects a voluntary transformation into a wolf by eating magical herbs. A later work by another distinguished Roman poet, Ovid's *Metamorphoses* includes the well-known story of Lycaon, the tyrannical king of Arcadia, who, when visited by the god Jupiter in disguise, outrages the deity by serving him a meal of human flesh. As a fitting punishment for his effrontery, Jupiter transforms Lycaon into a howling wolf to make the decadent monarch's appearance correspond with his moral appetites.

The first prose work to feature a werewolf was Petronius's *Satyricon,* written in A.D. 55. In Niceros's story (related in the section known as Trimalchio's Banquet) the servant of a rich merchant is passing by a moonlit graveyard when his companion, a young soldier, suddenly takes off all his clothes, lays them in a heap, and proceeds to urinate on them. At once he becomes a wolf, and after emitting a bloodcurdling howl runs off into the woods. Niceros learns afterward that a wolf has savaged the livestock on a nearby farm; the following morning he receives confirmation that it was his traveling companion who was responsible for the attack when a wound dealt the marauding beast is found reproduced on the soldier's body. While this hoary old yarn may seem insipid by today's standards, it is important, nonetheless, for having introduced certain key elements that have been incorporated into werewolf stories ever since.

The next milestone in the history of the werewolf story was the introduction of the motif into English literature at the end of the twelfth century. The story credited with this honor is "The Lay of the Bisclavaret" by Marie de France, which is best read in one of the modern prose versions. The hero of this famous romance is one of the most gallant knights in Brittany and is much loved by everyone, especially the king. His wife, however, becomes concerned when he regularly disappears for three days without offering any explanation; after questioning him repeatedly about this the knight reluctantly confesses that as a result of a curse he becomes a ravening werewolf during his absences. Pressed to reveal more he confides to his horrified wife that in order to effect the transformation he must remove all his clothes and conceal them in a safe hiding place; he also lets it be known that should he not be able to find them again, he would remain in his beastly form forever. Eventually, to the knight's cost, the location of the place of concealment is also coaxed out of him by his wife who, after hearing her husband's terrible confession, is afraid to live with him any longer. In order to get rid of him permanently, she persuades a former suitor to search out the werewolf's apparel and steal it away.

For more than a year nothing is seen or heard of the king's favorite, enabling the treacherous couple to marry and lay claim to the missing knight's lands and titles. One day while the king is hunting in the woods, he unknowingly encounters the transmogrified knight when a wolf he and his party have been hunting runs up to him and, with human gestures, pleads for protection. Marveling at the creature's actions, the king forbids anyone in his retinue to molest the supplicant, and he returns to his castle with the strange beast trotting tamely at his side. Thenceforth the wolf is treated like a pampered pet and earns the trust of the royal household by its friendly nature. One evening, however, at a great feast attended by all the nobility, the normally placid creature suddenly flies into a rage after encountering the man who had helped in his betrayal; on another occasion the transmogrified knight ferociously attacks his former wife and bites off her nose. These incidents seem inexplicable at the time, but suspicions are aroused when it is pointed out that the woman was once the wife of the missing knight. The couple are arrested and questioned under torture until a full confession is obtained. Soon thereafter the ensorcelled knight's clothes are retrieved and he regains his human form, much to the delight of the king, who restores all his friend's honors and banishes the disgraced wife and her accomplice from the kingdom forever.

The influence of Marie de France's lay is much in evidence in two other medieval werewolf tales, "Lai de Melion" and "Arthur and Gorlagon," both of which date from the thirteenth century. "Lai de Melion" is almost a carbon copy of "Bisclavaret," except that the setting has been transposed to Ireland, and King Arthur (of Round Table fame) has been substituted as the werewolf's royal protector. The legendary British monarch is also featured in "Arthur and Gorlagon," but his role in this recently rediscovered Celtic romance is only a passive one. The principal character is a king named Gorlagon, in whose garden a magic sapling is growing. He has kept this a secret, for he knows that should he, or anyone else, cut down the sapling and strike themselves on the head with the tip while reciting "Be a wolf and have the understanding of a wolf," they would be instantly transformed in compliance with the magic formula. The plot then heads in a familiar direction when Gorlagon's unfaithful wife wheedles the secret out of her husband and uses this knowledge to transform him into a wolf against his will. This act of treachery forces the bewitched monarch to flee into the forest, where he lives the life of an outcast. Meanwhile the perfidious queen uses her lord's absence as an excuse to install her lover as the kingdom's new ruler.

For more than two years the werewolf's furious attempts to extricate himself from his predicament end in failure, but his luck changes after he is befriended by the ruler of a neighboring kingdom. This king also has an adulterous wife, and the wolf's part in exposing her duplicity leads the cuckolded monarch to the conclusion that the beast's remarkable powers are attributable to it being, in reality, a man bewitched. The king shows his gratitude for the service rendered him by helping Gorlagon vanquish the usurpers, and the humbled queen is forced to remove the spell. In return, her life is spared on the condition that she must always carry in front of her the severed head of her lover, and that every time Gorlagon kisses the woman who has replaced her as his wife, she must do the same to the bloodstained head so that everyone is continually reminded of her treachery.

Perhaps the best known of all these medieval were-wolf narratives is the Old French romance *Guillaume de Palerne,* written in the last decade of the twelfth century. It was later translated into Middle English alliterative verse in 1350, and a modern English prose version was published in 1832. A long, complex narrative, *William and the Werewolf* (as it is otherwise known) is the first work of fiction to feature a benevolent werewolf. The character in the story who adopts this unusual role is Alphonse, heir to the Spanish throne, who has been bewitched by his wicked stepmother, Queen Braunde, who wants her own son to wear the crown in his stead. After his metamorphosis into a wolf, Alphonse becomes embroiled in a string of perilous adventures, during the course of which he befriends and acts as protector to two royal lovers, William and Melior. All ends happily with Alphonse regaining his human form and William becoming Emperor of Rome.

The Gothic Influence:
Early-Nineteenth-Century Stories

After the demise of the medieval romance, interest in the werewolf motif waned almost to the point of extinction and wasn't fully revived until the early nineteenth century. A glimpse of things to come is seen in Charles Maturin's last Gothic novel *The Albigenses* (1824). In an episode set in the dungeon of a French castle, the hero,

Sir Paladour, is confronted with a shapeless form howling and yelling: "I am a mad wolf . . . the hair grows inwards—the wolfish coat is within—the wolfish heart is within—the wolfish fangs are within!" The author then proceeds, with typical relish, to describe the horrors of the werewolf's lair.

Apart from this single instance, the werewolf is conspicuously absent from the pages of the Gothic novel and is rarely encountered in the lurid bluebooks and shilling shockers that followed in their wake. The earliest known short story from this era about a werewolf is reputed to be "The Wehr Wolf: A Legend of the Limousin," which was included in the first volume of Richard Thomson's three-volume collection *Tales of an Antiquary*, published in England in 1828. This appears to be identical to "The Severed Arm; or, The Wehrwolf of Limousin," which Peter Haining presented in his 1978 anthology *The Shilling Shockers*. In the introductory note Haining claims that the story originates from a bluebook titled *Tales of Superstition*, which he dates speculatively as c. 1820. I am inclined to the view, however, that this is a plagiarized version of Thomson's story and therefore postdates the original text. As the excellent introduction to Haining's anthology informs us, these slim, paper-covered chapbooks known as bluebooks or shilling shockers were notorious for appropriating the work of popular authors of Gothic fiction without their consent, and then cloaking this wholesale piracy by the scurrilous practice of retitling the stories and substituting "Anonymous" for the author's name.

Reprinted in *Tales of All Nations* in 1848, "The Severed Arm" tells the tragic story of Gaspar de Marcanville, a brave French knight falsely accused of treason by a former companion, Count de Saintefleur. Even the king, whose favorite Gaspar was, cannot save him from dishonor nor prevent the mark of a traitor being branded on his arm. After the further humiliation of banishment the embittered knight eventually settles in the woody province of Upper Limousin, where he leads the solitary life of a hunter. Shortly after his arrival, the inhabitants of the nearby town of St. Yrieux are alarmed by loud howlings coming from the woods at night, and their fears that werewolves have taken up residence in the neighborhood seem to be confirmed when the mutilated bodies of local children are found.

Some time later a badly wounded knight stumbles through the door of the local inn, carrying with him the huge paw of a wolf. As soon as he recovers sufficiently enough to answer questions, the knight (who turns out to be de Saintefleur) tells how this gruesome trophy came into his possession:

> "My tale is brief," answered the stranger: "The king is passing tonight through the Limousin, and with two of his attendants I rode forward to prepare for his coming; when, in the darkness of the wood, we were separated, and, as I galloped on alone, an enormous wolf, with fiery flashing eyes, leaped out of a brake before me, with the most fearful howlings, and

57

rushed on me with the speed of lightning. As the
wolf leaped upon my horse, I drew my couteau-de-
chasse, and severed that huge paw which you found
upon me: but as the violence of the blow made my
weapon fall, I caught up a large forked branch of a
tree, and struck the animal upon the forehead: upon
which, my horse began to rear and plunge; for,
where the wolf stood, I saw by a momentary glimpse
of moonlight the form of an ancient enemy, who had
long since been banished from France, and whom I
believed to have died of famine in the Hartz Forest."

Soon afterward the severed foreleg mysteriously
changes into a human arm cut off at the elbow and is
identified as that of the reclusive hunter by the brand
on it. Following this discovery a hunting party sets out
to apprehend the mutilated werewolf; but Gaspar is
not to be denied his last chance for vengeance and kills
de Saintefleur before meeting a similar fate himself
only moments later.

A severed limb also plays a pivotal role in Sutherland Menzies's "Hugues, the Wer-Wolf: A Kentish Legend of the Middle Ages," which first saw print in the
September 1838 issue of a Victorian periodical titled
The Court Magazine and Monthly Critic. The story
recounts the tragicomic story of Hugues Wulfric, the
last surviving member of an entire family shunned by
the local community for allegedly being werewolves.
Reduced to near-starvation after he is unable to find
work, Hugues dons the disguise of a werewolf in order
to frighten the neighborhood butcher into providing

him with a regular supply of fresh meat. However, his enterprising scheme backfires when the resentful victim, incensed by Hugues's persistent extortion, puts a stop to it by lopping off the fake werewolf's "paw." Nevertheless, the mutilated youth has the last laugh when his severed hand takes on a life of its own and torments the butcher incessantly, eventually driving him to suicide. Despite one or two farcical scenes, Menzies's story is generally grim in tone, and is chiefly notable for its strong historical background and revealing insight into the desperate plight of an outcast in the Middle Ages.

The female werewolf—a surprising absentee from the pages of supernatural fiction until the Victorian era—made her bow in "The Werewolf," a short story extracted from Frederick Marryat's novel *The Phantom Ship* (1839). Reprinted many times since, often under the alternative title of "The White Wolf of the Hartz Mountains," the tale chronicles the misfortunes of Krantz, a Hungarian nobleman's steward, who flees from Transylvania with his three children after murdering his unfaithful wife and her lover. The fugitive eventually finds refuge in a remote cottage in the Hartz Mountains, where he ekes out a sparse living for himself and his family by hunting and tilling the land.

One winter's day, while out hunting, Krantz rescues two fatigued travelers—Wilfred and his daughter Christina—and offers them shelter in his home. The young woman is exceedingly beautiful, with shiny flaxen hair, bright as a mirror; and her mouth, although somewhat large when open, displays the most brilliant teeth imaginable. There is, however, something about her eyes, sparkling as they are, that makes the children afraid and fills them with foreboding. Unaware of their misgivings, the love-blind Krantz finds Christina utterly adorable, and after a brief courtship asks Wilfred for her hand in marriage. Consent is readily given, and the couple are united in an unorthodox ceremony conducted by the bride's father, who makes the bridegroom promise not to harm his daughter in any way. In addition, he warns Krantz that should he fail to keep his word, the vengeance of the Spirits of the Mountains would fall upon him and his children, all of whom would perish horribly.

After Wilfred's sudden departure, the children soon come to fear the cruel ways of their stepmother—and her nocturnal wanderings arouse suspicions in their minds that she is a werewolf. But before they can pluck up the courage to tell their father what they have seen, Christina brutally kills two of the children and diverts suspicion from herself by putting the blame on a white wolf that has been seen prowling near the cottage. Her evil ways are finally exposed when the surviving child, the narrator of the story, finds his stepmother violating the grave of his little sister the night after her burial. Seeing his chance for revenge, he immediately runs back to the house and rouses his father from his sleep. He, thinking that the white wolf has returned, snatches up his gun and rushes outside to confront the beast.

> Imagine his horror, when (unprepared as he was for such a sight) he beheld, as he advanced towards the grave, not a wolf, but his wife, in her nightdress, on her hands and knees, crouching by the body of my sister, and tearing off large pieces of the flesh, and devouring them with all the avidity of a wolf. She was too busy to be aware of our approach. My father dropped his gun; his hair stood on end, so did mine; he breathed heavily, and then his breath for a time stopped. I picked up the gun and put it into his hand. Suddenly he appeared as if concentrated rage had restored him to double vigor; he leveled his piece, fired, and with a loud shriek down fell the wretch whom he had fostered in his bosom.

The shock causes Krantz to swoon, but when he recovers he is astonished to find that, instead of the body of his wife, the lifeless form lying over the mangled remains of his daughter's corpse is that of a huge white she-wolf. At last the scales fall from his eyes, and he realizes that all along he has been the victim of supernatural manipulation by dark forces inimical to mankind. The story concludes in the same grim fashion with Krantz and his eldest son both meeting horrible deaths after vainly trying to escape the wrath of the vengeful spirits.

Still popular today, this influential tale established a pattern for werewolf stories for the remainder of the nineteenth century, and variations on the climactic sequence where Christina is mortally wounded then changes into a wolf after death have appeared with undiminished regularity ever since, although it is usually considered more dramatic if the transformation occurs the opposite way around. The other innovative feature of "The Werewolf" was the introduction of an erotic element into the story by portraying the werewolf as a beautiful, alluring young woman. This innovation was also much imitated and subsequently became a staple of the werewolf genre.

A minor story from the same period is the anonymously written "The Wehr Wolf" (1833), about which little is known save that it was published in a long-forgotten magazine called *The Story-teller, or Journal of Fiction*. Another obscure periodical, *Hogg's Weekly Instructor*, carried Catherine Crowe's "A Story of a Weir-Wolf" (1846), which has also never been reprinted. However, according to the summary of this short story in Montague Summers's *The Werewolf*, the locale is a village of Auvergne in France in the late sixteenth century. The heroine, Francoise Thilouze, is falsely accused of witchcraft and of being a werewolf, and she and her father are condemned to be burned at the stake. Fortunately, they are reprieved at the last moment, and Francoise subsequently weds a young nobleman who secures her a pardon from the king. Summers, whose judgment was usually sound, describes this story as "a well-told and interesting narrative."

Crowe was considered to be an authority on the supernatural, and her compilations of ghost lore and legends enjoyed considerable popularity among Victorian readers. One of her best-known works, *Light and Darkness; or, Mysteries of Life* (1850), includes a chapter titled "The Lycanthropist," which is based on a report of the judicial investigations into a series of atrocities committed by a young French soldier, Sergeant François Bertrand, who was in the habit of digging up corpses from cemeteries in and around Paris and devouring the decaying flesh like a ghoul.

The first novel to have a werewolf as its principal character was George W. M. Reynolds's sprawling Gothic melodrama *Wagner, the Wehr-Wolf.* Based on the Faust legend and set in various exotic locales in Renaissance Europe, it catalogs the incredible adventures that befall Fernand Wagner, a feeble ninety-year-old shepherd, after he enters into a pact with the Devil. In return for a year's bondage, he is promised permanent rejuvenation, inexhaustible wealth, and increased intellectual powers. There is, however, an additional clause in the contract: it stipulates that for one day each month he must become a ravening werewolf. Undeterred by this prospect, Wagner willingly accepts the Devil's bargain and proceeds to take full advantage of his renewed youth and vigor by romancing a string of rich and beautiful women, as well as becoming involved in many violent and bloody escapades during those periods when he becomes a werewolf. On one occasion he is arrested in Florence by the officers of the Inquisition but uses his power to metamorphose into a wolf to make good his escape, leaving a trail of death and destruction in his wake. In another episode he is shipwrecked on an uninhabited island with his lover, the captivating Nisida, as his sole companion. She is unaware of Wagner's terrible secret, and to maintain her ignorance he has to climb over the mountains in the middle of the island every month so he can rage harmlessly on the other side. Again the Devil tries to tempt his reluctant bond-slave, thrice offering to help him out of his predicament if he will sell his soul. But Wagner will not yield, and the curse is eventually lifted after he is shown a way to achieve salvation by the venerable, semi-immortal Rosicrucian, Christian Rosenkreutz. Immediately after the curse is removed Wagner ages rapidly, undergoing a gruesome dissolution until his body is reduced to a lifeless husk.

Prior to its appearance in book form, *Wagner, the Wehr-Wolf* was serialized in *Reynolds's Miscellany,* commencing on November 6, 1846, and running until July 24, 1847. Interminably long and padded out with various subplots and other digressions, this novel is a prime example of the "penny blood," a term used in England during the 1840s to describe cheap, sensational fiction in its most extravagant form. Reynolds was acknowledged as the finest practitioner of this type of mass-produced literature and was possibly more widely read in his lifetime than Charles Dickens or other major novelists of the mid-nineteenth century. His writing style is distinguished by its vitality and unflagging enthusiasm but has little else worthy of commendation. Nonetheless, in *Wagner*, Reynolds compensates to some extent for any stylistic shortcomings by his lively imagination and enviable powers of invention as he weaves a tangled web of plot and counterplot, while at the same time keeping the action going with a welter of chases and escapes. The following extract—one of many transformation scenes—is typical of the novel's florid style:

> The young man, handsome and splendidly attired, has thrown himself upon the ground, where he writhes like a stricken serpent. He is the prey of a demoniac excitement; an appalling consternation is on him . . . madness is in his brain . . . his mind is on fire. Lightnings appear to gleam from his eyes . . . as if his soul were dismayed, and withering within his breast.
>
> Oh no! . . . No! he cries, with a piercing shriek, as if wrestling madly, furiously, but vainly, against some unseen fiend that holds him in his grasp. And the wood echoes to that terrible wail, and the startled bird flies fluttering from its bough. But lo! What awful change is taking place in the form of that doomed being? His handsome countenance elongates into one of a savage and brute-like shape; the rich garment which he wears becomes a rough, shaggy and wiry skin; his body loses its human contours, his arms and limbs take another form, and, with a frantic howl of misery, to which the woods give horribly faithful reverberations, and with a rush like a hurling wind, the wretch starts wildly away . . . no longer a man, but a monstrous wolf!

Although superior to the general run of these lurid thrillers—and, incidentally, one of the few "bloods" still obtainable today—*Wagner, the Wehr-Wolf* is nonetheless a crude, hastily written potboiler of negligible literary merit, and it should be mentioned that most readers today would find it a great struggle to wade through its seventy-seven chapters. However, for those undaunted by this prospect, the 1975 edition by Dover Press is definitely the best of the modern reprints.

A pact with the Devil also forms the basis for Alexandre Dumas's *The Wolf-Leader* (1857). An episodic historical romance that also utilizes the Faust motif, the tale is set in the late eighteenth century just prior to the French Revolution. The central character is Thibault, a handsome young shoemaker with ideas above his station, who lives a lonely existence on the estate of the tyrannical Baron de Vez. At odds with the nobleman after he is severely beaten for poaching, Thibault vows to gain his revenge and rashly invokes the Devil's aid. His prayers are answered when the archfiend's agent appears before him in the guise of a great black wolf with the power of speech. This results in a bargain being struck, whereby the shoemaker is granted his every wish in return for hairs from his head—one for the first wish, two for the second, four for the third, and so on, doubling the number of hairs for each wish granted. At first, Thibault regards this as a fair trade but soon discovers, to his horror, that the hairs, instead of disappearing, turn blood-red, branding him as one of the Devil's own. As his problems mount up, Thibault realizes, too late, that the magical powers he has acquired only make his life a misery. Eventually, after causing the death of his sweetheart and failing to get revenge on the baron, he becomes an outlaw in the forest, accompanied by a pack of wolves who do his bidding.

When all but one of the hairs on his head have been claimed by the Devil's color, Thibault realizes he is a lost soul and agrees to a new compact with his Satanic master, which involves taking the Black Wolf's place in return for vast wealth and dominion over all his fellow creatures. The Devil's agent explains that once Thibault has become a werewolf he will be virtually invulnerable; only once a year will he run the risk of death, when for twenty-four hours he will be subject to injury like any other living creature. Ironically, the day this proviso comes into effect he is chased by the baron's hounds and nearly torn to pieces. Salvation finally comes when Thibault encounters the funeral procession of his sweetheart, and in a moment of remorse wishes that he could sacrifice himself to bring her back to life. Through divine intervention this last wish is granted, and the repentant werewolf forfeits his life.

The first English translation of *The Wolf-Leader* was made in 1904, and a revised edition edited by L. Sprague de Camp was published by Prime Press in 1950. To be honest, this is not one of Dumas's major works, and anyone expecting something on the same level as *The Count of Monte Cristo* is bound to be disappointed.

That's not to say it is badly written—it just lacks the action and thrills one normally associates with this author.

One of the few whimsical werewolf tales from the Victorian era is Dudley Costello's "Lycanthropy in London; or, The Wehr-Wolf of Wilton Crescent," which was published in *Bentley's Miscellany* in 1855. In a brief reference to it in *The Werewolf*, Montague Summers describes the story as being "told with a sense of humour and brio that seem to be a particular Victorian quality for which we may look in vain today." Unfortunately, since there is no record of this story ever appearing in book form, it has to be regarded as another "lost" werewolf yarn.

A similar fate seems to have overtaken Mrs. Richard S. Greenough's "Monare," which has also slipped into an undeserved obscurity. One of four novelettes in her extremely rare collection *Arabesques: Monare, Apollyona, Domitia, Ombra* (1872), it chronicles the adventures of a medieval knight who embarks on a perilous quest to rescue a maiden held captive in Islam. Along the way he gets into a fight with a werewolf; and, after killing the monster, uses its blood to reanimate its victims.

An early example of the psychological werewolf story is "The Man-Wolf" by two writers from Alsace, Emile Erckmann and Alexandre Chatrian, who used the combined pen-name Erckmann-Chatrian on all their collaborations. Set in and around an ancient Black Forest castle, this novella centers on the strange bond between Count Von Nideck and a horrible old hag known as the Black Plague. The reader observes the unraveling mystery through the eyes of a young doctor, summoned to attend the count, who finds on his arrival that his patient is not only suffering from a most unusual complaint but also one that occurs with uncanny regularity. Every year, on the same day, at the same hour, the count foams at the mouth, his eyes bulge from their sockets; he shakes from head to foot and gnashes his teeth. The condition lasts for up to two weeks, during which the nobleman's countenance takes on a wolflike appearance. In one eerie scene fearful sounds awake the entire castle, and the count is found in his bedroom crouching on all fours and uttering loud, protracted howls.

The other main participant in the drama, the mysterious old woman, is seen in the vicinity of the castle only during the count's seizures and, for a time, is suspected of causing them. However, it eventually transpires that the lycanthropic madness afflicts both protagonists, and is caused by a hereditary curse passed down to them by a common ancestor, Hugh the Wolf, whose wife was a werewolf. A tragic outcome seems inevitable, but the sudden death of the old hag leads to the count's recovery and the lifting of the thousand-year-old curse.

"Hugues-le-Loup," to give the story its French title, was originally published in France in 1860. The first English translation was made in 1876 for *The Man-Wolf and Other Tales,* which was reprinted by Arno Press in 1976. The same story can also be found in *The Man-Wolf and Other Horrors* (1978) and *The Best Tales of Terror of Erckmann-Chatrian* (1981). In view of its popularity one might suppose that "The Man-Wolf" is a classic of its kind; on the contrary, its pedestrian pacing and lack of any really hair-raising moments considerably reduce its effectiveness.

A more realistic study of lycanthropic madness from the pen of a Continental author is "Le Loup" (1884) by Guy de Maupassant, in which the central character displays all the bestiality of a wolf without actually assuming the form of one. The title most often used in English translations is "The Wolf."

A phenomenon of the Victorian era in Great Britain was the rise to prominence of women writers, many of whom showed a great facility for fashioning tales of terror. One such "gentlewoman of evil" was The Hon. Mrs. Greene, who in 1885 wrote the neo-Gothic novel *Bound by a Spell; or, The Hunted Witch of the Forest,* in which there is a noted werewolf sequence.

The suspected witch, Christine Delemont, lives in a deserted cottage with her infant son. She is accused by the superstitious country folk of many terrible deeds and is also suspected of being in league with a werewolf after an incident involving a local farm laborer named Sylvestro. Staggering into town one hot summer's day, his shirt stained with gore and his sickle covered in blood, he tells the crowd that gathers around him that he had seen a wolf, "dark, large, and terrible to look at," dash from the witch's cottage with her child in its jaws. As it ran off into the woods, he had bravely given chase, and by doubling back on the four-legged kidnapper had come, for a moment, face to face with the brute:

> It turned, the great coward, as I drew my sickle from my belt, and fearing to meet me, it leaped over a low bush and made back with haste across the wooden bridge towards the house. I saw then what I had to deal with—no common brute such as God himself places in the forest, but one of those tailless monsters whose existence until now I had never believed in: a wicked werewolf, with slinking steps, whose every movement filled me with disgust. Full of some strange and ever-increasing strength, I followed after it, gaining each moment on its track, though it hurried forward with ever longer and more sinuous steps. At last, driven as it were almost to bay, it took the direct path towards the cottage, and, slinking through the narrow garden gate, passed in. At once I saw my advantage; I closed the gate with a sudden click that sent the hasp straight into the lock, and then, unless it dashed in at the open housedoor, it had no hole or possible outlet for escape. Round and round the garden I hunted it, my sharp sickle ever in my outstretched arm, until at last, with a kind of crying snarl, it dropped the child from its blood-stained jaws, and, turning with a sudden fury towards me, it sprang forward to meet me. It was its last hope, its last chance for life, and verily I gave myself up for lost; but seeing the child lie in a white heap on the gravel path, the same infant which had stood before me so lately in its purity and love, I thought of Him who carries the little lambs in His

bosom, and though the beast leaped on me, and as it were wrestled with me, and though I felt its jaws snap on my shoulder and its claws tear the flesh from my arm, still the good God guided the weapon in my hand so that I struck it right home to its craven heart, and with a kind of human cry it fell backwards upon the flower-beds behind us, and then rolled over on its side, dead.

To the astonishment of his audience, Sylvestro then describes how Christine Delemont suddenly rushed out of the cottage, and without any word or gesture of thanks picked up her son and hurriedly carried him indoors, adamantly refusing further help. Hearing this, some women in the crowd are quick to interpret the witch-woman's ingratitude as further proof of her wickedness. However, it emerges later on in the story that Christine is not the fiend people think she is but is possessed by an evil spirit, which had bound her to the werewolf against her will.

From Stevenson to Stenbock: Victorian Classics

A popular motif in Victorian supernatural fiction was the transformation, either physically or morally, of a respectable person into an evil, rapacious monster, such as occurs in Robert Louis Stevenson's celebrated dual-personality novel *The Strange Case of Dr. Jekyll and Mr. Hyde* (1886). This is not, strictly speaking, a werewolf story (the transformation being from one person into another rather than into a wolf or other ferocious animal), but there are undoubtedly many similarities between the squat, hairy Edward Hyde and the typical lycanthrope. The personification of the dark "other self" lurking within every man, Hyde is destructive, libidinous, and totally intoxicated with his own brutishness. He may not physically resemble a werewolf, but, nonetheless, the Mark of the Beast is indelibly stamped upon his face.

In common with other stories with a man-into-beast theme, *Jekyll and Hyde* concerns the conflict between good and evil going on inside the central character. In this instance, Dr. Henry Jekyll, a respected physician of great ability and probity, discovers a drug that will dissociate his personality, permitting his normally suppressed evil side to temporarily assume control of his mind and body, with the inevitable spiritual and material changes that this entails. For a while the two personalities alternate until, too late, Jekyll realizes that his malevolent alter ego is becoming the dominant personality. Finally, when his transformation into the monstrous Hyde begins to occur involuntarily, Jekyll realizes that he cannot avert the disastrous consequences of his foolhardy experiment and takes the only course of action open to him—self destruction.

Like many writers in the horror field, Stevenson was fascinated by the dual nature of humanity and used the "evil double" motif more than once. The basis for *Jekyll and Hyde* is the Darwinian notion that man is a descendant of the beasts and has a bestial inheritance within him, which he must learn to sublimate and restrain if order and reason are to prevail. By using the device of a chemical potion to effect the transformation, Stevenson suggests that the monster within us is waiting for the right catalyst to set it loose, so it can wreak havoc on those who seek to suppress it and place it in hiding. The physical change that occurs when the evil counterpart emerges indicates that Stevenson also subscribed to the theory that the body is the projection of the spirit, and that if one separates out the baser component of the spirit and allows it to become dominant, the body will reflect the change.

The popular view among literary critics is that *Jekyll and Hyde* is an allegory of the ordered conscious mind struggling with the violent unconscious for dominance, or what psychoanalysts describe as a battle between the superego and the id. It has also been suggested that, on another level, it was meant as an allegory of hypocritical Victorian society, which as we now know appeared respectable on the outside but was corrupt on the inside. Looked at from this standpoint, Jekyll represents reason and propriety, while Hyde, his hidden side, stands for lawlessness and depravity. Whatever the underlying meaning may be, most critics agree that this novel is one of the great masterpieces of macabre literature—one that leaves the reader in no doubt about the strength and ultimate triumph of evil once it is let loose.

Stevenson also utilized the werewolf motif in "Olalla" (1885), a superb novelette concerning the terrifying experiences of a wounded English officer convalescing at the home of a noble but impoverished Spanish family—a strange trio comprised of Felipe, the half-witted son; Olalla, the saintly daughter; and Doña Fernanda, the voluptuous and languid creature who is their mother. Forewarned about their aloofness, the Englishman has little contact with them at first but soon becomes aware of a brooding mystery pervading the *residencia* of his reluctant hosts. His unease grows when he hears bloodcurdling cries in the night but receives only evasive and unsatisfactory explanations when he questions Olalla and Felipe about the matter. The story reaches its dramatic climax when the young officer accidentally cuts himself and, not realizing the danger, shows the bleeding wounds to Doña Fernanda.

> Her great eyes opened wide, the pupils shrank into points; a veil seemed to fall from her face, and leave it sharply expressive and yet inscrutable. And as I stood still, marveling a little at her disturbance, she came swiftly up to me, and stooped and caught me by the hand, and the next moment my hand was to her mouth, and she had bitten me to the bone. The pang of the bite, the sudden spurting of blood, and the monstrous horror of the act flashed through me all in one, and I beat back; and she sprang at me again and again, with bestial cries, cries that I recognized, such cries as had awakened me on the night of the high wind. Her strength was like that of a madness; mine was rapidly ebbing with the loss of blood;

my mind besides was whirling with the abhorrent strangeness of the onslaught, and I was already forced against the wall, when Olalla ran between us, and Felipe, following at a bound, pinned down his mother on the floor.

The full horror of the situation is later revealed when Olalla confides to the wounded officer that her mother's violent behavior is triggered by a form of hereditary lycanthropy, and that she and her brother are also blighted by tainted blood passed down by previous generations.

Apart from the intensity of atmosphere, what makes "Olalla" such a brilliant story is the naturalistic manner in which the shocking events are depicted. In *The Supernatural in Fiction* (1952), Peter Penzoldt points to the author's penetrating knowledge of psychology, describing "Olalla" as "the first story in literature in which a case of insanity is not only correctly described but is also correctly diagnosed." This, he argues, makes it "probably the most convincing werewolf story there is."

By the late 1880s all the familiar elements of the werewolf story had been introduced, and for the next few decades there was an extensive repetition of plot devices and even a lingering impulse toward Gothicism. Typifying this old-fashioned approach is Sir Gilbert Campbell's "The White Wolf of Kostopchin" (*Wild and Weird*, 1889), which has similarities with Frederick Marryat's classic published fifty years earlier.

The story is set on the estate of Paul Sergevitch, where the discovery of the mutilated bodies of three serfs, each with the throat torn out, forces the young Russian nobleman to organize a search for the suspected perpetrator—a white she-wolf. Beaters sent to scour the surrounding woods eventually succeed in cornering their quarry in a thicket; but when they close in for the kill they are surprised to hear the sound of a human voice coming from the bushes imploring them not to shoot, followed by the sudden emergence of a young woman wrapped in a mantle of soft white fur. Exquisitely beautiful, with long Titian-red hair hanging in disheveled masses over her shoulders, she coolly tells the men surrounding her that the wolf they are pursuing had only moments before rushed past her and gone to ground in the center of the thicket, but when a search is made no trace of the beast can be found. This arouses suspicions about the woman among the beaters, but the gullible landowner, who has always had a weakness for a pretty face, is completely taken in by the stranger's story and invites her back to his residence at Kostopchin. There is a mixed reception for the newcomer from the lord's two motherless children, Alexis and Katrina: the boy takes an instant dislike to her, but his little sister is won over by the woman's soothing words. Naturally, Sergevitch is curious to know more about his mysterious guest, but all she is prepared to tell him is that her name is Ravina, and that she is a fugitive from the police.

Despite his guest's unusual behavior—refusing all food set before her and remaining locked in her room during the daylight hours—Paul soon finds himself falling in love, and it is not long before he asks her to become his wife. In reply, Ravina asks for a few weeks to consider his proposal, promising to give him her answer at a midnight rendezvous on the grounds of the estate. At the appointed hour the love-sick nobleman impatiently asks Ravina for her decision, to which she replies cryptically: "Do you give me your whole heart?" When he passionately responds "Yes, my heart is yours," she suddenly springs upon him with savage fury, knocking him to the ground.

> It was then that the full horror of his position came upon Paul Sergevitch, and he saw his fate clearly before him, but a terrible numbness prevented him from using his hands to free himself from the hideous embrace which was paralysing all his muscles. The face that was glaring into his seemed to be undergoing some fearful change, and the features to be losing their semblance of humanity. With a sudden, quick movement, she tore open his garments, and in another movement she had perforated his left breast with a ghastly wound, and, plunging in her delicate hands, tore out his heart and bit at it ravenously. Intent upon her hideous banquet she heeded not the convulsive struggles which agitated the dying form of the lord of Kostopchin. She was too much occupied to notice a diminutive form approaching, sheltering itself behind every tree and bush until it had arrived within ten paces of the scene of the terrible tragedy. Then the moonbeams

glistened upon the long shining barrel of a pistol, which the boy was leveling with both hands at the murderer. Then quick and sharp rang out the report, and with a wild shriek, in which there was something beast-like, Ravina leaped from the body of the dead man and staggered away to a thick clump of bushes some ten paces distant. The boy Alexis had heard the appointment that had been made, and dogged his father's footsteps to the trysting-place. After firing the fatal shot his courage had deserted him, and he fled backwards to the house, uttering loud shrieks for help. The startled servants were soon in the presence of their slaughtered master, but aid was of no avail, for the lord of Kostopchin had passed away. With fear and trembling the superstitious peasants searched the clump of bushes, and started back in horror as they perceived a huge white wolf, lying stark and dead, with a half-devoured human heart clasped between its forepaws.

The ironic ending of "The White Wolf of Kostopchin" is neatly handled, helping to make it one of the most enjoyable stories from the heyday of the old-fashioned werewolf yarn. On reflection it seems a pity that Hammer Films never got around to filming it, because the storyline and old-world setting are perfect for the type of horror movies associated with this famous British studio.

Arthur Conan Doyle, now chiefly remembered as the creator of the immortal Sherlock Holmes, also produced a number of excellent horror stories early in his career. One that seems to have escaped the attention of anthologists is "A Pastoral Horror" (1890), in which a seemingly devout priest is revealed as the perpetrator of a series of horrific murders, committed during fits of lycanthropic madness.

A superb story about metempsychosis (the transmigration of souls) that is often classified as belonging to the werewolf canon is Rudyard Kipling's "The Mark of the Beast" (*Life's Handicap*, 1891). Set in India, it describes the misfortunes that befall an Englishman after he gets drunk on New Year's Eve and desecrates a Hindu temple by grinding the ashes of his cigar butt into the stone image of Hanuman, the monkey-god. In revenge, a leper priest puts a curse on him, causing a beast's soul to take possession of his body. A vivid description of the victim's gradual transformation into a wolf culminates in the final harrowing scene, when the Hindu priest is compelled by torture to lift the curse.

Human transformation into members of the cat family—especially the big cats like tigers and leopards—is another popular variant on the shapeshifting theme. One of the strangest stories in this category is "The Eyes of the Panther" by Ambrose Bierce, from his collection of short stories *In the Midst of Life* (1898). Concerning an unusual form of possession, it has as its setting the wilds of North America in the days when small communities of settlers lived in isolated cabins surrounded by vast forests infested with wild animals. A young woman living among these hardy folk confides to a would-be suitor that shortly before she was born her mother (who died giving birth to her) was "marked" by a panther, which had stared at her through the cabin window until she went insane with fear. As a result of this incident the dead woman's daughter is doomed to become a panther at night, terrifying other settlers by peering into their windows. These nocturnal prowlings are finally terminated when the girl is shot dead.

The classic werewolf tale of the late nineteenth century is undoubtedly Clemence Housman's novelette "The Were-Wolf," which has met with critical acclaim ever since its first appearance in book form in 1896. Told in a pseudoarchaic, heavily rhythmic prose and set against the bleak, snow-covered landscape of medieval Scandinavia, the tale recounts the tragic events that occur after evil—in its most alluring form—is innocently invited into the home of simple, god-fearing folk.

One cold winter's evening as the occupants of a great farmhouse are busy with their household tasks, a ghostly voice pleads for admittance on three separate occasions, but each time that Sweyn—the boldest of those present—opens the door to investigate, there is no one there. Later that night, after another knock is heard, a fur-clad young woman is found on the doorstep seeking shelter for the night; but no sooner has she stepped over the threshold than she is viciously attacked by Tyr, the wolfhound. Reacting swiftly, the girl lithely evades the dog's sharp fangs and in the same movement snatches from her girdle a small two-edged axe, which she would have used in her defense had not Sweyn forcibly dragged the snarling beast away.

Sweyn, a mighty hunter, is impressed by the woman's strength and agility, and discovers, when she loosens the furs about her face, that she is also stunningly beautiful. His apology for such an unfriendly reception is accepted by the stranger, who reveals that her name is White Fell, and that she has traveled for many leagues across hostile territory to visit distant relatives. Sweyn marvels that she has undertaken such a dangerous journey alone, but White Fell, proud and independent, boasts that she fears neither man nor beast, and adds that a few fear her.

Sweyn's twin brother, Christian, who has been absent all day, observes on his return home that there are wolf tracks leading up to the door of the homestead but none going away. When he goes inside he sees the beautiful stranger and knows intuitively that she is a werewolf. Christian warns his brother about his suspicions, but Sweyn, who is enamored of White Fell, just laughs and mocks his twin for believing in old wives' tales. Even when two much-loved members of the family, Rol and Trella, are mysteriously abducted and never seen alive again, Sweyn stubbornly refuses to believe that White Fell has had any part in their disappearance. His refusal to accept the possibility of the supernatural materialized is based on his belief that no living beast could ever be other than palpably bestial. The wild and fearful legends whose veracity he blindly accepted as a child now seem to him to be built upon distorted facts, overlaid by imagination. In contrast, Christian feels that all life is a spiritual mystery, veiled from full understanding by the density of flesh. He therefore finds it no great effort to believe that White Fell is a Thing of Evil cloaked in womanly beauty, and he sets about converting other members of the family to his point of view. Most telling is his charge that the missing pair had both received a kiss from White Fell, the significance of which is not lost on those present who are familiar with their country's legends about werewolves. Predictably, Christian's actions—which include a failed attempt to throw holy water over the suspected werewolf—bring him into conflict with his brother; but when blows are exchanged, Sweyn, the stronger of the two, prevails.

Matters reach a head when Christian catches Sweyn in a passionate embrace with White Fell and, realizing that his brother is the next one marked for death, resolves to destroy the werewolf before she can claim another victim. Learning of Christian's intentions, White Fell attempts to escape, and a dramatic chase across the snowy wastes ensues. A key factor in the outcome is Christian's fleetness of foot:

> Never before had Christian so rejoiced in his powers. The gift of speed, and the training of use and endurance were priceless to him now. Though midnight was hours away, he was confident that, go where that Fell Thing would, hasten as she would, she

could not outstrip him nor escape from him. Then, when came the time for transformation, when the woman's form made no longer a shield against a man's hand, he could slay or be slain to save Sweyn. He had struck his dear brother in dire extremity, but he could not, though reason urged, strike a woman.

For one mile, for two miles they ran: White Fell ever foremost, Christian ever at equal distance from her side, so near that, now and again, her out-flying furs touched him. She spoke no word, nor he. She never turned her head to look at him, nor swerved to evade him; but, with set face looking forward, sped straight on, over rough, over smooth, aware of his nearness by the regular beat of his feet, and the sound of his breath behind.

In a while she quickened her pace. From the first, Christian had judged of her speed as admirable, yet with exulting security in his own excelling and enduring whatever her efforts. But, when the pace increased, he found himself put to the test as never had he been before in any race. Her feet, indeed, flew faster than his; it was only by the length of stride that he kept his place at her side. But his heart was high and resolute, and he did not fear failure yet.

So the desperate race flew on . . . White Fell held on without slack. She, it was evident, with confidence in her speed proving matchless, as resolute to out-run her pursuer as he to endure till midnight and fulfill his purpose. And Christian held on, still self-assured. He could not fail; he would not fail. To avenge Rol and Trella was motive enough for him to do what man could do; but for Sweyn more. She had kissed Sweyn, but he should not die too: with Sweyn to save he could not fail.

On and on they race, until at length the relentless pace begins to take its toll on Christian; and from then on it is only his indomitable will that keeps him going. His resolve is further tested when a blow from White Fell's axe shatters the bones in his left hand, making him drop his spear; later another blow renders his right arm powerless. As the pain becomes almost unbearable, he begins to hallucinate and imagines that the trees and snow-covered mounds take on grotesque forms and join in the chase.

As the midnight hour rapidly approaches, White Fell seems likely to triumph when an escape route suddenly comes into view, but with one last desperate effort Christian surges past her and turns, defiantly barring the way:

> She came hurling desperate, with a feint to the right hand, and then launched herself upon him with a spring like a wild beast when it leaps to kill. And he with one strong arm and a hand that could not hold, and one strong hand and an arm that could not guide and sustain, he caught and held her even so. And they fell together. And because he felt his whole arm slipping, and his whole hand loosing, to slack the dreadful agony of the wrenched bone above, he caught and held with his teeth the tunic at her knee, as she struggled up and wrung off his hands to overleap him victorious.
>
> Like lightning she snatched her axe, and struck him on the neck, deep—once, twice—his life-blood gushed out staining her feet.
>
> The stars touched midnight.

The death scream he heard was not his, for his set teeth had hardly yet relaxed when it rang out; and the dreadful cry began with a woman's shriek, and changed and ended as the yell of a beast. And before the final blank overtook his dying eyes, he saw that She gave place to It; he saw more, that Life gave place to Death—causelessly, incomprehensibly.

For he did not presume that no holy water could be more holy, more potent to destroy an evil thing than the life-blood of a pure heart poured out for another in willing devotion.

The following morning, when Sweyn follows the tracks made by the two implacable adversaries, he finds Christian's frozen corpse with the arms rigidly outstretched in the shape of a cross, and beside him is the carcass of a great white she-wolf. Now, at last, Sweyn realizes that White Fell was, after all, the dreadful creature that his brother had claimed her to be, and that Christian had selflessly sacrificed his life in order to save him from a similar fate.

Although clearly intended as a Christian allegory, with the salvation-through-love motif predominant, the sheer beauty of the prose and the author's considerable gifts as a storyteller ensure that "The Were-Wolf" is much more than a moralistic tale. In his introduction to this story in *Masters of Horror* (1968), fantasy historian Sam Moskowitz expressed the opinion that "it may quite likely be the single greatest work of fiction yet written on the theme of lycanthropy . . . so like pure poetry that it carries the reader with dramatic intensity toward an ultimate horror that threatens both body and spirit." Other anthologies that have reprinted this story include *Book of the Werewolf* (1973), edited by Brian J. Frost, and *Barbarians* (1986), edited by Robert Adams, Martin H. Greenberg, and Charles G. Waugh.

Another story rooted in Norse mythology is Eugene Field's "The Werewolf" (*The Second Book of Tales,* 1896), whose hero, a handsome youth named Harold, periodically metamorphoses into a wolf as a result of a hereditary curse. In a cruel twist of fate he is mortally wounded in his beast form by a magic spear thrown by his sweetheart, who is unaware that she has caused the death of the man she loves until his body is later found with an identical wound.

Some of the best supernatural stories from the Victorian era were originally published in periodicals. The June 1893 issue of *The Spirit Lamp,* for instance, carried the dreamlike werewolf tale "The Other Side" by Count Eric Stenbock. Based on an old Breton legend, it features a lycanthropous brook, bounded by a village on one side and a dark, shadowy domain on the other. None of the villagers dares cross to the "other side" because it is reputed to be inhabited by werewolves. One moonlit evening the story's hero, a boy called Gabriel, is wandering by the brook when he sees a large deep blue flower on the opposite bank, hanging over the water. Its strong intoxicating perfume fills him with an irresistible desire to pluck it and, ignoring the warnings of his elders, he leaps over the brook into the mysterious realm beyond:

> Then the moon breaking from a cloud shone with unusual brilliance, and he saw, stretching before him, long reaches of strange blue flowers each one lovelier than the last, till, not being able to make up his mind which one flower to take or whether to take several, he went on and on, and the moon shone very brightly, and a strange unseen bird, somewhat like a nightingale, but louder and lovelier, sang, and his heart was filled with longing for he knew not what, and the moon shone and the nightingale sang. But on a sudden a black cloud covered the moon entirely, and all was black, utter darkness, and through the darkness he heard wolves howling and shrieking in the hideous ardour of the chase, and there passed before him a horrible procession of wolves (black wolves with red fiery eyes), and with them men that had the heads of wolves and wolves that had the heads of men, and above them flew owls (black owls with red fiery eyes), and bats and long serpentine black things, and last of all seated on an enormous black ram with hideous human face the wolf-keeper on whose face was eternal shadow; but they continued their horrid chase and passed by him, and when they had passed the moon shone out more beautiful than ever, and the strange nightingale sang again, and the strange intense blue flowers were in long reaches in front to the right and to the left. But one thing was there which had not been before, among the deep blue

flowers walked one with long gleaming golden hair, and she turned once round and her eyes were of the same color as the strange blue flowers, and she walked on and Gabriel could not choose but follow. But when a cloud passed over the moon he saw no beautiful woman but a wolf, so in utter terror he turned and fled, plucking one of the strange blue flowers on the way, and leapt again over the brook and ran home.

Despite his nightmarish experiences, Gabriel cannot get the wolf-woman out of his mind; one night he returns with her to the "other side," where he spends his days in languid contentment, his will subjugated and his vitality sapped by a drug made from the blue flowers. At length, Gabriel realizes what is happening to him and tries to return home, only to discover, when he sees his reflection in the brook, that he has been transformed into a wolf. He is eventually restored to his human form by the local priest, who is instrumental in bringing about the destruction of the "other side" and all its denizens.

The author of this strangely beautiful tale was a Russian nobleman living in England, and his chief claim to fame is as the author of a handful of short stories dealing with witchcraft and diabolism, the best of which were collected in *Studies of Death* (1894). Literary biographers describe Stenbock as an eccentric homosexual whose obsession with the dark side of life eventually brought on bouts of madness. This gave him such an evil disposition that another *fin de siècle* author, Arthur Symons, once described Stenbock as "one of the most inhuman beings I have ever encountered." Inevitably the count's dissolute lifestyle finally caught up with him, and he died prematurely, at the age of thirty-five.

Two other stories from the final decade of the nineteenth century are H. Beaugrand's "The Werwolves" (1898) and Eden Phillpotts's "Loup Garou!" (1899). The earlier story, which takes place in eighteenth-century Canada, concerns a scary incident witnessed by an old trapper, who claims to have come across a group of Indians with heads and tails like wolves, dancing around a campfire. In contrast, Phillpotts's story is set on the West Indian island of Dominica, where loups-garous and jumbies are much feared by the native population. Disappointingly, it turns out to be an improbable tale of subterfuge, in which the villain dons the disguise of a werewolf in an effort to scare off a rival claimant to the family fortune.

The only novel from this period with a significant werewolf element is S. R. Crockett's historical romance *The Black Douglas* (1899). A tale of political intrigue and black magic in the fifteenth century, it begins with the betrayal of William, Earl of Douglas, the most powerful man in Scotland, who is lured to his death in Edinburgh castle by a French witch called La Meffraye. William's sister and her companion, Lady Maud, are subsequently kidnapped on the orders of the infamous necromancer Gilles de Retz and taken to his estate in France, where he and the witch-woman command a pack of werewolves. La Meffraye also has shapeshifting powers and alternates between her human form and that of a huge shaggy she-wolf called Astarte. When not slinking around the castle in her beast form, she procures children for sacrifice at de Retz's Black Masses, through which he seeks to obtain perpetual youth. The young Scotswomen are saved from a similar fate when members of the Douglas clan make a successful bid to rescue them, vanquishing the werewolves and killing the witch-woman in the process. In his day, Crockett was regarded as "the British Alexandre Dumas," but on the evidence of this tepid novel he was only a pale imitation of the original.

One other piece from the nineteenth century worth a brief mention is Graham R. Tomson's "A Ballad of the Were-wolf," a grim poem in broad Scots dialect about the severing of a werewolf's hand. Originally published in *Macmillan's Magazine*, September 1890, it was reprinted in 1970 in the paperback anthology *Demon Lovers*, edited by Lucy Berman.

These, then, are the known works of fiction from the nineteenth century with a werewolf motif. Regrettably, there are many minor stories—perhaps even a few gems—that have been lost, and we can only hope that the small band of dedicated researchers currently delving into obscure periodicals and chapbooks will eventually unearth some of these.

Tales from the Edwardian Era and the 1920s

Werewolf stories from the early years of the twentieth century are generally similar in style and structure to those produced during the last two decades of the nineteenth century. One of the best known, Commander F. G. Loring's "The Tomb of Sarah," from the December 1900 issue of *Pall Mall Magazine,* tells of a dead vampiress who recommences her nocturnal attacks on the living in the form of a wolf after workmen disturb her tomb. Two other specimens of the form from long-defunct British periodicals are Fred Whishaw's "The Were-Wolf," a story based on Russian folklore from the November 1902 issue of *Temple Bar,* in which a roguish cowherd pretends to be the victim of a curse placed on him by the spirits of the forest in order to cover up his nefarious activities; and Alan Sullivan's "Loup Garou" (*Windsor Magazine,* July 1905), which is set in the wilds of Canada. All three stories provide first-rate entertainment for those who enjoy storytelling of the good, old-fashioned kind.

Barry Pain, whose literary output in the Edwardian era included satirical novels as well as several collections of weird stories, made a memorable contribution to the werewolf canon with his short story "The Undying Thing" (*Stories in the Dark,* 1901). Creating and sustaining a mood of inevitable and deadly menace, it concerns the plight of an aristocratic family faced with imminent extinction due to the fulfillment of an eighteenth-century ancestral curse. A baby born to the wife of one of their ancestors, the wicked Sir Edric Vanquerest, was prenatally marked after its pregnant mother was frightened by a pack of wolves kept by her husband. The child was then abandoned in nearby woods after the sudden death of its mother, and by some mysterious process metamorphosed into a deathless were-creature. A century and a half later the moment has come when it will have its desire for retribution fulfilled. Considered fresh at the time, the plot has since become hackneyed through repeated use.

In another top-notch story from this period, Algernon Blackwood's "The Camp of the Dog" (*John Silence, Physician Extraordinary,* 1908), a mixed party of campers spending their summer vacation on an idyllic island wilderness in Sweden gets the jitters when their sleep is repeatedly disturbed by the nocturnal prowlings of a large, unidentified beast. To solve the mystery the leader of the party sends for John Silence, a noted psychic detective, whose investigations lead him to the conclusion that Peter Sangree, a Canadian member of the group, is the source of the problem. Dr. Silence's theory that the young man is the unwitting victim of atavistic forces unleashed by his strong physical desire for a young female camper is borne out when the figure of a large hound bearing the visage of Sangree materializes on the campsite one evening, causing consternation among the onlookers. Among them is the story's narrator, who observes the incident with a mixture of disbelief and wonderment:

> Yet the harder I stared, the clearer appeared the amazing and monstrous apparition. For, after all, it was Sangree and yet it was not Sangree. It was the head and face of an animal, and yet it was the face of Sangree; the face of a wild dog, a wolf, and yet his face. The eyes were sharper, narrower, more fiery, yet they were his eyes—his eyes run wild; the teeth were larger, whiter, more pointed—yet they were his teeth, his teeth grown cruel; the expression was flaming, terrible, exultant—yet it was his expression carried to the border of savagery—his expression as I had already surprised it more than once, only dominant now, fully released from human constraint, with the mad yearning of a hungry and importunate soul. It was the soul of Sangree, expressed in its single and intense desire—pure utterly and utterly wonderful.

The true nature of the phenomenon is revealed when Sangree's etheric double is observed leaving his tent in the shape of a huge, wolfish dog, while his slumbering flesh-and-blood body remains on its bunk, curiously deflated. This provides John Silence with conclusive evidence that Sangree's conscious ego-identity is being attacked with increasing force by a savage and seemingly alien self, which has been buried in his unconscious all his life; and because of its present dominance he is able to participate in both erotic and violent experiences denied him by his modern, self-effacing persona. Eventually the wolflike simulacrum is shot, and Sangree awakens with "psychic wounds" on his body, the only cure for which is a promise of marriage from the woman he loves.

What makes "The Camp of the Dog" different from other stories written at that time is the way it treats the werewolf as a psychical creature with whom the reader can sympathize. According to Peter Penzoldt, who was in contact with the author shortly before his death, Blackwood was convinced that the superstition of the werewolf was a true psychical reality of profound importance: the projection of the slumbering, untamed, sanguinary instincts in men, which he thought strong enough to materialize and assume what he called "the body of desire."

"Gabriel-Ernest" by Saki (pseudonym of H. H. Munro) is a subtle blend of irony and sardonic humor in which the werewolf myth is used obliquely to satirize Edwardian society's reluctance to accept unpalatable reality. The eponymous hero, a savage youth, unexpectedly appears on the country estate of Van Cheele, who, to his surprise, finds the naked interloper lying by a pool "drying his wet brown limbs luxuriously in the sun." The youth candidly tells the wealthy landowner that he sleeps during the day and eats at night, his diet consisting of rabbits, poultry, and the occasional young child. Although told to leave immediately, he later invades the drawing room of the manor and ingratiates himself with Van Cheele's aunt. After adopting the foundling, whom she christens Gabriel-Ernest, the blinkered matriarch entrusts an orphaned boy into his care; when screams are later heard and discarded clothing found by the millstream, it is presumed that the child had fallen in the water and drowned, and the youth had perished trying to save him. The more likely explanation, that Gabriel-Ernest is a werewolf and has absconded after devouring his young charge, is too dreadful even to be considered a possibility. Originally published in *The Westminster Gazette* (May 29, 1909), this famous story has been anthologized many times since. In the 1980s it was included in *Young Monsters* (1985) and *Asimov's Ghosts and Monsters* (1988), both of which were edited by that formidable triumvirate, Isaac Asimov, Martin H. Greenberg, and Charles G. Waugh.

On more traditional lines is R. H. Benson's "Father Meuron's Tale," in which a peasant woman who exhibits symptoms of lycanthropy is restored to her normal self by exorcism. This story comes from the rare collection *A Mirror of Shalott* (1907), which contains fourteen stories with a religious background.

Werewolf novels from the early years of the twentieth century are few in number and not particularly interesting. In one of the dullest, Richard Bagot's *A Roman Mystery* (1902), a young Englishwoman marries an Italian nobleman and discovers that his elder brother is secretly locked away in an unused part of the family's castle to prevent the outside world from finding out that he is afflicted by wolf-mania. More original, at least, is *For the Soul of a Witch* (1910) by

J. W. Brodie-Innes, whose capricious heroine alternates between two contrasting personalities. At times she is a saintly mystic; at others a devil-worshiper who, under extreme emotional stress, becomes a werewolf. A female shapechanger is also featured in *Tamar Curze* (1908) by Berthe St. Luz. Low-level twaddle about a beautiful femme fatale who metamorphoses into a were-leopard, it was disparagingly described in E. F. Bleiler's *The Guide to Supernatural Fiction* as "shopgirl theriomorphy."

A landmark work of macabre fiction from the second decade of the twentieth century is Frank Norris's posthumously published novel *Vandover and the Brute* (1914). One of the grimmest, most terrifying accounts of the moral degeneration of a soul ever penned, it documents the gradual descent into madness of a fine, sensitive young man, who becomes so deranged that he imagines he has been physically transformed into a wolf and runs naked on all fours about his room howling "wolf, wolf!"

With this novel the werewolf had finally been taken out of the shadow-world of superstition and into the realm of reality. Not since Stevenson's "Olalla" had anyone presented lycanthropy in such a stark, uncompromising manner or dared to show the utter degradation to which someone in the grip of this terrible delusion might fall. Just how much this great novel was ahead of its time was recently revealed when fantasy historian Sam Moskowitz disclosed that the writing was actually begun as early as 1894, and when finished the manuscript was temporarily lost. Unfortunately, by the time the manuscript was recovered Frank Norris was no longer alive, having died from a ruptured appendix in 1902, at the age of thirty-two.

A contemporaneous novel, *The Door of the Unreal* (1919) by Gerald Biss, has dated badly and would probably be forgotten today had not H. P. Lovecraft made some favorable comments about it in his scholarly survey *Supernatural Horror in Literature*. The clichéd plot concerns the mysterious disappearances of members of the public, all of whom have been involved in automobile accidents on a particular stretch of the Brighton Road in southern England. Two private citizens take on the role of detectives and connect these multiple abductions to a sinister German botanist and his beautiful stepdaughter, both of whom turn out to be werewolves. The professor (aptly named Wolff) is eventually killed, but the young woman is spared after it is discovered that she was transformed into a werewolf against her will. She is later restored to normality when the elemental responsible for her condition is exorcised.

Short stories with werewolf motifs written in the years leading up to and including World War I are few in number. They include Bram Stoker's "Dracula's Guest" (1914), wherein Count Dracula appears in the guise of a wolf; Bernard Capes's "The Thing in the Forest" (1915), which features Hungarian werewolves; and Sir Arthur Gray's "The Necromancer" (1919), an old-fashioned yarn concerning black magic and were-wolfery in the seventeenth century. Stoker's story—originally a chapter in *Dracula* but omitted from the published version for reasons of length—is available in numerous anthologies. Bernard Capes's story can be found in *100 Hair-raising Little Horror Stories* (1993), edited by Al Sarrantonio and Martin H. Greenberg; and Sir Arthur Gray's evocative piece, which had long been unavailable, made a welcome reappearance in *100 Creepy Little Creature Stories* (1994), edited by Stefan R. Dziemianowicz, Robert Weinberg, and Martin H. Greenberg.

After World War I, horror stories fell sharply out of favor with the reading public, whose antipathy was due partly to the way authors were continually regurgitating stale plots instead of hatching new, original ideas. Another significant factor in this temporary decline was the growing popularity of crime and mystery novels, which had gained such a stranglehold on the literary market by the late twenties that they constituted half the total output of books in the United States and Great Britain. Forced to adapt to this change in the public's taste, horror novelists increasingly made use of the mystery-story format, until eventually the line of demarcation between the horror and mystery genres became blurred.

A prime example of this literary hybrid is *The Undying Monster* (1922) by Jessie Douglas Kerruish. Set, like so many other thrillers of this period, in an English country house, the plot concerns a curse that manifests itself in successive generations of an upper-crust family. At regular intervals the eldest male member of the family suffers from psychic attacks during which he unknowingly assumes lupine form. When Oliver Hammand, who currently occupies this position, becomes similarly afflicted, his sister enlists the services of a psychic investigator, Luna Bartendale, who decides that the only way to effect a permanent cure is to discover the origin of the curse.

After deciphering ancient inscriptions found in a sealed room in the Hammands' ancestral home, Miss Bartendale learns that the curse is punishment for a sinful deed committed by one of Oliver Hammand's ancestors. To put her findings to the test she conducts an experiment in hypnotic regression, taking Oliver back through time to the Bronze Age. This leads to the revelation that the Hammand family are descendants of Sigmund the Volsung, whose well-known bout of wolf-mania had been recorded in the Elder Edda. So powerful was this experience that it is reproduced from time to time in the minds of Sigmund's male descendants, awakened by some outer circumstances similar to that in which the original impression was recorded.

To bring this harrowing experiment to a satisfactory conclusion, Oliver is hypnotized again and persuaded by Luna Bartendale that he is his own ancestor, Sigmund, with all the recollections connected with him. After a spectacular sequence of events in which Oliver—as Sigmund—witnesses the Twilight of the Gods, the wolf-mania is considered to have worked itself out, and the curse is rescinded. However, despite this grandstand finish, the rest of the narrative is tedious in the extreme, and one can well understand why the manuscript was initially rejected by every publisher to whom it was submitted.

In contrast, David Garnett's *Lady into Fox,* which was published in the same year as Kerruish's overrated potboiler, is brilliantly conceived and developed. This prize-winning novel centers on the plight of a married couple whose lives are dramatically changed when the wife suddenly metamorphoses into a vixen while they are watching a fox-hunt. Although dismayed by this unexpected turn of events, the husband remains unswervingly loyal to his wife and continues to love and protect her. As time passes, however, the woman's personality gradually changes to that of a fox, until the last vestiges of humanity finally disappear. In the end she is killed by a pack of hounds after deserting her husband for a dog-fox.

Three minor British werewolf novels from the 1920s are *The Wolf Trail* (1923) by Roger S. Pocock, *The Soul of the Wolf* (1923) by E. O. Carolin, and *"Ware Wolf!"* (1928) by E. Lascelles Forester. Cliché-ridden potboilers, they are deservedly forgotten today.

Other werewolf novels from the same decade are also fairly routine, offering little in the way of new ideas. *The Thing in the Woods* (1924) by Harper Williams tells of a series of murders committed by an unknown assailant in the woodlands of Pennsylvania; the murders are revealed to be the work of a mentally challenged individual who is shot dead while in wolf form. *The House of Fear* (1927) by Robert W. Service concerns a similar spate of killings on a country estate in France, the perpetrator of which is a wolfish creature under the control of a descendant of the fifteenth-century Satanist Gilles de Rais. In *The White Robe* (1928) by James Branch Cabell, the hero is transformed into a wolf after applying witches' ointment and putting on a wolf skin; and in *Werewolf* (1928) by Charles Lee Swem, a bedridden old man is sporadically afflicted by bouts of homicidal frenzy after donning a wolf skin.

One of the few serious works of fiction to deal with lycanthropy is *Steppenwolf* (1927; English translation 1929) by the German-born writer Hermann Hesse. This controversial book depicts in psychoanalytical terms the despair a man who imagines himself to be half man, half wolf feels as his wolfish instincts and cultured intellect clash. Essentially a meditation on transcendence, this novel quickly gained a cult following when it was reissued in the 1960s.

Algernon Blackwood's main contribution to the werewolf canon in the 1920s was "Running Wolf," from *The Wolves of God and Other Fey Stories* (1921). Based on Native American folklore, "Running Wolf" is the story of a young man who has killed a wolf—the totem animal of his tribe—and is doomed after death to appear as a phantom werewolf until he has made full atonement for his crime. Another unusual story from the same collection is "The Empty Sleeve," in which the "desire body" of a violent man assumes the form of a giant catlike being. Theriomorphy is also the central theme of Oliver Onions's atmospheric novelette "The Master of the House" (*The Painted Face*, 1929), the plot of which hinges on the discovery that the manservant of a reclusive old gentleman is secretly dabbling in Oriental magic and has acquired the ability to meta-morphose into a foul-smelling Alsatian dog.

A modest little collection of short stories by Arthur L. Salmon, *The Ferry of Souls* (1927), contains "The Were-Wolf," which is a titillating mixture of horror and eroticism. A young man, accompanied by his faithful dog, is journeying through a forest as night approaches when the distant howl of a wolf makes him tremble with fear. Amid the gloom he spies a small cottage in a clearing and, seeing a light in one of the windows, knocks on the door. The sole occupant, a voluptuous young woman, warmly invites him in and offers him shelter for the night; but she takes an instant dislike to his dog and insists that he tie it up in a back room. The youth is instantly attracted to his sensual hostess and has to stifle a strong urge to take her in his arms as she takes her leave of him before retiring to her bedchamber. The youth finally falls asleep by the hearth . . . but later that night:

He was aroused by the sudden sharp bay of a wolf, so close to the window that it seemed within the room itself; the dog replied to it, howling. A stealthy sensation, half of fear, half of some nameless expectancy, crept over him. There was a curious sound overhead, and the quiet opening of a door; he imagined he heard footsteps on the staircase. Was she coming down to him? He sat up and listened breathless. Who and what was she, living thus in this solitude? There was still a red gleam from the embers, and in this faint light he saw her steal into the room. She had come undraped from her bed, naked, shameless, entrancing; the glimmering light caught the tips of her beautiful breasts, and kissed ripe curvings of her limbs. As she drew near he waited for her tremblingly; all other thought had gone from him but a hungry drinking of her beauty, an utter abandonment of the soul to this intoxicating draught of vision, the more magical because so much was only half-seen or wholly concealed. He was hers so absolutely that she laughed aloud, as she glided to him with open arms—there was something almost wolf-like in the laugh; her teeth gleamed white through lips that were as red as blood. And then those lips were fastened on his own, voluptuously, nay fiercely; he had a single moment of ecstasy, and then—a sudden awakening of horror. Instead of his arms closing eagerly around an exquisite figure of firm warm womanhood, he found himself struggling with a powerful wolf. His lip was bleeding from its first rapid bite; his arms were grasping its throat with a frenzied endeavor to hold its fangs away; the hot breath that came was nauseating. Rousing all his strength, he staggered to his feet; but he could not keep the beast from him—one of his hands was savagely bitten, the clutch of the other on the animal's throat was failing; he cried aloud in helpless pain and terror. The dog answered with howlings and fierce barks. So swift a change from the delirium of joy to this nightmare of unutterable extremity! He was growing weaker—he was slipping backward—the beast's foul jaws were about to close on his face, and then, when the very smell of death seemed in his nostrils, the dog, whose frantic teeth had torn its cords, rushed into the room and dashed at the beast's neck, holding grimly. Powerful as the wolf was, the dog had it at a fatal advantage.

Gashed, bleeding, weakened with a sickening horror, the youth dragged himself from beneath the wolf's quivering paws; the dog needed no help now. He groped for means to strike a light, and found them. The transformation, or the illusion, returned again. There in front of the hearth lay a beautiful unclad figure, the dog's fangs fixed in her blood-stained throat. She no longer stirred. Far off in the forest was the retreating cry of a wolf; and then utter silence.

Other little-known stories hidden away in long-forgotten hardcover collections from the 1920s are W. James Wintle's "The Voice in the Night" (*Ghost Gleams*, 1921), Duncan Campbell Scott's "The Witching Hour" (*The Witching of Elspie*, 1923), Lord Castletown's "Once Upon a Time" (*A Bundle of Lies*, 1925), and Alan Sullivan's "The Eyes of Sebastian" (*Under the Northern Lights*, 1926). No doubt there are many others waiting to be rediscovered.

4

A New Approach

The Werewolf Theme in the Pulp Magazines

In the period immediately after World War I it might
have seemed to most observers that the werewolf story
had run its course and had no further capacity for development. However, there was a phenomenon taking
place in the United States that would not only rekindle
interest in the theme but greatly broaden its scope.

The main source of light reading matter for mil-
lions of Americans during the interwar years was not
hardcover books or quality periodicals; instead, what
they preferred was the exciting type of fiction that
could be found only in the pages of pulp magazines,
whose rise to prominence and eventual domination of
the all-fiction market had been made possible by the
introduction of mass distribution techniques. The

twentieth-century equivalent of the Victorian chap-books, these luridly illustrated periodicals were cheaply printed on paper manufactured from chemically treated wood pulp (hence their popular appellation) and could be found on every newsstand and bookstall across the nation, selling for as little as a dime. Aimed primarily at the educated working classes but attracting readers from all walks of life, the pulps provided their many devotees with a regular diet of escapist fiction, catering to every possible taste. As far as magazines in the fantasy category were concerned, none was more important or influential than the legendary *Weird Tales,* which had the distinction of being the first pulp-sized magazine to devote the whole of its contents to fantasy fiction. Launched in March 1923, the magazine was the brainchild of an enterprising businessman named Jacob Clark Henneberger, whose main reason for founding "The Unique Magazine" (as *Weird Tales* was appropriately subtitled) was to provide a regular market for off-trail material that no other publisher would accept at that time.

Within a few years *Weird Tales* had established itself as the world's leading purveyor of weird-fantasy fiction, for which most of the credit must be attributed to the inspired editorship of Farnsworth Wright, who was appointed to the post in 1924. A cultured man, he always insisted on the maintenance of high literary standards despite the magazine's cheap format. More importantly, he discovered and developed the talents of many young American writers who later went on to become major figures in the fantasy genre.

This new crop of fantasists brought a fresh approach to weird fiction, saving it from what would otherwise have been a slow death. Sweeping away the old-fashioned ideas of their predecessors, they adopted a different, more exciting narrative technique where the emphasis was on fast-paced action and audacious plots. They also breathed new life into well-worn themes and were the first group of writers to appreciate the untapped potential of the werewolf theme. The most gifted of Wright's young protégés was Robert E. Howard, whose action-packed tales of Conan, the barbarian adventurer, are still hugely popular today. In July 1925, while still at college, the young Texan made his professional debut in "The Unique Magazine" with a story called "Spear and Fang," which was quickly followed a month later by "In the Forest of Villefere," a brief werewolf tale set in medieval France. Both were plainly juvenile efforts, and their reception at the time was less than enthusiastic.

Howard's standing with the readers of *Weird Tales* improved considerably, however, following the publication of "Wolfshead" (April 1926), a sequel to his earlier werewolf yarn and a much more mature work than anything he had previously produced. The exotic setting for this thrilling story is a Portuguese colonial castle on the West Coast of Africa, where a spate of brutal killings and mutilations are initially thought to be the handiwork of a crazed follower of the local leopard cult. The real culprit, however, is a French cavalier staying at the castle, who has suffered from the curse of lycanthropy ever since he slew a werewolf in a fight to the death. The unusual form this particular curse takes is that every full moon the ghostly outline of a wolf's head appears and hovers above the Frenchman; then it slowly descends and merges with him until he is transformed into the ravening beast. Ironically, had the cavalier killed the demon in its wolf form all would have been well, but because it was slain in the half-form of a man, its ghost is destined to haunt him forever.

According to Howard, a true werewolf is not a man who has the power to take the form of a wolf, but rather a wolf who takes the shape of a man. Wolves, the author asserts, are half animal, half demon and have the power to take the form—or half-form—of a man during the time of the full moon; but when the moon hovers at its zenith the wolf spirit regains ascendancy, and the werewolf becomes a true wolf once more. A fascinating account of the origin of werewolves is also incorporated into the narrative, making this a story of more than usual interest.

Howard's "The Lost Race" (January 1927) and "The Hyena" (March 1928) are further variations on the shapeshifting theme. In "The Lost Race" a young Celtic warrior encounters a wolf fighting a losing battle with a panther and goes to its aid. Later, when the youth is captured by enemy tribesmen, he is saved from being burned alive as a human sacrifice by one of his captors, who is the wolf in human form. In contrast, "The Hyena" is set in the nineteenth century and tells of an African witch doctor with shapeshifting powers.

Another author inseparably associated with *Weird Tales* is Seabury Quinn, who was the magazine's most popular and regular contributor with no fewer than 145 stories to his credit. Formerly a lawyer before turning to writing, he made an auspicious debut in the October 1923 issue with "The Phantom Farmhouse," a poignant tale of forbidden love narrated by John Weatherby, a young clergyman convalescing at a sanitarium in Maine. One evening he ventures into the nearby woods, where he discovers a secluded farmhouse and makes friends with the occupants, an elderly couple and their daughter, Mildred. All is not what it seems, however, for unbeknown to the clergyman all three are were-wolves, and the farmhouse is merely an illusion created by glamour. During the day the undead trio must repose in their graves, but at night they are free to roam abroad in search of prey, both animal and human. The one restriction on their nocturnal activities is that when the moon is shining they are obliged to appear in human form, but on those occasions when the moon hides its light behind a cloud they have the power to assume lupine form.

Over the next few weeks the clergyman becomes a regular visitor at the farmhouse, irresistibly drawn by his love for the young woman, who he senses has similar feelings for him. When, at length, he plucks up the courage to tell her of his love and tries to seal it with a kiss, her reaction stuns him:

> With a cry that was half scream, half weeping, she thrust me suddenly from her, pressing her hands against my breast and lowering her head until her face was hidden between her outstretched arms. I, too, started back, for in the instant our lips were about to meet, hers had writhed back from her teeth, like a dog's when he is about to spring, and a low, harsh noise, almost a growl, had risen in her throat.
>
> "For God's sake," she whispered hoarsely, agony in every note of her shaking voice, "never do that again! Oh, my dear, dear love, you don't know how near to a horror worse than death you were."
>
> "A—horror—worse—than—death?" I echoed dully, pressing her cold little hands in mine. "What do you mean, Mildred?"
>
> "Loose my hands," she commanded with a quaint reversion to the speech of our ancestors, "and hear me. I do love you. I love you better than life, better than death. I love you so much I have overcome something stronger than the walls of the grave for your sake; but John, my very love, this is our last night together. We can never meet again."

Despite the clergyman's protestations, Mildred makes him promise to return early the next morning with his prayer book and read the office for the burial of the dead over three graves at the back of the farmhouse. "At last I shall have peace, and you shall bring it to me," she tells him.

Quinn's next significant contribution to *Weird Tales* was a story he wrote for the October 1925 issue, "The Horror on the Links," which introduced his most famous creation, the mercurial psychic investigator Jules de Grandin. Egotistical and highly principled, the dapper little Frenchman has an explosive personality, and when annoyed invariably resorts to Gallic expletives to vent his anger. The list of de Grandin's vocations and avocations is long and varied: apart from being a criminologist and phantom-fighter, he is also a surgeon and physician, a deeply learned occultist, and a student of all branches of the supernatural. Among the great detective's many other accomplishments—which seemed to grow as the series progressed—he is an expert fencer, skilled in jujitsu and the art of foot-boxing, and a crack marksman with rifle as well as pistol. Originally from Paris where he was connected with the Service de Sûreté, de Grandin has taken up permanent residence in Harrisonville, New Jersey, and is a member of the household of Dr. Samuel Trowbridge, who acts as his loyal assistant.

In ninety-three cases, written between 1925 and 1951, Jules de Grandin proved to be an implacable foe of evil in whatever form it might take and was never squeamish when it came to handing out just deserts to his adversaries, whether they were of the human kind or denizens of the phantom world. His first brush with a werewolf was in "The Blood Flower" (March 1927), in which a young woman comes under an evil spell after wearing a hellish bloom, which has the property of transforming people into wolves. The blood-colored flower, which grows only on the Transylvanian Alps, was given to her by an evil relative who has become a werewolf by the same process and now wants her for his mate. A high point of the narrative is the chilling description of the man-wolf:

> Not human, nor yet wholly bestial it was, but partook grotesquely of both, so that it was at once a foul caricature of each. The forehead was low and narrow, and sloped back to a thatch of short, nondescript-colored hair resembling an animal's fur. The nose was elongated out of all semblance to a human feature and resembled the pointed snout of some animal of the canine tribe except that it curved sharply down at the tip like the beak of some unclean bird of prey. Thin, cruel lips were drawn sneeringly back from the double row of tusklike teeth which gleamed horridly in the dim reflection of the open fire, and a pair of round, baleful eyes, green as the luminescence from a rotting carcass in a midnight swamp, glared at us across the windowsill.

One of the grimmest werewolf stories ever to appear in *Weird Tales* was "The Werewolf of Ponkert" by H. Warner Munn. Published in the July 1925 issue, it was the author's first sale to a pulp magazine, written as a result of a letter to the readers' column from H. P. Lovecraft, in which he bemoaned the fact that no one had ever attempted to tell a story from the werewolf's viewpoint. The remarkable tale that the young New Englander produced in response is in the form of a document written in the late fifteenth century by someone called Wladislaw Brenryk. A resident of the village of Ponkert in Transylvania, he recounts his harrowing experiences after being pressed into becoming a member of a pack of werewolves, whose leader is a horribly shrunken dwarf with a face like "a crinkled, seamed piece of time-worn parchment, coalblack with age." Known to his minions as the Master, the near-immortal warlock assumes the form of a black wolf at night and rampages across the countryside with his six bond-slaves, preying on livestock and vulnerable travelers. The Master is essentially vampiric by nature; he initiates new members into his brotherhood by drinking their blood, giving him an unbreakable power over that person. After their enforced initiation, Brenryk and the other recruits also begin to show vampiric tendencies:

> Although I have called myself a *vampyr*, I was not one in the true sense of the word. Neither were any of the rest of my companions, except the Master, for although we ate human flesh, drank blood, and cracked bones to extract the last particle of nourishment therefrom, we did so to assuage our fierce hunger more than because it was necessary for our continued existence. We ate heartily of human food also, in man form, but more and more we found it unsatisfying appetite, which only flesh and blood could conquer. Gradually we were leaving even this for a diet consisting solely of blood.

Brenryk's intense dislike of his new way of life makes him long to be a normal person again; but when he tries to foster opposition and revolt among the other werewolves, the Master finds out and exacts a terrible vengeance by forcing the rebel to kill his wife and deliver his infant daughter into the clutches of the wolf pack. After this, Brenryk loses the will to live and confesses his crimes to the authorities, as a result of which the king's soldiers ambush the other werewolves and kill all of them with the exception of the Master, who makes good his escape. The document concludes with Brenryk reflecting on the fate in store for him—the only certainty being that he will be flayed alive, have his hide tanned like a beast, and his dark and gloomy history written upon it for all to read.

Encouraged by the enthusiastic response to his story, Munn went on to write more episodes in the evil warlock's sanguinary career. The sequel, appropriately titled "The Return of the Master" (July 1927), was, however, somewhat disappointing, possibly because the diminutive shapeshifter abandoned his lupine guise in favor of a variety of other forms, one of which was a giant bat. Similarly, in the third story in the trilogy, "The Werewolf's Daughter" (serialized in three parts, October–December 1928), the werewolf element is almost nonexistent. As was intimated at the end of the original story, Brenryk's daughter, Ivga, was not killed by the werewolves as he had supposed but had survived her ordeal unscathed and is living in Ponkert with her foster father, the former captain of the guards who had taken her natural father into custody. Ivga, now a grown woman, is unaware of her past but is nonetheless treated as an outcast by the rest of the villagers, who blame her for every misfortune that befalls them. Matters come to a head when a local resident is found dead from wounds similar to those made by a wolf, and Ivga is immediately suspected. She escapes the wrath of the lynch mob that comes after her only by entering into a pact with the Master, to whom she promises that at least one of her descendants from each succeeding generation of her family will serve him. The only element of surprise in an otherwise predictable narrative is the revelation that the Master is not of human—or even demonic—origin but is an extraterrestrial being who was summoned to Earth centuries ago by a powerful Babylonian witch and imprisoned in the misshapen body of her servant, whose soul he has displaced. This has had the effect of making the Master hostile to the entire human race, on which he has vowed to sow misery and discord for the rest of his unnatural existence.

The only female writer to rival the top male contributors in popularity during *Weird Tales'* formative years was Greye La Spina, a formidable hawk-faced lady from Massachusetts whose best-known contribution to the magazine is the werewolf novella "Invaders from the Dark" (serialized in three parts, April–June 1925). Reading like the scenario for an old "B" movie, it concerns the conflict between Portia Delorme, a young white witch, and her rival in love, a glamorous Russian princess. When Portia's fiancé is enticed away from her, she suspects the influence of malign forces, and further investigations lead to the discovery that the Russian princess is a werewolf. The rest of the highly improbable plot revolves around Portia's attempts to prize her ex-boyfriend from the werewolf's clutches and prevent him from being similarly transformed.

The female werewolf in this story has all the classic features of the femme fatale and is a lot easier on the eye than her male counterpart in Seabury Quinn's "The Blood Flower." For instance,

> there were the beryl green eyes that in the dusk gleamed like garnets; the sharp white teeth; the small, low-set ears, pointed above . . . the over-red lips . . . eyebrows that narrowed down to meet at the top of the nose. There were the oval, tinted, highly-polished nails on the slender fingers, with the third finger so abnormally long. Even the princess's slinking walk, by its resemblance to the tireless gait of the wolf, would have betrayed her real personality to an expert.

In its day this novella received a great deal of acclaim and reputedly helped boost the magazine's circulation. One enthusiastic reader declared: "Greater than *Dracula*!"; another described it as "the most wonderful werewolf story ever written." Today's horror fans, however, are unlikely to be impressed by the trite plot and paucity of weird atmosphere.

Fedor Sologub's "The White Dog," in the February 1926 issue of *Weird Tales*, originally came from an obscure hardcover collection, *The Sweet-Scented Name,* published in 1915. In this deceptively simple story, which defies conventional categorization, a lonely, frustrated spinster employed as a seamstress in a small Russian town comes under the baleful influence of the moon, resulting in bouts of aberrational behavior. One night she dashes out of doors, strips naked, and lies down in the grass; then raising herself on her elbows, she lifts her face toward the moon and gives a long drawn-out whine. A young boy and his uncle arrive on the scene, drawn by the eerie sound, but their perception of what they are witnessing is distorted by their overstimulated imaginations:

> Near the bathhouse, in the grass, lay a huge white dog, whining piteously. Its head, black on the crown, was raised to the moon, which pursued its way in the cold sky; its hind legs were strangely thrown backward, while the front ones, firm and straight, pressed hard against the ground. In the pale green and unreal light of the moon it seemed enormous. So huge a dog was surely never seen on earth. It was thick and fat. The black spot, which began at the head and stretched in uneven strands down the entire spine, seemed like a woman's loosened hair. No tail was visible; presumably it was turned under. The fur on the body was so short that in the distance the dog seemed wholly naked, and its hide shone dimly in the moonlight, so that altogether it resembled the body of a nude woman, who lay in the grass and bayed at the moon.

Convinced that it is a werewolf, the older of the two onlookers raises his rifle and shoots, and the naked woman, her body covered in blood, jumps up and starts to run, all the while groaning and raising cries of distress. The boy and his uncle, meanwhile, throw themselves onto the ground and begin to moan in wild terror.

Other werewolf stories that appeared in *Weird Tales* during the 1920s were "The Ghost-Eater" by C. M. Eddy Jr. (April 1924); "The Wolf of the Campagna" by Harry Bailey (February 1925); "The Girdle" by Joseph McCord (February 1927); and "Loup-Garou" by Wallace West (October 1927). All are fairly competent commercial work but lack the invention and originality of some of the stories mentioned earlier.

Although *Weird Tales* was the main vehicle for werewolf stories, some also appeared in other pulp magazines. These included "Wolf of the Steppes" by Greye La Spina (*The Thrill Book*, March 1919); "Between Two Worlds" by Ada Louvie Evans (*The Thrill Book*, October 1919); "The Werewolf" by Max Brand (*Western Story Magazine*, December 1926); "Werewolf" by Cassie H. MacLaury (*Ghost Stories*, March 1927); and "The Wolf Man" by Mont Hurst (*Ghost Stories*, July 1928).

Monster Delights: Stories from *Weird Tales'* Heyday

By the early 1930s *Weird Tales* was firmly established in the affections of its loyal band of readers and had acquired a coterie of authors who regularly contributed well-crafted stories, many of which are now considered classics of their kind. As in the previous decade the author who most consistently topped the readers' preference poll was Seabury Quinn, and any issue that did not contain a story about his lovable creation, Jules de Grandin, invariably drew howls of protest from his army of admirers. And Quinn, knowing when he was on to a sure thing, was more than willing to oblige with further exploits, including two involving lycanthropy.

The first of these, "The Wolf of St. Bonnot" (December 1930), was inspired by historical accounts of the alleged crimes of Gilles Garnier, a sixteenth-century lycanthrope dubbed "The Wolf of St. Bonnot." During a séance at a social gathering the participants inadvertently make contact with the notorious wolfman's malevolent spirit, which has remained earthbound for four and a half centuries. All this time the spirit has been seeking an opportunity to materialize and has been attracted by the "unholy thoughts" in the subconscious of one of the guests, a pregnant young woman whose condition makes her easy to manipulate. Slipping in through the psychic door conveniently left ajar, Garnier's discarnate spirit seizes the opportunity to fabricate a corporeal body for itself from the ectoplasm radiated by the sitters at the séance, making it possible for the former lycanthrope to resume his nefarious activities in the modern world—with the young woman as his accomplice. Thereafter she involuntarily changes into a wolf and joins Garnier on his nocturnal questing for forbidden sustenance, which includes an unsuccessful attempt to rob a grave and devour the grisly contents. To rectify the situation de Grandin resorts to a magical ceremony of his own devising, at which the participants at the original séance are seated inside a pentagram. Then, by a combination of chanting and other occult techniques, the werewolf is summoned into the sitters' presence and the stolen ectoplasm reabsorbed into their bodies, forcing the disembodied revenant to return to the spirit world. This ceremony also releases the werewolf's accomplice from her obsession, and she is restored to the bosom of her family none the worse for her ordeal.

Jules de Grandin's unrivaled experience at dealing with occult phenomena also stood him in good stead in "The Thing in the Fog" (March 1933), in which the indomitable phantom-fighter is once again called upon to rescue a damsel in distress. His client in this intriguing case is a young American woman named Sarah Leigh, whose life is constantly blighted by the unwanted attentions of a former lover—a situation made even more alarming by the fact that he is a werewolf. Miss Leigh explains to de Grandin that it all started when she was an impressionable teenager living in Turkey, where her father was attached to the consulate at Smyrna. She reveals that it was there she met and became infatuated with a handsome Greek secret agent, George Athanasakos, who claimed to be the last of a very ancient clan. At a midnight rendezvous he had persuaded her to take part in a prenuptial ritual, during which they both wore wolf-skin cloaks. After a while Sarah found herself drifting into a dreamlike state during which she vividly remembers changing into a wolf and joining forces with a male wolf in an orgy of killing. When she regained her senses, Sarah's lover triumphantly announced that she was now the mate of a *vrykolakas*—which is the Greek word for werewolf— and to seal the bond he would put his mark on her. Tearing open Sarah's upper garments he savagely bit her below the armpit in direct line with her left breast, leaving a small whitened cicatrix from which, ever since, a tuft of long, grayish-brown hair has grown. Athanasakos then told her: "You belong to me now, and no-one shall take you from me. Anyone who tries will die!"

After this, Sarah wants nothing more to do with the sinister Greek and returns to the United States to escape further harassment. Undeterred, Athanasakos doggedly follows her and tries to kill the man she is engaged to. He is thwarted, however, by de Grandin, who is again on hand to drive off the *vrykolakas* when he attempts to disrupt the couple's wedding. The persistent villain still refuses to be diverted from his purpose, and, while Sarah is on her honeymoon, he tricks her into accepting a gift of perfume made from the sap of wolf-flowers, which, once applied, transforms her into a werewolf. As such she must obey the call of the *vrykolakas* and join him on his nighttime questing. A satisfactory outcome to the case is ultimately achieved when the wily detective shoots the villain in his wolf form after cornering him in his lair; he then performs an occult ritual to lift the spell from his client.

It is typical of de Grandin's unorthodox methods that in this story he uses an ordinary bullet to dispatch the werewolf and not, as tradition dictates, a silver one. When challenged about this he replies:

> Strong and ferocious, cunning and malicious as the werewolf is, he can be killed as easily as any natural wolf. A sharp sword will slay him, and a well-aimed bullet puts an end to his career; the wood of the thorn-bush and the mountain ash are so repugnant to him that he will shrink away if beaten or merely threatened with a switch of either. Weapons efficacious against an ordinary physical foe are potent against him, while charms and exorcisms which would put a true demon to flight are powerless.

In the late thirties, Seabury Quinn produced a number of stories unconnected with the "Jules de Grandin" series, most of which revealed the full extent of this underrated writer's considerable talents. Along with highly entertaining novelettes such as "The Globe of Memories" and "Roads," they included a couple of excellent werewolf tales set in the Middle Ages. In the earlier of the two, "Fortune's Fools" (July 1938), the hero, a young soldier of fortune named Ramon de Grandin—Jules's thirteenth-century ancestor—becomes romantically entangled with a voluptuous dancing girl named Basta during their imprisonment in the castle of Count Otto von Wolfberg, the tyrannical leader of a band of werewolves who prey upon the local serfs and any rich travelers who happen to pass by.

The lovers eventually succeed in escaping from the fortress, but the count and his henchmen give chase and head them off, forcing the valiant duo to make a stand. Despite putting up a brave fight, they are soon overwhelmed by sheer force of numbers. Then, just as the giant wolf-leader is about to tear out the hero's throat, a wild cry echoes through the woods:

> The wolves heard it and were afraid. For the first time in their savage, man-beast lives they knew the paralysing grip of sheer, stark terror. And even as they turned in fright they knew the realization of their fear, for, apparently from nowhere, a dreadful thing was in their midst. It was a creature like a cata-mountain, but four times larger, with rippling soot-black fur and flashing eyes of green, and teeth like scimitars and claws like sabers. It rushed among them, spreading death so swift it might have been a lightning bolt. At a single blow from its great paw a wolf lay belly-down with twitching legs and whimpering breath, its back snapped like a rotten twig; a sweep of its sword-studded talons, and skin and flesh and pelage ripped away from staring bones. The creature seized a great wolf in its jaws and shook it as a cat might shake a mouse, then tossed the carcass by contemptuously and struck two more beasts from its path as it made for the wolf-thing that worried at de Grandin's throat.

Moments later, Otto and his fellow werewolves have all been killed by the cat-monster, which, to Ramon's surprise, turns out to be the beast form assumed by his lovely companion—the transformation having suddenly occurred after she had eaten the flower of a plant with shapeshifting properties. Sadly, this brings an abrupt end to the couple's romantic aspirations, as Basta is doomed to remain in her feline guise for three years.

Quinn's other werewolf tale from the late 1930s, "Uncanonized" (November 1939), tells the tragic story of two German peasants, Wolfgang and Gertruda, whose happiness is destroyed when the lord of the land, Count Otho, gatecrashes their marriage celebrations and claims the *droit du seigneur,* an old custom that permits him to sleep with his vassal's wife on her wedding night. The bridegroom, a boyhood companion of the count—whose life he once saved—pleads with him to waive this ancient privilege, but the arrogant nobleman refuses and orders Wolfgang to be thrown into the dungeon. That night, after a dramatic confrontation with Otho in the bridal chamber, Gertruda flings herself from the window rather than submit to her lord's caresses, and she is killed on the rocks below.

As was the fate of all suicides in those days, Gertruda's broken body is buried at the crossroads in an unblessed grave, signifying the Church's disapproval of her blasphemous act. Unable to rest, she returns from the dead as a werewolf and in this terrifying form gains a fitting revenge on Count Otho by forcing her way into his bedchamber on his own wedding night and hurling him from the window to his death.

In stories of this kind, Quinn always stretched himself to the limit of his capabilities, and we now know that he did a considerable amount of research before putting pen to paper. In "Uncanonized" this is particularly evident from his erudite knowledge of the European feudal system and its customs, and the historical authenticity of the story is further enhanced by the use of archaic words and phrases, which make it one of the most literate works of fiction to appear in the pulps.

The only author to seriously challenge Quinn's preeminence in the 1930s was Robert E. Howard, who achieved enormous popularity during this decade with his prototypal "sword-and-sorcery" tales about Conan the Cimmerian. Although these made up the bulk of his contributions to *Weird Tales,* Howard still continued to submit the occasional horror yarn. One of the most memorable is "Black Hound of Death" (November 1936), a gruesome thriller about the terrible disfigurement inflicted upon a white man by the black monks of Inner Mongolia. After he was betrayed into their hands by a fellow American, the fiendish devil-worshipers did not put their captive to death (as they usually did with outsiders); instead they played a cruel jest on him by using their damnable arts to remold his face so that it resembled that of a wolf. Ears, forehead, and eyes were left untouched, but nose, mouth, and jaws were hideously elongated into a muzzle. Thereafter, a corresponding change takes place in the victim's personality, changing him from a rational human being into a ruthless werewolf whose sole motivation is the desire for revenge. The ingenious method by which this is ultimately achieved forms the gripping conclusion to a narrative full of gory incidents and spine-chilling horror.

H. Warner Munn's main contribution to *Weird Tales* in the thirties was an additional series of short stories featuring the Master. Known collectively as "Tales of the Werewolf Clan," each story chronicles the misadventures of descendants of the author's original werewolf character, Wladislaw Brenryk, and concerns some catastrophe for which the Master is indirectly responsible. "The Master Strikes" (November 1930) is set at the time of the massacre of the Huguenots in sixteenth-century France; "The Master Fights" (December 1930) concerns the wrecking of the Spanish Armada off the coast of Ireland; and the final story, "The Master Has a Narrow Escape" (January 1931), covers the period of the Great Plague in central Europe, then switches to America for the trial of the first witch executed in New England. Not particularly weird—and having little to do with shapeshifting—the stories in this second trilogy are noteworthy only for the authenticity of their historical backgrounds.

While Munn had found it difficult to repeat his earlier success, Greye La Spina's return to the werewolf theme in "The Devil's Pool" (June 1932) was greeted with a chorus of approval. Hugely entertaining, this wonderful slice of hokum recounts the strange events that occur after an elderly farmer enters into a pact with the Devil's agent, a tall, gaunt-looking man who poses as the hired hand. Mason Hardy, the story's resourceful hero, is sent to the farm to investigate the disappearance of his best friend's fiancée, who has not been seen since she was hired to look after the farmer's bedridden granddaughter. He finds that she and a young man similarly employed are virtual prisoners of the "hired man." It turns out that the curse of lycanthropy has been inflicted on the young couple after they fell into a pool of tainted crystalline water in a nearby quarry, which had miraculously appeared shortly after the hired man's arrival. Each time there is a full moon the bewitched couple and the hired hand metamorphose into wolves and are observed by the hero slinking into the woods where they hunt wild animals to satisfy their hunger for raw flesh; on one occasion they even bring back a baby boy with the intention of devouring him. The conclusion to this incident-packed story concerns the hero's attempt to break the hold the Devil's agent has over the couple and restore them to their former selves. The most memorable scene in the story—brilliantly captured by J. Allen St. John in his cover painting—is undoubtedly the one where the female werewolf crouches in front of a full-length mirror, but the image reflected is not that of a wolf but a naked woman on all fours.

Several other female writers made their mark in *Weird Tales* in the thirties. One of the most prolific was

G. G. Pendarves (pseudonym of British author Gladys Gordon Trenery), who is probably best remembered for that oft-reprinted classic "The Eighth Green Man." Her only stab at a werewolf story—and a good one at that—was "Werewolf of the Sahara" (August/September 1936), in which the hero is magically transformed into a wolf whenever he attempts to challenge the authority of his master, a powerful Arab sorcerer.

Grace M. Campbell's "The Law of the Hills" (August 1930) has a more traditional setting. Played out against the rugged backdrop of the North American pine forests, this is the poignant tale of a newly married couple whose happiness is shattered when the bride, a beautiful blonde-haired Norwegian girl, becomes afflicted by the curse of hereditary lycanthropy. At night she sneaks away from her husband's side and roams the surrounding hills in the guise of a slender white wolf, which is frequently seen running with a pack of gray timber wolves. The husband's suspicions about the real identity of the she-wolf are tragically confirmed when it is killed, and his wife never returns home.

The finest werewolf story by a woman writer ever to appear in "The Unique Magazine" was Everil Worrell Murphy's "Norn" (February 1936), published under her "Lireve Monet" pseudonym—one of many she employed during a long and productive writing career. Strongly plotted and charged with emotional power, "Norn" is told from the viewpoint of an impressionable young woman who witnesses strange events within her family circle. At the center is her domineering aunt, known to all her relatives by the nickname of Norn. A tall, rangy woman with cold, gray eyes whose black pupils never dilate or contract, Norn exerts a powerful influence over the rest of the family. The narrator reveals that when she was a child she idolized her aunt but now that she is grown up and with a child of her own, she sees a sinister side to Norn's nature. Her concern grows as she observes the gradual alienation of her daughter's affections as Norn starts to impose her will upon the infant. The conflict intensifies when Norn comes to live with her niece after marrying the latter's widowed father. Soon afterward, Norn's lover, the significantly named Mr. Wolf, is invited as a houseguest, adding to the tension in the household. It is at this point that Norn's true nature is finally revealed. During a violent argument between the two women over the child's upbringing, Norn suddenly undergoes a terrifying transformation into the beast her soul symbolizes:

> I watched those awful changes—the dizzy swimming of the air between us, through which I yet saw clearly the fast-changing, definite outlines—Norn, growing in stature, assuming a leaping posture—her face reaching out before her, the long jaws still elongating, the fixed pale gaze of her wide eyes with the unchanging pupils now seeming to come to life, to shoot red sparks . . . the long arms hanging down, now, before her—those strangely awkward feet and hands seeming at last at ease, wildly graceful, *the hands turning to wolf's paws* . . .

While the change from woman to wolf is still only partial, the gaunt form hurls itself upon its transfigured victim:

> Over me, muzzle near to my face, eyes gleaming red in the dusky gloom, bent the wolf-head. I *saw* the claws that tore at my face and body—but what I felt was the large, bony hands of a woman, tearing and clawing as the claws of the beast should have done, but so much more ineffectually that I was not mangled, as the evidence of my sense of sight told my frantic brain from second to second I was about to be.
>
> Those claws tore at my face and I felt scratches; but only the scratches of fingernails. Bony fingers closed around my left eyeball in its socket, as though they would tear it from its place. It was the sort of attack which could only be made by human hands and fingers prompted by the workings of a mind gone down to the level of a beast. Then, just as I uttered a despairing cry at the sharpness of the pain shooting from the back of my eyeball to the top and back of my head, the grip shifted, and the brutish hands, that still were only hands, tore at my breast, and beat and tore and mauled my body. I screamed out loud, and a tiny form was upon me—my little girl, rushing to my defense in spite of the spell that was upon her. The hands loosed their hold, and I staggered to my feet, circled, crouched low, got away—and dashed through the rooms of the dark and silent house.

The young mother's harrowing ordeal comes to an abrupt end when Norn and Mr. Wolf tear each other to pieces in a fight to the death, after Wolf, a fellow lycanthrope, becomes jealous of his mistress's obsessive love for the child.

Whether viewed as a story of obsessive love worked out in a supernatural context, or as a domestic feud that gets out of hand, there is no arguing that the sense of gradually escalating menace in "Norn" is superbly handled. The characterizations of the leading protagonists in the drama are full and rich—the lycanthropic aunt being especially memorable—and the introduction of the supernatural at the end of the story is perfectly timed to achieve maximum impact. Today, the author of this unsung classic is remembered chiefly for her much-admired vampire story "The Canal," but there is no doubt in my own mind that "Norn" is her masterpiece.

The greatest, and also the most popular author among *Weird Tales'* roster of female contributors, was C. L. Moore. Following her sensational debut in the November 1933 issue with the thrilling vampire yarn "Shambleau," in which she introduced her most famous creation, the hard-bitten space-outlaw Northwest Smith, Moore had submitted a werewolf story titled "Werewoman" to *Weird Tales* as the next story in the series, but Farnsworth Wright rejected it. The story eventually saw print in the fall 1938 issue of *Leaves,* an amateur magazine published by R. H. Barlow. Atypical of the Northwest Smith stories, the plot revolves around the space-outlaw's transformation into a werewolf after straying onto an accursed moor that is a safe haven for all the half-real beings that haunt mankind. Although not one of Moore's best stories, it was deservedly rescued from obscurity by Sam Moskowitz, who included it in his 1971 anthology *Horrors Unknown*.

A story from *Weird Tales* that is difficult to categorize is "Placide's Wife" by Kirk Mashburn. It was described on the cover of the November 1931 issue as "a startling vampire story," yet the bloodsucking spouse of the title, Nita Duboin, frequently appears in wolf form and, to add to the confusion, is called a "loup-garou" at one point in the narrative. In the sequel, "The Last of Placide's Wife" (September 1932), the undead femme fatale has an entire pack of werewolves at her beck and call, but here she prefers to run around in the nude.

Val Lewton, the producer of the classic horror movie *Cat People* (1942), had earlier utilized the shape-shifting theme in a story he wrote for the July 1930 issue of *Weird Tales*. Titled "The Bagheeta," it concerns a supernatural creature, half leopard and half woman, which is said to be the reincarnation of a virgin who died from wrongs inflicted upon her by sinful men, and who comes again to the world so that she may prey upon the flocks of the sinful. Only a pure youth, one who has not had carnal knowledge of a woman, can hope to slay the mystic beast. He must ride out against her with only a sword at his side and a prayer on his lips. At his coming, the Bagheeta, so the legend goes, will change into a beautiful woman and attempt to seduce him. If she is successful his life is forfeit, and after changing back into a black leopard the Bagheeta will tear him limb from limb. Only if the youth remains steadfast in his purity can he hope to triumph. In an ironic conclusion to the story, the youth chosen to face the Bagheeta discovers that the legend is without substance, but he claims to have vanquished the monster—just as others before him have done—and is hailed as a hero.

An equally fascinating legend forms the basis of Arlton Eadie's "The Wolf-Girl of Josselin" (August 1938), in which a young Englishman vacationing in northern France falls in love with a girl from the village of Josselin, unaware that she harbors a dark secret. When it is announced that they are to be married, a local historian approaches the Englishman and warns him that it is not wise to choose his bride from among the women of Josselin. To support this advice he explains that two hundred years ago a beggar-woman with a baby boy had begged for food from the women of the village but had been driven away. Shortly thereafter the baby died, and in revenge its mother called down a curse upon those who refused them succor, using the following words: "May ye be cursed unto the tenth generation. Like ravening wolves have ye denied us food, like baying hounds have ye driven us from your doors. Henceforth, ye women of Josselin, ye shall be dogs and wolves in very truth." And so saying, she died. That night all the women erupted in a frenzy, tearing off their garments and howling like wolves. The following morning it was discovered that they had killed all their male children; and since that day, according to local belief, succeeding generations of women from the village have inherited the curse.

Choosing to ignore the warning the Englishman goes ahead with the wedding, and for a while nothing untoward occurs. But when the couple have a baby—a son and heir—the curse begins to take effect, and the infant's life becomes endangered when its mother periodically metamorphoses into a wolf. In the end, however, mother-love triumphs and no harm befalls the child.

An ingenious method of nullifying the werewolf's curse is employed in "The Woman at Loon Point" (December 1936) by August Derleth and Mark Schorer. This well-spun yarn describes the ordeal experienced by a brother and sister while on vacation at Loon Point in the backwoods of Michigan's Upper Peninsula. After being bitten by a werewolf that roams the woods, the young man is similarly afflicted, experiencing an overpowering urge to join his assailant on its nocturnal questing. He reasons, however, that if he can be kept from tasting blood the spell will be weakened and eventually broken. Each night, therefore, just prior to his transformation into a wolf, he persuades his sister to chain him up securely so that escape into the woods is impossible. This proves a successful stratagem and ultimately leads to the lifting of the spell.

The Arctic wastes of Canada is the bleak setting for "The Silver Knife" by Ralph Allen Lang. In this suspenseful story from the January 1932 issue, Wolf Dahlgren, a fugitive from the law, is heading for civilization and a life of luxury after dishonestly acquiring a priceless Native American sacrificial knife made of silver and with a pair of large rubies set in the ornamental hilt. However, throughout the journey he is constantly trailed by a huge timber wolf that attacks his dog-team, reducing their number by one each night. Bullets fired at the beast fail to harm it, adding to Dahlgren's alarm; and after all the huskies have been killed he is forced to take refuge in an abandoned cabin, where he fearfully awaits the inevitable showdown with his nemesis. Dahlgren's body is later found with the throat torn out, and lying beside it is the body of a wrinkled old medicine man with the silver knife embedded in his chest.

In Howard Wandrei's "The Hand of the O'Mecca" (April 1935) a lonely farmer courts a local girl, unaware that she is a werewolf. Impatient to be wed, he asks for her hand in marriage but gets a nasty shock when he literally receives the girl's hand when he wrenches it off after she attacks him in her wolf form.

A stalwart of *Weird Tales* for most of its lifetime was the popular fantasist Manly Wade Wellman, who made his debut in 1927 and was still writing for the magazine in the early 1950s. His initial foray into the realm of the werewolf was in "The Horror Undying" (May 1936), which is based on the old belief that if a man who was a werewolf dies painlessly and his body is left whole, he can still live on as a vampire. This was followed by "The Werewolf Snarls" (March 1937), a short but effective tale in which a man attending a social gathering leaves hurriedly after an unnerving conversation with one of the other guests, who confidentially discloses that he is a werewolf. The next morning the newspapers are full of reports about the brutal murders that had taken place at the party later that evening.

Under the pseudonym "Gans T. Field," Wellman also wrote a werewolf serial, "The Hairy Ones Shall Dance" (January–March 1938), the first of a quartet of stories featuring the psychic investigator Judge Pursuivant. The narrator is Talbot Wills, a former stage magician, who has given up his career to study psychic phenomena. His initial skepticism is diminished after meeting Doctor Otto Zoberg, a lecturing expert on spiritism and other occult subjects. Zoberg, seeking to convert Wills, arranges for him to take part in a séance at which all of the participants are shackled to their chairs to ensure fair play. An abrupt end to the eerie proceedings occurs, however, when a strange wolflike shape suddenly materializes and attacks one of the sitters, rending him to death. When the police arrive they ridicule Wills's version of events and accuse him of the murder, on the grounds that as a trained escapologist he was the only person in the sealed room with the ability to free himself from the manacles.

After Wills is placed under arrest a mob gathers outside the prison, threatening to lynch him; but he manages to escape from his cell and finds shelter in a mysterious grove on the edge of town called the Devil's Croft, which custom and local law forbid anyone to enter. In its depths Wills encounters and fights with the same wolf-thing that had materialized at the séance, and after stunning it with a lucky blow he is horrified to see the creature gradually turning human. Not stopping to see the completion of the transformation, Wills flees from the grove and finds sanctuary in the house of a scholarly recluse, Judge Keith Pursuivant, who shows him by logic and quotation of distinguished authorities that a werewolf can be explained by the spiritist theory of ectoplasmic materialization.

The final installment of the serial concerns Pursuivant's quest to discover the identity of the werewolf, and it concludes with the revelation that Dr. Zoberg is the villain. After being apprehended he confesses that he has mastered the ability to exude ectoplasm at will—the supernatural substance acting as the agent for his controlled transformation into a wolf.

Robert Bloch's first werewolf story for *Weird Tales* was "The Hound of Pedro" in the November 1938 issue. Set in old Mexico during the early period of Spanish rule, it tells the story of Black Pedro Dominguez, the tyrannical leader of a band of freebooters who terrorize the native Indians. Totally merciless, he and a Moorish wizard enter into a pact with the Devil, which brings them wealth and occult powers in exchange for the souls of their victims. Every month when the moon is full, the Indians are forced to hand over a maiden, who is used as a human sacrifice in an occult rite in which the evil Spaniard and his constant companion, a huge black hound, exchange souls after drinking the girl's blood. Thus endowed with human intelligence and able to walk upright, the fearsome beast goes on a rampage in search of souls for Black Pedro's Satanic master.

Minor werewolf stories published in *Weird Tales* in the thirties include Jeremy Ellis's "Silver Bullets" (April 1930); Theda Kenyon's "The House of the Golden Eyes" (September 1930); Howard Wandrei's "In the Triangle" (January 1934); Brooke Byrne's "The Werewolf's Howl" (December 1934); and Captain S. P. Meek's "The Curse of the Valedi" (July 1935). *Weird Tales* also published an abridged version of Alexandre Dumas's novel *The Wolf-Leader*, running it as an eight-part serial from August 1931 to March 1932. Two were-tiger stories, Bassett Morgan's "Tiger Dust" (April 1933) and Vennette Herron's "Toean Matjan" (January 1938), are also worthy of mention as is Nathan Hindin's "Fangs of Vengeance" (April 1937), a melodramatic circus yarn about were-leopards that would have made a great vehicle for Boris Karloff—had it been adapted for the screen.

Each issue of *Weird Tales* also contained two or three pieces of weird poetry. Most were merely space fillers, but the better ones were accorded more prominence and often accompanied by illustrations. Among the latter was H. P. Lovecraft's "Psychopompos," published in the September 1937 issue, shortly after his death. A long narrative ballad in couplets, it tells of a medieval baron who terrorizes his vassals in the guise of a wolf. Three shorter poems that utilized the werewolf motif were Henry Kuttner's "Ballad of the Wolf" (June 1936), C. Edgar Bolen's "Lycanthropus" (August/September 1936), and Leah Bodine Drake's "They Run Again" (June/July 1939).

Weird Tales' main competitor during the early thirties was Clayton Magazines' *Strange Tales of Mystery and Terror,* which had a brief seven-issue run from September 1931 to January 1933. Similar in content to its illustrious rival, it rose rapidly to prominence by securing the services of most of the top authors in the horror field, who were enticed by the offer of two cents a word for their best material, a rate that *Weird Tales* could not match.

A notable story from the January 1932 issue is Jack Williamson's "Wolves of Darkness," which set a precedent by postulating a pseudoscientific explanation of the werewolf myth. Like many of the early science fiction stories in the pulps, it concerns an attempt by aliens to take over the world. In this instance a horde of abominable entities—described in typically extravagant fashion as "dark masses of fetid, reeking blackness"—find ingress into our dimension and, by possessing the minds and bodies of human beings, turn them into wolflike monsters. Fortunately for the human race the aliens fear light, and by exploiting this fatal weakness the hero eventually brings about their downfall. Nevertheless, the story ends on a note of caution, with the narrator suggesting this is not the first—nor probably the last—incursion into our dimension by these unwelcome visitors. This notion is emphasized even further in the epilogue, which claims that through some cosmic accident these beings have invaded our world before; and the widespread legends about werewolves are folk-memories of horrors visited upon Earth by these hideous monstrosities in times past.

Strange Tales also published a cracking were-tiger story, Bassett Morgan's "Tiger" (March 1932), in which the white owner of a plantation in Sumatra becomes a marked man after giving his number-one boy money to buy himself a young dancing girl to replace his aging wife. The rejected spouse gets her revenge by enlisting the aid of a powerful relative, a temple priest known as the tiger-lord, who menaces the plantation owner in the form of a tiger.

In the mid-1930s the emergence of a range of lurid magazines known collectively as "Weird Menace" pulps ushered in a slightly unsavory chapter in American popular fiction. Aimed specifically at the least intellectual section of the reading public, these notorious periodicals mostly featured mystery-terror stories with a strong element of sex and sadism. All contributors were required to follow a strict formula; no matter how bizarre or supernatural the situations they concocted seemed, the plots always had to be resolved with rational explanations. Invariably they involved a lovely young woman falling into the clutches of a maniacal villain, who then proceeded to subject his terrified victim to some ingenious form of torture and/or various sexual indignities.

Not surprisingly, werewolves were rarely encountered in the pages of these magazines, and the few that did appear were usually of the fake variety. A story that typifies the way the phenomenon was represented is Wayne Rogers's "Beast-Women Stalk at Night" (*Horror Stories,* August/September 1937), in which an epidemic of lycanthropy is suspected when a pack of nude, ravening beast-women run amok and pursue their victims with the ferocity of wolves. In the same author's "Hell's Brew" (*Thrilling Mystery,* January 1936), a large black beast resembling a werewolf plays a part in the grisly proceedings; and a giant, bloodsucking wolf is featured in "The Death Beast" by Norvell Page (*Dime Mystery Magazine,* December 1933).

Other stories in the Weird Menace pulps that utilize the werewolf theme are "Nightmare!" by John H. Knox (*Dime Mystery Magazine,* May 1934); "Accursed Thirst" by Norvell Page (*Terror Tales,* September 1935); "The Werewolf of Wall Street" by Edith and Ejler Jacobson (*Dime Mystery Magazine,* July 1938); "Master of the Werewolves" by Gabriel Wilson (*Terror Tales,* July/August 1939); and "Wooed by a Werewolf" by Robert Leslie Bellem (*Uncanny Tales,* November 1939).

Worth a brief mention are three stories from pulps not belonging to the Weird Menace range: "The Wolf in the Dark" by J. Paul Suter (*Ghost Stories,* February 1931); "Rescued by Satan" by Richard B. Sale (*Mystery Adventures,* May 1936); and "Flowers from the Moon" by Tarleton Fiske [Robert Bloch] (*Strange Stories,* August 1939), which tells of a species of orchid found on the moon that induces lycanthropy when brought back to earth.

5

The Beast Within

Freudian Overtones in Endore's Classic

The vigor and inventiveness of the pulp stories found few echoes in the werewolf novels of the 1930s, most of which were routine potboilers revolving around stock situations. One of the few to rise above the general mediocrity was *The Wolf's Bride* (1930) by the Finnish author Madame Aino Kallas. Imitating the style and language of the old Norse chronicles, it tells of the tragic events that occur after Pridiik the hunter takes the lovely maiden Aolo for his bride. For a while the couple are blissfully happy, but the situation changes dramatically after the Forest-Daemon magically transforms Aolo into a werewolf. By day she is the same gentle, loving wife that she was before, but at night she undergoes a terrifying metamorphosis and runs with the wolf pack, committing acts of wanton savagery. The double life of the enchanted spouse is finally terminated when her husband learns her dreadful secret and shoots her with a gun that fires silver bullets.

Alfred H. Bill's popular historical thriller *The Wolf in the Garden* (1931) treats the theme in a more stereotypical fashion. Set in the early 1800s, the story centers on the sinister activities of a French nobleman, Le Comte de Saint Loup, who has come to live in America after fleeing from the French Revolution. Shortly after his arrival in a quiet town in northern New York State, several local residents are attacked by a giant wolf that, strangely enough, seems to pick only on those who have shown animosity toward the count. This leads the local minister to suspect that the disagreeable newcomer is a werewolf, and when confirmation of this is finally obtained he uses his knowledge of the occult to help a group of townspeople put a stop to the shape-changer's reign of terror.

The most famous werewolf novel from the 1930s is undoubtedly Guy Endore's *The Werewolf of Paris,* which has rarely been out of print since its initial publication in 1933. Regarded by critics as the only modern werewolf text of any literary quality, it now enjoys the same preeminence that Bram Stoker's *Dracula* achieved in its particular field. Another common denominator is that both novels were inspired by the inhuman deeds of real people. In *Dracula* it was the ruthless fifteenth-century Wallachian warlord Vlad Tepes who was the model for the central character, while in Endore's *magnum opus* it was the equally notorious Sergeant François Bertrand, the nineteenth-century French soldier who robbed graves of their corpses and devoured the rotting flesh. Although generally regarded as a ghoul, Bertrand's link with lycanthropy emerged during his trial, at which he claimed that he turned into a wolf while committing his atrocities.

Bertrand Caillet, the hero of *The Werewolf of Paris*, is a more sympathetic character than his real-life counterpart. Born on Christmas Eve, the bastard son of a lecherous priest, Caillet's life is cursed from the outset by tainted ancestry. Even as an infant his appearance has a marked canine resemblance, and during his early childhood he develops peculiar physical characteristics, such as hairy palms, thick eyebrows that meet above the nose, interlocking teeth, and, most tellingly, a tendency to howl like a wolf. By the time he has reached adolescence he begins to experience realistic dreams in which he assumes lupine form. At the same time his condition is further aggravated by his emerging sexual urges.

Bertrand's guardian, Aymar Galliez, has his suspicions about his ward's lycanthropic nature confirmed after the local forest warden wounds a marauding wolf with a silver bullet, and this projectile is later found embedded in the boy's leg. After this incident, Aymar locks the youngster in his room at night and tries to appease his craving for blood by putting him on a diet of raw meat. But these precautions only postpone the inevitable, for once Bertrand has reached manhood his wolfish nature reasserts itself.

After sexually assaulting his mother and brutally murdering the forest warden, Bertrand flees to Paris to escape prosecution. From then on his affliction gets worse, and his subsequent one-man crime wave (which includes the violation of graves and the mutilation of the corpses within) brings even more horror to a city already in a state of turmoil following the collapse of the Third Empire and the commencement of a bloody struggle for power. As a cover for his activities, Bertrand joins the National Guard and rents a cheap basement room, conveniently located at the rear of the house. A window, which he leaves open at night, allows him to depart and return unnoticed. He is by this time fully aware of his condition and always knows when an attack is coming on:

> During the day he would have no appetite. In the evening he would feel tense and both tired and sleepless. Then he would lock his door, and having taken his precautions, he would lie down. Frequently he would wake in the morning, in bed, with no recollection of what had happened at night. Only a wretched stiffness in the neck, a lassitude in his limbs, that could come from nothing but miles of running; scratches on his hands, and feet, and an acrid taste in his mouth argued that he had spent the night elsewhere. On such occasions, however, full

conviction awaited him when he rose. Under his bed he caught a flash of white. It was a human forearm! A man's. The fingers were clutched tightly into a fist. Hair, as if torn from a fur coat, protruded from the interstices between the fingers.

Just when it seems that his excesses are certain to bring about his capture, Caillet meets and falls in love with the beautiful Sophie de Blumenberg. A bizarre sadomasochistic relationship quickly develops, and Sophie willingly yields some of her blood while they make love. This new focus in Bertrand's life miraculously brings about the sudden cessation of his lycanthropic seizures and reveals the true nature of his affliction. It shows that he is not irredeemably evil but is one of those anguished individuals in whom the soul of man and beast are constantly at war. Whatever weakens the human soul, either sin or darkness, solitude or cold, brings the wolf to the fore; and whatever weakens the beastly soul, either virtue or daylight, warmth or the companionship of another human being, raises and strengthens the human soul.

For a while it seems that Sophie's love will be the means of Bertrand's salvation, but his incessant demands for larger quantities of his lover's blood eventually place her life in jeopardy. At night, as they lie in each other's arms, Bertrand constantly fights against the overwhelming desire to sink his teeth into Sophie's carotid artery and drink his fill. One evening, when the torment becomes unbearable, he rushes out into the street and attacks the first person who comes along. But the intended victim, who happens to be a fellow soldier, fights off his attacker and puts him under arrest. Declared insane at his court-martial, Bertrand is incarcerated in an asylum, where he finally puts an end to his miserable existence by committing suicide. Years later when his coffin is disinterred, the skeleton of a wolf is found inside.

One of the most intriguing aspects of this novel is the way the author links cruelty with sexuality. Bertrand, for instance, represents the sadist whose desire to dominate his partner manifests itself in a compulsion to injure, to torture—to inflict pain. Sophie, on the other hand, displays masochistic tendencies and derives pleasure from pain, which is brilliantly depicted in the passage describing the lovers' first meeting. At Bertrand's tentative attempt to show affection, Sophie rebukes him: "Don't hurt me! Oh please don't hurt me!" But when he releases her from his embrace she is filled with contrition and implores him to embrace her once more:

> "You must hold me tighter," she said. "Tighter still," she whispered. Such a bliss flowed through her from his body pressed close to hers that her head grew dizzy, her breath came and went. Her body tensed and then seemed about to dissolve in liquid. If only he would press harder. If only he would crush her, tear her! Mutilate her! In desperation she cried out: "Hurt me! Bertrand, hurt me!"

On reflection, it seems strange that, prior to this novel, so few werewolf stories had stressed the psycho-sexual aspect of lycanthropy. In the mid-nineteenth century the French and English "Decadents" had con-cluded that the sadistic component of the sexual in-stinct is ideally represented by the werewolf. Baude-laire, for instance, maintained that lycanthropy was merely another name for sadism; and the idea of pain as an integral part of sexual pleasure was a major obses-sion of the whole Romantic movement.

Translated into Freudian terms, Bertrand's violent behavior patterns point to him being psychologically arrested at the oral stage of sexuality. This is particu-larly evident in his lovemaking, during which he makes small incisions in Sophie's naked body with a sharp knife and sucks out the blood. Later this lust for the warm fluid of life becomes almost vampiric as he strives to extract ever larger amounts. For like all individuals in the thrall of oral desire, Bertrand has what psycho-analysts describe as an unconscious desire to devour the beloved object; and though he struggles valiantly against it, he realizes toward the end that these power-ful urges must ultimately triumph.

Significantly, the author who had the greatest in-fluence on Endore was the infamous German writer Hanns Heinz Ewers, whose classic horror novel *Vampire* (1922) revolves around an almost identical sadomasoch-istic relationship. Another similarity between the two novels is that, like Frank Braun in *Vampire,* Endore's hero has been divested of all the supernatural attributes associated with the monster he represents, thereby giving greater credibility to his actions. There is also no attempt by the author to sensationalize the events in the story, which adds to its believability and gives parts of the narrative a documentary realism. There are, for instance, no theatrical transformation scenes nor are there any graphic descriptions of Bertrand's grave-robbing activities. Nevertheless, there are occasions when this understated approach seems inappropriate, and several potentially horrific scenes are told in such a matter-of-fact manner that they lack any shock value. Readers used to the gross violence of contemporary horror novels may find the opening chapters here too bland for their liking; but the latter half of the book, which has its fair share of "blood and gore," will certainly repay their perseverance. Finding a copy should not be a problem either, since there have been several paperback editions published in recent years.

Compared to this innovative work, F. Layland-Barratt's *Lycanthia* (1935) is positively anachronistic. The highly derivative plot revolves around the activities of a female werewolf, Lycanthia Kritzulescu, the daughter of a Polish count and an Englishwoman. After her father's death Lycanthia goes to live with her aunt in England, who has no idea that she has invited a flesh-eating monster into her home. Following the usual pattern of such stories, Lycanthia proceeds to prey on the local community in the form of a wolf.

Equally predictably she is shot and mortally wounded during one of her nocturnal rampages, and after death, reverts to human form.

Meatier fare is provided by J. U. Nicolson's *Fingers of Fear* (1937), in which the residents of a secluded English mansion all suffer from a form of homicidal pseudo-lycanthropy. Inevitably this leads to a succession of horrific incidents, including some very grisly murders. If this weren't enough to keep the proverbial pot boiling, the author deems it necessary to introduce ghosts, hidden corpses, vampire-women, and a living portrait into the plot. Unfortunately, by letting his imagination run riot in this way, Nicolson spreads on the horror with too heavy a hand so that the reader's credulity is stretched much too far.

Another novel with a typically British setting is *Grey Shapes* by Jack Mann. Published in 1938, this is one of a series of crime thrillers featuring Gregory George Gordon Green, a private investigator specializing in bizarre cases, who is known to his friends and associates as Gees. On this occasion a wealthy landowner hires him to exterminate wolflike creatures that have been attacking his flock of sheep. As a result of his investigations, Gees becomes suspicious of his client's reclusive neighbors, Diarmid and Gyda McCoul, who live nearby in a half-ruined castle. When more killings occur, including that of a shepherd, Gees sets a trap for the perpetrators, and both werewolves are killed. The dead forms then assume human shape and are identified as the McCouls.

It is later revealed that the werewolves were seven hundred years old and had lived at their ancestral home since the reign of Henry III of England.

Two thrillers in a similar mold—except that they have rationalized endings—are John Dickson Carr's *It Walks by Night* (1930) and Eden Phillpotts's *Lycanthrope: The Mystery of Sir William Wolf* (1937).

Most of the short stories published in the 1930s with a werewolf motif have already been mentioned in the previous section about the pulp magazines, but a few found their way into hardcover collections. The majority of these, however, were run-of-the-mill and are deservedly forgotten today. A rare gem among the dross is Peter Fleming's "The Kill" (*Creeps by Night*, 1931), which is justly famous for its surprise ending. As the story opens, two men are sitting in the otherwise deserted waiting room of a small provincial railway station in the West of England. Fog has delayed the arrival of their train, and the younger of the two men decides to engage the other in conversation. To pass the time he tells the stranger about the misfortunes that have lately beset his uncle, Lord Fleer, with whom he has been staying. The wealthy nobleman, who lives in a castle on a nearby country estate is, the young man explains, a bachelor, but had an adopted daughter who would have been his heir had she not been recently murdered. Disturbingly, Lord Fleer's troubles had started a few weeks previously with reports that an unidentified predator had been killing sheep on his land, recalling to mind events that had taken place a quarter of a century earlier. The narrator reveals that in his youth the nobleman had been involved in a brief fling with his fiery Welsh housekeeper, but when he found out she expected him to marry her, he abruptly broke off the relationship. Packed off to an unused wing of the castle, the spurned mistress later gave birth to a son, then she died almost immediately afterward. With her dying breath she warned Lord Fleer that there was a curse embodied in the child, which would fall on anyone who was made heir over his head; to add to Fleer's alarm he subsequently discovered that the infant had a physical peculiarity: the third finger on each hand was longer than the second, signifying—according to ancient superstition—that he would become a werewolf.

Disowned by his father and fostered by a local woman, the motherless child ran away when he was ten. Now, some fifteen years later, Lord Fleer suspects the young man-wolf has returned to get revenge and claim his inheritance. Determined to stop him, the rich landowner and his nephew, together with a posse of retainers, scour the woods on the estate, but the werewolf is nowhere to be seen. On their return, however, the nobleman's fears are realized when the dead, mutilated body of his adopted daughter is found lying on the drive outside the house.

The final twist in the story is precipitated by the storyteller's final revelation, and the stranger's unexpected reaction to it:

"It is a wild and improbable story," he said. "I do not expect you to believe the whole of it. For me, perhaps, the reality of its implications has obscured its almost ludicrous lack of verisimilitude. You see, by the death of my uncle's daughter I am heir to Fleer."

The stranger smiled: a slow, but no longer abstracted smile. His honey-colored eyes were bright. Under his long black overcoat his body seemed to be stretching itself in sensual anticipation. He rose silently to his feet.

The other found a sharp, cold fear drilling into his vitals. Something behind those shining eyes threatened him with appalling immediacy, like a sword at his heart. He was sweating. He dared not move.

The stranger's smile was now a grin, a ravening convulsion of the face. His eyes blazed with a hard and purposeful delight. A thread of saliva dangled from the corner of his mouth.

Very slowly he lifted one hand and removed his bowler hat. Of the fingers crooked about its brim, the young man saw that the third was longer than the second.

Several stories by other British writers showed a similar subtlety in their treatment of the theme. In Hugh Walpole's "Tarnhelm" (*All Souls' Night,* 1933) an elderly warlock living in a quiet suburban neighborhood in England is able to transform himself into an evil-looking mongrel dog by placing on his head a small gray skullcap, which he calls his tarnhelm (a reference to the shapeshifting device in *The Ring of the Nibelungs*). More exotic in their choice of locale are two stories by Lewis Spence, "Enchantment on the Unicorn" and "The Temple of the Jaguars," both of which come from his collection *The Archer in the Arras and Other Tales of Mystery* (1932). In "Enchantment on the Unicorn" the crew of a ship manned by Scotsmen fleeing from their disastrous defeat by the English in 1745 is plagued by an outbreak of lycanthropy after one of them is bitten by Mexican natives belonging to a jaguar cult. "The Temple of the Jaguars" is set in Central America and features a lycanthrope whose condition is caused by a virus. C. H. B. Kitchin's adult fairy tale "Beauty and the Beast" (*A Century of Creepy Stories,* 1934) has the novelty of a woman-panther and a man-tiger as its enchanted protagonists; while H. Russell Wakefield's African voodoo tale "Death of a Poacher" (*A Ghostly Company,* 1935) boasts a were-hyena. "Taboo" by Geoffrey Household, in which lycanthropy is depicted as a mental illness, was probably inspired by the real-life case of Denke the Butcher, which scandalized Europe in the years immediately following World War I. Originally from the collection *The Salvation of Pisco Gabar and Other Stories* (1939), this tale appeared more recently in *Realms of Darkness* (Chartwell Books, 1988). Household also wrote a routine yarn called "The Night of the Werewolf" (1938), which has sunk into oblivion—a fate also shared by Mrs. L. Baillie Reynolds's "The Terrible Baron" (*The Terrible Baron and Other Stories,* 1933), and E. H. Visiak's "In the Mangrove

Hall," which has not been seen since its appearance in the bumper anthology *Masterpiece of Thrills* (1936).

Shifting Tastes: The Influence of *Unknown* in the 1940s

In common with the previous decade, werewolf stories from the 1940s can be divided into two groups: those that appeared in hardcover books (i.e., anthologies and single-author collections) and those from the pages of the weird-fantasy magazines. In the United States the latter again formed the majority and were generally superior to their upmarket counterparts.

As in the thirties the pick of the werewolf stories from the pulps were published in *Weird Tales,* which continued to be the primary forum for masters of macabre fiction, despite the fact that some of the legendary authors associated with the magazine were either dead or had moved on to better-paying markets. One prominent member of the old guard who was not lured away was the ever-popular Seabury Quinn, whose numerous contributions to *Weird Tales* in the forties included two additional werewolf stories, bringing his tally to eight in all. The first of these, "The Gentle Werewolf" (July 1940), is set in the Holy Land in the period following the Crusades and centers on the plight of a Frankish maiden, Sylvanette de Gavaret, who is transformed into a wolf by a witch whose wrath she has incurred. To add to her woes the unfortunate young woman is told that she is doomed to remain in this form until "some noble lord shall kiss thy hairy beast's-lips and declare his love for thee." Despite her savage appearance, the newly created werewolf loses none of her innate gentleness, and after being forced to flee into the wilderness finds she hasn't the heart to kill animals for food. She becomes a scavenger and exists by helping herself to the remains of kills made by real wolves. After many trials and tribulations the curse is eventually lifted when the "gentle werewolf" comes to the rescue of a former suitor, who fulfills the condition of the curse by rewarding his savior with a kiss.

Quinn's last werewolf story for *Weird Tales* was "Bon Voyage, Michele" (January 1944), which, unusually for him, takes place in the future. Prejudging the outcome of World War II—which was still in progress when the story was written—it concerns a revanchist plot by a group of German were-folk, who have been secretly stockpiling weapons to mount a resistance to the Allied Army of Occupation. Reluctantly drawn into their machinations the story's plucky heroine, Michele Mikhailovitch, is transformed into a wolf against her will and valiantly tries to prevent her lover from suffering a similar fate.

Both of the above-mentioned stories were included in *Is the Devil a Gentleman?* (Mirage Press, 1970), a collection of Quinn's best stories selected by the great man himself. One suspects, however, that most of Quinn's fans, had they been given the same opportunity to select his two finest werewolf stories, would have chosen "The Phantom Farmhouse" and "Uncanonized."

The incomparable Clark Ashton Smith, whose exotic fantasies had helped to give *Weird Tales* its unique flavor in the 1930s, rarely wrote about werewolves, preferring monsters of his own creation. One of the few occasions he made use of the theme was in "The Enchantress of Sylaire" (July 1941), which is set in a magical land ruled by a glamorous femme fatale. One of her discarded lovers is a wizard named Malachie du Marais, who has been magically transformed into a werewolf after being duped into drinking water from a lycanthropous pool. Although this has greatly diminished his occult powers, he is able to throw off his wolf-shape temporarily by eating wild garlic.

Outstanding though Smith's decadent other-world fantasy is, it was not typical of the werewolf tales then in vogue. Most of the other stories used contemporary settings, and humor and clever wordplay were much more in evidence as authors increasingly searched for new and unusual angles on which to base their stories. Epitomizing this new trend were the stories in *Unknown* (later retitled *Unknown Worlds*), which was the only fantasy magazine to seriously challenge *Weird Tales'* supremacy during the 1940s. More literary than its legendary counterpart, it broke new ground by publishing slick stories satirizing standard weird-fantasy themes. A typical example is Anthony Boucher's novelette "The Compleat Werewolf" (April 1942), a delightfully wacky romp in which the unlikely hero, a professor of Old German, gets involved in some hilarious adventures when he discovers he can metamorphose into a wolf simply by saying the word "Absarka." Morally unaffected by the change from man to beast, he demonstrates his public spiritedness by helping the authorities round up a Nazi spy ring.

Another story from *Unknown* with a World War II setting is Jane Rice's "The Refugee" (October 1943). An ingenious reworking of Saki's "Gabriel-Ernest," but with a much punchier ending, it concerns a battle of wits between a resourceful American woman living in war-torn France and a naked young man found lurking in her garden. The interloper claims to be a refugee, but he is really a hungry werewolf who plans to devour the woman after sundown. However, she adroitly turns the tables on him with a cunning stratagem. Boldly inviting the stranger into her house and lulling him into a relaxed mood, she nonchalantly drops a chocolate into his mouth while at the same time jabbing him violently with a hairpin. The shock forces the werewolf to swallow the innocent-looking confection; but unbeknown to him a silver bullet is hidden inside it, and within a few minutes he is dead. Now, at last, the full import of the heroine's actions become clear: By killing the werewolf before sundown she has not only disposed of a serious threat to her life but has also acquired a welcome supply of a rare commodity in those troubled times—fresh meat!

Some of the most innovative works of fiction published in *Unknown/Unknown Worlds* resulted from the magazine's policy of encouraging authors to submit stories that demythologized well-known myths. For example, traditionally supernatural monsters like vampires and werewolves were rendered more believable by giving them a quasi-scientific rationale. A classic example is Jack Williamson's novel *Darker Than You Think* (December 1940), which is based on the premise that in the remote past there existed another humanoid species on earth called *Homo lycanthropus,* identical in appearance to *Homo sapiens* but genetically different. Predatory and rapacious by nature, the males feasted on the flesh of true men and impregnated their womenfolk. Their dominion over the more numerous *Homo sapiens* was due to their magical powers, chiefly the ability to assume the shape of any animal by using a technique similar to astral projection. The witch-folk, as they were known, were also able to communicate by telepathy and possessed other such highly developed mental faculties as clairvoyance and the gift of prophecy. Undisputed masters of the earth, they looked down on primitive humankind, whom they enslaved and used as a source of food. Despite their apparent invincibility, the witch-folk's reign of terror came to an end when ways to counteract their magic were discovered; the turning point in the long struggle came when true men acquired a weapon that brought about the virtual extermination of their oppressors.

The intriguing presumption made by this thought-provoking novel is that the long period of terror and subjugation endured by our early ancestors before their deliverance has left an indelible impression on our unconscious minds, and consequently every myth about vampires, werewolves, and evil spirits that has come down to us is a racial memory of this dark period in human history.

The bizarre events depicted in *Darker Than You Think* take place in the twentieth century and are set in motion by the return to the United States of the Humane Research Foundation expedition, which has spent two years in a remote part of the Gobi Desert excavating prehistoric burial sites. On their arrival at the airport, the leader of the team of scientists, Dr. Mondrick, dramatically reveals to the waiting reporters that they have brought back with them a sealed wooden box whose contents will have an earth-shattering impact on the way we view the origin of human life. But, before he can add any more to this statement, he suddenly chokes to death for no apparent reason.

The hero, Will Barbee, who is one of the newsmen covering the return of the expedition, finds himself drawn into the mystery surrounding the noted anthropologist's death after meeting a beautiful redhead named April Bell, who claims to be a witch. Taking Barbee into her confidence she reveals that she belongs to an underground movement whose members are descendants of the outlawed race of shapeshifters, and she makes no bones about the fact that she used her magical powers to kill Mondrick. What's more, she intends to permanently silence the other members of the expedition and destroy the contents of the wooden box, which is thought to contain the ancient weapon used so successfully against the witch-folk. Although shocked to hear about her plans—especially since members of the Humane Research Foundation are his friends—Barbee becomes more amenable to April's viewpoint when he discovers that he, too, has the blood of the witch-folk flowing through his veins.

When April awakens powers in him similar to her own, Barbee begins to experience realistic "dreams" in which he leaves his body behind and joins the witch-woman in hunting down and killing the remaining expedition members while in a variety of fearsome animal guises. The first time this happens he metamorphoses into a wolf, and April changes into a white she-wolf. On another occasion he takes the form of a saber-toothed tiger, and the flame-haired femme fatale sits astride him in the nude, urging him on as he pursues his terrified victim.

As Barbee learns more about the witch-folk, he discovers that they have infiltrated all walks of life, and those in high positions have secretly manipulated the course of history to the advantage of their species. In the centuries since their downfall they have built up their numbers by crossbreeding with humans, and now they are ready to reassert themselves and establish a new order, which will be ushered in by the coming of a Messiah—the Child of Night. In a final twist it emerges that Barbee has been specially bred to take on this role.

Clearly a lot of research and deep thought went into the writing of *Darker Than You Think,* and it must be acknowledged that the theories advanced to substantiate the novel's premise are convincingly presented, to the extent that one could almost believe they have a basis in fact. The novel's only flaw is that it is difficult to sympathize with the hero, who not only goes around bumping off his friends but is also in league with a subversive group who are plotting to seize power from the human race and place them in bondage.

An expanded version of Williamson's novel was published in hardcover by Fantasy Press in 1948, and several paperback editions have appeared since.

The refreshingly different stories featured in *Unknown* soon caught on with the fans, and other weird-fiction magazines—including *Weird Tales*—felt obliged to introduce stories in a similar vein. Among the regular contributors to *Weird Tales* in the 1940s the one best equipped to counter the challenge from *Unknown* was Robert Bloch, who had abandoned the corny Lovecraft pastiches of his youth and was well on the way to developing his own inimitable style. Some of Bloch's best stories from this period involve ingenious murder plots, with one spouse in an unhappy marriage trying to kill the other but ultimately suffering the fate intended for their partner when their plans go horribly wrong. A prime example is "The Man Who Cried 'Wolf'!" (*Weird Tales*, May 1945), in which a writer begins an illicit love affair with a beautiful Indian girl while on vacation with his nagging wife in the Canadian backwoods. Eager to make this new relationship a permanent one, the writer hatches a plan to drive his wife insane by making her believe she is being stalked by a werewolf. However, he had not bargained for the unexpected discovery that his lover is, in reality, a werewolf, finding out on the night of the full moon when she suddenly transforms in his presence. Nonetheless, being a writer he takes it all in, mentally recording every detail:

> It was fascinating to watch her skull change shape—as though the hands of an invisible sculptor were kneading and molding the living clay, squeezing the very bony structure into new conformations.
> The elongated head seemed miraculously shorn of curls for the moment, and then the fine fur sprang up, the ears flared outward, the pinkish tips twitched along a thickened neck.
> Her eyes slitted upward, while the features of the face convulsed, then converged into a protuberant muzzle. The grimace of involuntary rictus became a snarl, and fangs jutted forth.
> Her skin darkened perceptibly—so that her

image was akin to that of an over-developed photographic print "coming up" in the hypo bath.

Lisa's clothing had dropped away, and I watched the melting of the limbs as they foreshortened, furred, and flexed anew. The hands that had pawed the earth in agony now became paws.

Once over the shock, the writer sees this unexpected development as an advantage in his efforts to get rid of his wife. But his carefully laid plans start to go wrong when the besotted wolf-girl becomes jealous of the woman she hopes to displace and bites her on the throat. Although not fatal, the attack leads to a police investigation, which culminates in the "wolf" being hunted down and killed. The bullet-riddled body then undergoes a transformation into human form, but a more shocking change occurs when the dead girl rapidly ages to a hideous old hag. Shortly afterward the unfaithful husband makes a full confession to his wife, but any hope of a reconciliation is dashed when the wound on her throat finally takes effect, and she metamorphoses into a raging wolf bent on revenge.

Bloch's fondness for things that go bite in the night provided him with the inspiration for two other stories in the forties. In the first of these, "Nursemaid to Nightmares" (November 1942), a man encounters a werewolf and other mythical creatures when an eccentric collector hires him to look after his private zoo. In the other story, "The Bogey Man Will Get You" (March 1946), the heroine meets a sticky end when she pokes her nose into the affairs of her handsome neighbor. Mistakenly, she believes the signs all point to him being a vampire but discovers, too late, that he is a werewolf.

One author capable of matching Bloch when it came to thinking up offbeat plots was Manly Banister. He had seven stories published in *Weird Tales* in the forties, four of which had a werewolf theme—"Satan's Bondage" (September 1942), "Devil Dog" (July 1945), "Loup-Garou" (May 1947), and "Eena" (September 1947). When "Satan's Bondage" appeared in the magazine the editor heralded it as "a werewolf western" and appended the following caption: "You're going to get the werewolf's slant on life—as you read how these accursed man-beasts roam the American West in a hellish quest for human food!" A bogus piece of werewolf lore common to this story and "Devil Dog" is that the lycanthropes must bathe in a certain stream in order to transform into wolves, and bathe again in the same stretch of water before sunrise to avoid having to remain in lupine form until the following evening.

There are some splendidly macabre moments in all of Banister's werewolf stories, but his masterpiece of the form is undoubtedly "Eena." In this poignant tale a sensitive writer named Joel Cameron, who lives among homesteaders in the vicinity of Wolf Lake, sows the seeds of tragedy when he takes in and rears a stray albino wolf cub against the advice of his neighbors. Despite the strong bond that develops between them, Eena (as the foundling is called) escapes from her compound upon reaching maturity; and soon stories arise about a great white she-wolf, who has been seen leading a pack of gray wolves in raids on the homesteaders' livestock. The plot then takes a dramatic turn when Eena suddenly changes into a beautiful young woman and henceforward alternates between human and wolf form.

In her sensual womanly guise Eena embarks on a passionate relationship with her former protector, who is completely unaware of her real identity. The truth finally emerges as a result of the irate homesteaders joining forces to stop the white wolf's attacks on their cattle. As the hunters close in for the kill the sound of their guns brings Joel to his cabin door, just in time to see the enormous, pale form of a wolf leap from the forest edge and charge toward him. Mistakenly thinking his life is in danger Joel shoots the oncoming beast, which falls mortally wounded at his feet. Then, to his dismay, the wolf metamorphoses into the form of his lover; and he is overwhelmed by despair as she dies cradled in his arms. This final scene is extremely moving and makes a memorable climax to one of the best werewolf stories ever written.

The first pulp story to challenge the stereotypical image of the werewolf was Fritz Leiber's "The Hound" (*Weird Tales*, November 1942), which has a modern urban setting. The werewolf-like monster is depicted as a shadowy creature of uncertain appearance, making it difficult to codify or define. To its intended victim it is the monster of his dreams made flesh and blood—similar to a wolf, yet malformed and giving off a sickening stench—but seen through the eyes of a witness to the attack the creature seems so outlandish it is impossible to describe.

A few original touches are also to be found in other pulp stories of the period. In Paul Selonke's "Beast of the Island" (*Strange Stories*, October 1940) the hero hits on an effective substitute for silver bullets by slaying a werewolf with a silver crucifix fired from his gun; Carl Jacobi's "The Phantom Pistol" (*Weird Tales*, May 1941) tells of a firearms' collector who possesses a pistol expressly designed for killing werewolves; and in Henry Kuttner's "The Seal of Sin" (*Strange Stories*, August 1940) a ring bearing the seal of Solomon gives a scheming occultist the power to recruit a gang of lupine henchmen. Further variations on the man-into-beast theme can be found in E. A. Grosser's "The Psychomorph" (*Unknown*, February 1940); Emerson Graves's "When the Werewolf Howls" (*Horror Stories*, May 1940); and Clifford Ball's "The Werewolf Howls" (*Weird Tales*, November 1941).

Included in *Prince Godfrey* (1946), a little-known collection of short stories by the Polish author Halina Gorska, is a remarkable story grandly titled "Prince Godfrey Frees Mountain Dwellers and Little Shepherds from a Savage Werewolf and from Witches." The voracious werewolf mentioned in the title—which is virtually a story in itself—consumes numerous goats, sheep, cows, and a bull, not to mention two shepherds and several children. He also sports what appears to be a pair of hoofs, but these turn out to be outsized bunions!

The best-known werewolf novel from the 1940s is Franklin Gregory's *The White Wolf* (1941). Purportedly an attempt at an adult treatment of the theme, it centers on the evil activities of a wealthy businessman's daughter, Sara de Camp d'Avesnes, who goes on a killing spree in the form of a white wolf after getting involved with a Satanic cult. Sara's father, who is alarmed by the sudden change in her personality, stumbles upon the truth about his daughter's double life when he consults ancient family records. These reveal that she was predestined to become a werewolf as part of a deal made with the Devil by a twelfth-century ancestor (predictably called Hugues) who was granted occult powers after accepting the condition that every seventh heir of his family would inherit the curse of lycanthropy.

Two fantasy novels with a werewolf element that appeared in pulp magazines prior to book publication are Henry Kuttner's *The Dark World* (*Startling Stories,* summer 1946) and L. Sprague de Camp and Fletcher Pratt's *The Castle of Iron* (*Unknown,* April 1941).

An interesting fragment dealing with Asian shapeshifting is "The Fox Woman" by the great fantasy writer A. Merritt. This uncompleted novel was discovered after the author's sudden death in 1943. Set in Yunnun in China, the story chronicles the strange experiences of an American woman after she is rescued from a band of thugs by a supernatural being called a Fox Woman—a class of nature spirit peculiar to the Far East, which Merritt describes as follows:

> These spirits have certain powers far exceeding the human. They can assume two earthly shapes only— that of a fox and that of a beautiful woman. There are fox men, too, but the weight of the legends are upon the women. Since for them time does not exist, they are mistresses of time. To those who come under their power, they can cause a day to seem like a thousand years, or a thousand years like a day. They can open the doors to other worlds—worlds of terror, worlds of delight. They can create other illusions. Phantoms, perhaps—but if so, phantoms whose blows maim or kill. They are capricious, bestowing good fortune or ill regardless of the virtue or lack of it of the recipient. They are peculiarly favorable to women with child. They can, by invitation, enter a woman, passing through her breasts or beneath her fingernails. They can enter an unborn child, or rather a child about to be born. In such cases the mother dies—nor is the manner of birth the normal one. They cannot oust the soul of the child, but they can dwell beside it, influencing it.

This fragment was later completed by Hannes Bok and published as *The Fox Woman and the Blue Pagoda* in 1946. The original version appeared in a collection titled *The Fox Woman and Other Stories* (1949), which contained all of Merritt's short fiction. One of the "other stories" in this volume was "The Drone," in which a group of explorers recount the uncanny experiences they have had with the phenomenon of shapeshifting in various parts of the globe. During the course of their anecdotes about were-hyenas, leopard men, bird people, and the like, one of the explorers conjectures that "man's consciousness may share the brain with other consciousnesses—beast or bird or what not." He further speculates that "all life is one . . . a thinking and conscious force of which the trees, the beasts, the flowers, germs and man and everything living are parts, just as the billions of living cells in a man are parts of him. And that under certain conditions the parts may be interchangeable." This, he thinks, may be the source of the ancient tales of the dryads and the nymphs, the harpies, and the werewolves and other were-beasts.

Changing with the Times: Postwar Trends

The immediate postwar era marked the beginning of the end for the pulp magazines, and by the early 1950s most had ceased publication. Taking their place initially were handier digest-sized magazines, which would in turn face stiff competition from pocket-sized paperback books later on in the decade. In the weird-fantasy genre, as in other forms of popular fiction, authors had to contend with an increasingly sophisticated readership no longer content to be fobbed off with stale plots and outdated images. Werewolf stories were no exception and needed to change with the times in order to retain their appeal. Out went supernatural monsters and rural settings, and in came a new breed of werewolf who stalked his victims among the streets and alleys of modern cities. Werewolves also invaded the pages of science fiction magazines, invariably disguised as shapeshifting aliens.

One of the best short stories from this period is Bruce Elliott's "Wolves Don't Cry" (*The Magazine of Fantasy and Science Fiction*, April 1954). Written from a nonhuman perspective, it centers on the dilemma faced by a natural wolf when he suddenly metamorphoses into a human being. Up to this point, Lobo (as the wolf is called) had reconciled himself to a life of captivity in a zoo; but following the miraculous change in appearance his reasonably contented existence is irrevocably destroyed. Thereafter he has to cope with learning to wear clothes and adapting to alien modes of behavior. He cannot understand, for instance, why he has to do such absurd things as encumber his legs with cloth that flaps about and gets in his way, or why he needs to balance precariously on his hind legs. It transpires, however, that Lobo's transformation is only skin deep, for when he impregnates a young woman she gives birth to a baby werewolf.

The offbeat humor of Elliott's yarn is reflected in other stories from the 1950s. In Frank Robinson's "The Night Shift," a story from the February/March 1953 issue of *Fantasy Magazine*, a vampire sets the fur flying when he tries to muscle in on the werewolves who control Chicago. Theodore Cogswell's "Wolfie" (*Beyond Fantasy Fiction*, January 1954) concerns a man who wants to become a werewolf for a limited period. A doctor, whose contract allows his patients to commit crimes by supernatural methods, helps him to achieve his odd objective. In Anthony Boucher's "The Ambassadors" (*Startling Stories,* June 1952), the lupine Martians loathe primate Earthmen but manage to maintain diplomatic contact by exchanging werewolves and wereapes as ambassadors. Another futuristic story with a sting in the tail is Clark Ashton Smith's "A Prophecy of Monsters" (*The Magazine of Fantasy and Science Fiction,* October 1954). Set in the twenty-first century, where werewolves and vampires have survived as a consequence of mass skepticism, the story relates how a werewolf meets his match when he attacks an android.

The most famous werewolf story from the 1950s, James Blish's "There Shall Be No Darkness" (*Thrilling Wonder Stories,* April 1950), bucked the trend by utilizing one of the most clichéd formulas in popular fiction. Like countless murder mysteries of the 1920s and 1930s, all the action takes place in and around an isolated country house where a party is being held. Two of the guests, an artist named Paul Foote and Christian Lundgren, an eminent psychiatrist, observe that one of their number, the great Polish pianist Jarmoskowski, exhibits all the stigmata associated with the werewolf—eyes bloodshot with moonrise, first and second fingers of equal length, pointed ears, domed prefrontal bones, and elongated upper cuspids. When challenged later that evening, Jarmoskowski metamorphoses into a wolf, but he is forced to flee from the house and hide in the woods, where he evades an attempt by the others to capture him.

As a precaution, traditional werewolf repellents are placed around the house to ward off nocturnal attacks, but the following morning everyone is shocked by the discovery of Lundgren's horribly mutilated body. Taking charge of proceedings, Foote gathers all the remaining houseguests together to discuss the situation; he then stuns them by announcing that Lundgren was not killed by the obvious suspect but by another werewolf— someone who has become afflicted after accidentally coming into contact with Jarmoskowski's tainted blood. As he is about to examine their hands for telltale cuts, the unknown werewolf's identity is startlingly revealed when a woman in the group suddenly takes on wolf form and becomes a raging monster. But before she can do any serious harm, she is bludgeoned to death with a heavy silver candlestick. Jarmoskowski's unnatural existence is eventually terminated when he is shot by Foote, who catches him unawares as he is attempting to recruit another houseguest to his cause.

The only fresh idea in "There Shall Be No Darkness" is the pseudoscientific theory the author has devised to explain the existence of werewolves. At one point in the narrative, Lundgren (an expert on hormone-created insanity) claims that lycanthropy is caused by a rare aberration of the pea-sized pineal gland in the brain. Asked how a werewolf maintains his lupine shape, he replies:

"Oh, that's the easiest part. You know how water takes the shape of a vessel it sits in? Well protoplasm is a liquid. The pineal hormone lowers the surface tension of the cells and at the same time short circuits the sympathetic nervous system directly to the cerebral cortex. Result, a plastic, malleable body within limits. A wolf is easiest because the skeletons are similar."

A favorite with anthologists, this suspenseful novelette has been reprinted a number of times. One of its most recent appearances was in *Masters of Fantasy*, edited by Terry Carr and Martin H. Greenberg (Galahad Books, 1992).

August Derleth's "The Adventure of the Tottenham Werewolf" (in *Memoirs of Solar Pons,* 1951) is a tongue-in-cheek Sherlock Holmes pastiche, in which a string of grisly murders are thought to be the work of a werewolf. The prime suspect is Septimus Grayle, who suffers from seizures during which he gets down on all fours and howls like a wolf; but the real culprit, his scheming sister, is duly unmasked by the brilliant detective. In contrast, A. Bertram Chandler's novelette "The Frontier of the Dark" (*Astounding Science Fiction,* September 1952) is set in the far future, when the Mannschenn Drive has made traveling faster than light a reality. Unfortunately it has an unforseen side effect, causing humans to revert to the bestial form of their own legendary ancestry. In Will F. Jenkins's suspenseful "Night Drive" (*Today's Woman,* March 1950), a werewolf poses as a female hitchhiker and attacks women drivers who give him a lift. A voluptuous female were-wolf is encountered in Manly Wade Wellman's "The Last Grave of Lill Warran" (*Weird Tales,* May 1951), which is based on the old belief that a werewolf killed in its wolf shape will become a vampire after death; and in Charles G. Finney's "The Black Retriever" (*The Magazine of Fantasy and Science Fiction,* October 1958), residents of a quiet suburban neighborhood suspect a local spinster is really a shapeshifting witch after they are terrorized by a phantom dog. Not quite in the same class but still enjoyable are Manly Banister's "Cry Wolf!" (*The Nekromantikon,* spring 1950); Steve Benedict's "Come, My Sweet" (*The Nekromantikon,* mid-year 1951); Jerome Bixby's "The Young One" (*Fantastic,* April 1954); Poul Anderson's "Operation Afreet" (*The Magazine of Fantasy and Science Fiction,* September 1956); Brian Aldiss's "Flowers of the Forest" (*Science Fantasy,* August 1957); and Gordon Dickson's "The Girl Who Played Wolf" (*Fantastic,* August 1958). Low-grade stories from the same decade include Ray Cosmic's "Lycanthrope" (*Supernatural Stories,* May 1954); Bernard L. Calmus's "The Howl of the Werewolf" (*Phantom,* April 1957); R. L. Fanthorpe's "Call of the Werewolf" (*Out of This World,* August 1958); Charles D. Hammer's "The Man Who Believed in Werewolves" (*Monster Parade,* November 1958); Gordon Fry's "Seven Curses of Lust" (*Monster Parade,* November 1958); Ralph Thornton's "I Was a Teenage Werewolf" (*Screen Chills and Macabre Stories,* November 1957); Joseph E.

Kelleam's "Revenge of the Were-Thing" (*Monsters and Things,* January 1959); and Leo Brett's "White Wolf" (*Supernatural Stories,* July 1959).

The only werewolf novel from this period worth remembering is Mario Pei's *The Sparrows of Paris* (1958). Slightly farcical, it concerns a plot to subvert American culture by means of drugs. Behind this criminal conspiracy is an organization called the Sparrows of Paris, whose leader, a renegade scientist, has dishonestly obtained rare medieval manuscripts from the Bibliothèque Nationale in Paris. The manuscripts contain formulas for powerful narcotic potions capable of inducing theriomorphic transformations. For a time the fate of civilization hangs in the balance, but the forces of law and order step in and save the day.

Werewolves called Wargs are among the denizens of Middle-Earth, the imaginary world of J. R. R. Tolkien's famous *The Lord of the Rings* trilogy, which was originally published in England in the mid-1950s. The books tell us that the Wargs appeared in Middle-Earth during the Third Age and have remained to plague the wilderness ever after. Unlike true wolves they are phantasms and become real only after dark.

Paranoia and Madness in the 1960s

After being stuck in the doldrums for several years, weird fiction enjoyed a modest resurgence in the 1960s. As in the latter half of the previous decade, regular professional markets for authors were still limited, but the emergence of a number of small press publications helped to alleviate this situation. The genre also received a boost from the growing popularity of paperback horror anthologies, although the contents of these were predominantly reprints.

For reasons not easy to pinpoint, the popularity of werewolf stories was still at a fairly low ebb, but the adaptability of the theme guaranteed its survival. As ever, traditional stories continued to appear, but alongside them were others that explored strange and abnormal states of mind, offering stark presentations of man against the beast within. A superb example of this approach is Joseph Payne Brennan's short story "Diary of a Werewolf" (*Macabre,* winter 1960), which interprets the protagonist's affliction as a hallucinatory psychosis. The man in question, a vain supercilious aesthete, retreats to the countryside to recuperate from excessive drug abuse; but some mysterious force in the surrounding landscape transforms him into a flesh-eating predator. His wild thoughts about his condition are regularly recorded in a diary, with the most significant entry reading as follows:

> I suppose [those who read this] will be expecting me to report the growth of long hair on my legs, a sudden increase in the length of my canine teeth, etc. This is all nonsense dreamed up by hack fictioneers— melodramatic trappings, nothing more. But I am convinced that werewolves like myself have existed for centuries. Harassed peasants may have invented

some of the trappings in the first place, but I can clearly see now that there is a solid basis of fact for the many legends which have come down through the ages. There must have been many like me! External trappings invented for effect are as nothing compared to the hidden horrors which exist unseen in convolutions of our brains—brains subjected to who knows what monstrous pressures, derangements, diseases, hereditary taints!

At length, the crazed lycanthrope is captured and narrowly escapes being lynched by the irate townsfolk. Declared insane at his trial, he is sentenced to life in an asylum.

In Larry Eugene Meredith's "The Last Letter from Norman Underwood" (in *Magazine of Horror*, January 1968), the story's mounting horror is conveyed through a series of letters written by a reclusive young man whose only close companion is his German shepherd dog, Heff. The letters (which are received over a period of weeks by a boyhood chum) graphically detail the letter writer's growing unease about his new neighbor—a Mr. Groff—who seems to have all the characteristics of a werewolf. Norman's suspicions are eventually confirmed when he is awakened one night by a commotion beneath his bedroom window. He rushes downstairs to investigate and grabs the only weapon at hand—a silver fork. When he gets outside he is confronted by the sight of a wolf attacking a woman, whose terrified screams spur Norman to rush to her aid. After a fierce struggle, in which the faithful Heff plays a crucial part, the wolf is stabbed to death; by the following morning it has changed into the lifeless form of Mr. Groff.

Any hopes that this is the end of the matter are dashed when three brutal murders are committed in the neighborhood, each victim torn apart as if by a savage animal. Norman is convinced that he must be responsible for these outrages, reasoning that the scratches he received in the fight with the werewolf have afflicted him with the dreaded curse. Intending to do away with himself if his worst fears are confirmed, Norman arms himself with a gun that fires silver bullets; but, as his last letter reveals, he has badly misinterpreted the situation. Written on bloodstained paper, the letter describes how he was savagely attacked in his home by a large hunched man whose naked body was covered with coarse brown hair. In his account of the violent struggle that ensued, Norman tells his friend that he had managed to shoot and mortally wound his assailant but had sustained terrible injuries himself, which he fears will eventually prove fatal. Norman's lifeless body is eventually found lying beside the mailbox, and the identity of his attacker is finally revealed when the body of his faithful dog, Heff, is found with a silver bullet lodged in its throat.

One of the most sensational werewolf stories of the decade, Dale C. Donaldson's "Pia!" (*Coven 13*, November 1969), starts off promisingly, then descends into the sort of gimmicky plot twists associated with lurid horror comics. In a scenario borrowed from "There Shall Be No Darkness," a group of old friends attending a house party are shocked when the host suddenly announces that, in the opinion of an expert on the occult who lives in the apartment above, one of the people present is a werewolf. The news fills everyone with a sense of unease, which quickly escalates into panic when one of the guests is horribly murdered after the lights suddenly go out. The killer—who is subsequently revealed to be one of the female guests—is shot dead after she unexpectedly metamorphoses into a wolf. Soon the tension climbs to an even higher level when a second female partygoer transforms into a wolf and terrorizes the other guests. She, too, is fatally wounded; but before she dies she points an accusing finger at the story's narrator, claiming that he is also a werewolf.

In David Case's masterly novella "The Cell" (1969) the unnamed protagonist convinces his wife that he poses a danger to her—and the community at large—after developing the typical symptoms of lycanthropy. To counter this threat the couple construct a special padded cell in the basement of their house, and during each full moon the lycanthrope voluntarily submits to being locked inside it so that he can undergo his transformation without hurting anyone. The protagonist's mental instability remains untreated, however, and his gradual descent into madness and paranoia is evident from the tone of the notes in his journal. Nonetheless, he occasionally shows flashes of inspiration, as the following observation about the nature of his affliction reveals:

> The disease must be carried in the blood or, more likely, in the genes. I suppose that it is passed on to one's children in a recessive state, waiting, lurking latently in man after man down through the generations until, once every century . . . once every thousand years perhaps . . . there is the proper combination to turn it into a dominant trait. And then it becomes a malignant, raging disease, growing stronger as the victim grows older, gaining strength from the body that it shares, and tries to destroy.

After two women are brutally murdered in the neighborhood, the wife keeps her husband permanently locked up; but she, too, becomes mentally unhinged after observing her husband's transformation into a raving monster through a hole she had cut in the wall of his cell. Years later the contents of the journal come to light when the dead couple's nephew inherits the house. In a final twist, which brings the story to a suitably chilling close, the young man realizes that he is also afflicted with the family curse.

This story originally appeared in *The Cell, and Other Tales of Horror* (Macdonald, 1969), which also contains "The Hunter," an atmospheric werewolf novella set on mist-shrouded Dartmoor. This tale allegedly formed the basis of the 1974 movie *Scream of the Wolf,* but the resemblance between the two is only superficial.

The humorous side of shapeshifting is cleverly exploited in Dan Lindsay's "The Beatnik Werewolf" (*The*

Magazine of Fantasy and Science Fiction, April 1961). An amusing skit on the alternative lifestyle adopted by the Beat Generation, it features a beatnik werewolf who enlists the aid of a horror-story writer to sort out a personal dilemma. Having convinced the writer that he really is a werewolf, he tells him: "My problem is simple. I'm making it with this chick, see? She wouldn't dig this werewolf bit at all. Man, she'd blow! After 200 years I'm beat. I want to retire like anybody else . . . maybe have cubs . . . you know. It's square but I'm playing it by ear." A further shock in store for the writer is that the "chick" in question turns out to be his regular girlfriend.

Another story with the accent on humor rather than horror is Peter S. Beagle's "Farrell and Lila the Werewolf" (*Guabi,* 1969). Set in New York toward the end of the psychedelic sixties, it features a hippy female werewolf who attracts every male dog in the neighborhood when she is "in heat." The ensuing mayhem culminates in a hilarious chase sequence in which the metamorphosed heroine is frantically pursued through the alleys and backstreets of the city by a bunch of irate dog owners.

In stark contrast, "Mrs. Kaye" by Beverly Haaf (*Startling Mystery Stories,* winter 1968/69) has not even a glimmer of humor about it. A dark, depressing narrative with the quality of a morbid nightmare, it successfully holds the reader's attention by concealing the identity of the werewolf until the final paragraph.

Other stories from the 1960s include "Werewolf at Large" by Lionel Fanthorpe (*Supernatural Stories,* November 1960); "Wolf Man's Vengeance" by Pel Torro (*Supernatural Stories,* February 1961); "The Werewolf Lover" by Geoffrey Van Loan Jr. (*Thriller,* February 1962); "Werewolves Are Furry" by Sandor Szabo (*Thriller,* July 1962); "Howl at the Moon" by A. J. Merak (*Supernatural Stories,* July 1963); "Moon Wolf" by Lionel Fanthorpe (*Supernatural Stories,* June 1963); "The House by the Crab Apple Tree" by S. S. Johnson (1964); "Wolf" by Michael Moorcock, writing as James Colvin (*The Deep Fix;* Compact, 1966); "Full Sun" by Brian W. Aldiss (*Orbit 2,* edited by Damon Knight; Putnam, 1967); "Once Upon a Werewolf" by R. L. Davis (*Coven 13,* November 1969); and "The Werewolf of St. Claude" by Ronald Seth (*50 Great Horror Stories,* edited by John Canning; Hamlyn/Odhams, 1969).

None of the werewolf novels published in the 1960s are particularly outstanding. More original than most is Adam Lukens's *Sons of the Wolf* (Avalon, 1961), in which a group of werewolves from the Middle Ages are mysteriously relocated in the twenty-first century and find themselves thrust into an alien environment. In another science fiction novel of the period, Andre Norton's *Moon of Three Rings* (Viking, 1966), werewolf-like beasts are encountered on another planet. Clifford Simak's *The Werewolf Principle* (Putnam, 1967; Berkley, 1968) rationalizes shapeshifting in terms of alien psi talents and features an android with multiple personalities, only one of which is wolflike. More like the genuine article are Leslie H. Whitten's *Moon of the Wolf* (Doubleday, 1967; Ace, 1968), a mystery-suspense novel about a lycanthropic serial killer, which one unimpressed critic described as "a museum of clichés," and Peter Saxon's *The Disorientated Man* (Mayflower, 1966), in which a mad scientist creates a seemingly invulnerable werewolf. Other sixties novels that utilized the theme were Leonard Holton's *Deliver Us from Wolves* (Dell, 1963); John E. Muller's *Mark of the Beast* (Badger, 1964); Kenneth Robeson's *Brand of the Werewolf* (Bantam, 1965); Barbara Michaels's *Sons of the Wolf* (Herbert Jenkins, 1968); and Salambo Forest's *Night of the Wolf* (Ophelia Press, 1969).

6

The Boom Years

A Howling Success: 1970s Blockbusters

In the 1970s a sudden groundswell in the popularity of horror novels and films had publishers and producers snapping up virtually every property they could lay their hands on in an effort to feed the momentarily insatiable appetite of the reading and viewing public. A welcome bonus for werewolf fans was the corresponding increase in the number of werewolf novels being produced. Unfortunately, only a few were of any significance; the rest were blatantly commercial, relying on stomach-turning scenes of gratuitous violence for their impact.

One of the best werewolf novels from the seventies, Whitley Strieber's *The Wolfen* (Morrow, 1978; Bantam, 1979), successfully revived the idea first mooted in Jack

Williamson's *Darker Than You Think*—that werewolves are a separate intelligent species residing, unsuspected, among us. Evidence of their existence initially
surfaces when two New York patrolmen are brutally
murdered and half-devoured by unknown assailants.
The two detectives assigned to track down their killers
subsequently discover that they belong to an ancient
race of wolflike predators called the Wolfen, who have
secretly coexisted with the human race throughout history. In parts of the narrative written from the Wolfen's
viewpoint, we find that they live in small packs scattered around the globe, and their preferred habitat
since the advent of the industrial era has been the dark,
desolate sections of large cities. During the day they
sleep in carefully concealed lairs—usually in base-
ments of abandoned buildings—and do most of their
hunting at night, preying on the dregs of society. The
chances of survival for anyone targeted as a victim is
negligible; not only are the Wolfen ferociously strong
but they are also equipped with razor-sharp fangs and
claws, and they move with incredible swiftness.

It is of paramount importance to the Wolfen that
they maintain the status quo at all costs. Anyone who
accidentally finds out about them is immediately
bumped off; if one of their own kind is killed or fatally
wounded, other members of the pack devour the body
so that no evidence is left behind to arouse suspicion.
Disastrously for the Wolfen, the detectives on their trail
survive all attempts to silence them, and in the novel's

gripping climax the evidence needed to convince the authorities of their existence is finally obtained.

The ending of *The Wolfen* suggests that Strieber may have had a sequel in mind, but so far it has failed to materialize. Until it does, we can only speculate about the steps that might have been taken to resolve the situation. For instance, would the governments of the world have suppressed the news to avoid panic among the general public, and perhaps come to some accommodation with their new-found foe? Or would they have collectively embarked on a ruthless extermination of the Wolfen, who would surely have succumbed, in the end, to the weapons of their human adversaries? Whichever course of action was chosen it would undoubtedly make a fascinating story and lend itself for adaptation into a multimillion-dollar blockbuster movie.

The biggest-selling werewolf novel of the modern era, Gary Brandner's *The Howling* (Fawcett Gold Medal, 1977), also depicts werewolves living secretly in our midst, albeit on a much smaller scale. After a young married woman, Karyn Beatty, is brutally raped in her own home, her husband rents a house in the quiet woodland village of Drago to help her recover from the ordeal, little realizing that he is putting her in even greater danger. On the surface the inhabitants of this sleepy backwater seem quite friendly, but it is not long before a succession of frightening incidents begin to disturb the newcomers' peace of mind. First, the couple's pet dog is savagely killed by an unknown predator; next, a young couple visiting the area are found murdered; and finally, most alarming of all, a woman from a nearby town turns up on Karyn's doorstep and warns her that Drago might be harboring a werewolf. After this last incident various townspeople come under suspicion; but it turns out that they are all werewolves. And if this weren't enough to cope with, Karyn's plight gets even worse when her husband becomes one of them and joins the other members of the werewolf colony in trying to stop his wife from making a last-ditch attempt to escape from Drago. Two inferior sequels, *The Howling II* and *The Howling III*, were published by Fawcett in 1978 and 1985 respectively.

Another highly regarded novel from this period is Thomas Tessier's *The Nightwalker* (Macmillan, 1979; Berkley, 1981), which may well be one of the grimmest, most pitiless accounts of lycanthropy ever written. The doomed hero, Bobby Ives, a young American living in London, begins to suspect something is wrong with his physical and mental health when he experiences bouts of migraine and sudden violent seizures. To make matters worse he is also plagued by recurring nightmares about a former life in which he was transformed into a zombie. As his condition deteriorates, Ives begins to experience an overpowering desire to attack people and tear their bodies to pieces, leading him to commit a string of brutal murders. In desperation he seeks help from a clairvoyant, who correctly diagnoses that he is suffering from lycanthropy. After initial misgivings the young seeress agrees to help her tormented client, but her experimental treatment—which involves keeping him locked up in a cell and putting him on a strictly controlled diet—fails to alleviate the condition. During a particularly violent seizure Ives breaks loose from his cell but is eventually tracked down by the police and killed.

Shortly after *The Nightwalker* was published, Stephen King hailed it as "perhaps the finest werewolf novel of the last twenty years." While respecting King's opinion, it should be pointed out that this novel is not exactly swimming with original ideas. For instance, it follows the same pattern as previous stories about lycanthropic serial killers, and the sequence where Ives is incarcerated to prevent him harming anyone was obviously inspired by a similar situation in David Case's "The Cell." Therefore, any praise due to this novel should rightfully be directed at the way the author has transcended the limitations of the form and made his narrative utterly convincing.

Although novels that placed the werewolf in a modern context were gaining in popularity, there were still traditional ones around as well as others which had a foot in both camps. One firmly in the traditional mold, *The Black Wolf* (Donald M. Grant, 1979) by Galad Elflandsson, is set in the backwoods of New England and revolves around the machinations of an immortal witch who reanimates deceased members of an ancient family to lead an army of werewolves against the inhabitants of a small rural town. Frank Belknap Long's *The Night of the Wolf* (Popular Library, 1972) features a giant werewolf and is a mixture of magic and lycanthropy; while Jay Callahan's similarly titled *Night of the Wolf* (Leisure, 1979) is an atmospheric thriller in which the residents of a close-knit rural community in Tennessee have learned to accommodate the werewolves who live in their midst. The English moors are the traditional setting for Guy N. Smith's *Werewolf by Moonlight* (New English Library, 1974), which spawned two sequels, *The Return of the Werewolf* (NEL, 1977) and *The Son of the Werewolf* (NEL, 1978).

The popularity of novelizations of horror movies and the contemporaneous vogue for Gothic romances exemplified the diversity of weird fiction in the seventies. Among the plethora of titles in the former category were *Legend of the Werewolf* (Sphere, 1976) by Robert Black; *The Werewolf of London* (Berkley, 1977) by Carl Dreadstone (Walter Harris); *The Wolfman* (Berkley, 1977) by Carl Dreadstone (Ramsey Campbell); and *The Werewolf vs. the Vampire Woman* (Guild-Hartford, 1972) by Arthur N. Scarm. This last-named novel is quite appallingly written and, in my opinion, has the dubious honor of being the worst werewolf novel ever to appear in print. Werewolf novels in the Gothic romance category included *The Wolves of Craywood* (Lancer, 1970) by Jan Alexander; *Doomway* (Beagle,

1971) by Evelyn Bond; and *The Eve of the Hound* (Zebra Books, 1977) by Deborah Lewis (pseudonym of Charles L. Grant). Aimed primarily at women readers, these novels are strong on love interest and have rationalized endings.

Only the merest hint of the supernatural is present in John Gardner's espionage novel *The Werewolf Trace* (Doubleday, 1977), which concerns undercover surveillance rather than shapeshifting. Michael Avallone's *The Werewolf Walks Tonight* (Warner, 1974) also belies its title, as the "werewolf" is only a deformed madman. More bizarrely, a robot with a split personality metaphorically substitutes for a werewolf in Dean R. Koontz's *A Werewolf among Us* (Ballantine, 1973). And in David Bischoff's *Nightworld* (Ballantine, 1979) mandroidal werewolves serve a computerized Prince of Darkness.

Other werewolf novels from the 1970s include *The Other People* (Powell, 1970) by Pat A. Briscoe; *Cry Wolf!* (Darkroom Reader, 1970) by Kyle Roxbury; *The Curse of the Concullens* (World Publishing, 1970; Signet, 1972) by Florence Stevenson; *Operation Chaos* (Doubleday, 1971) by Poul Anderson; *The Werewolf* (Vanguard, 1972) by Bruce Lowery; *Lady Sativa* (Curtis, 1973) by Frank Lauria; *Hawkshaw* (Doubleday, 1972) by Ron Goulart; *The Curse of Leo* (Pinnacle, 1974) by Robert Lory; *Lisa Kane* (Bobbs-Merrill, 1976) by Richard Lupoff; and *The Werewolf's Prey* (Fawcett, 1977) by Robert Arthur Smith.

It is also worth mentioning that a werewolf character, Quentin Collins, was featured in eighteen of the "Dark Shadows" novels by Marilyn Ross. All published in rapid succession by Paperback Library, the titles are: *Barnabas Collins and Quentin's Demon* (1969); *Barnabas, Quentin, and the Mummy's Curse* (1970); *Barnabas, Quentin, and the Avenging Ghost* (1970); *Barnabas, Quentin, and the Nightmare Assassin* (1970); *Barnabas, Quentin, and the Crystal Coffin* (1970); *Barnabas, Quentin, and the Witch's Curse* (1970); *Barnabas, Quentin, and the Haunted Cave* (1970); *Barnabas, Quentin, and the Frightened Bride* (1970); *Barnabas, Quentin, and the Scorpio Curse* (1970); *Barnabas, Quentin, and the Serpent* (1970); *Barnabas, Quentin, and the Magic Potion* (1970); *Barnabas, Quentin, and the Body Snatchers* (1970); *Barnabas, Quentin, and Dr. Jekyll's Son* (1970); *Barnabas, Quentin, and the Grave Robbers* (1971); *Barnabas, Quentin, and the Sea Ghost* (1971); *Barnabas, Quentin, and the Mad Magician* (1971); *Barnabas, Quentin, and the Hidden Tomb* (1971); and finally, *Barnabas, Quentin, and the Vampire Beauty* (1972).

Werewolf fiction in the shorter form also enjoyed something of a resurgence in the 1970s, although, unlike previous decades, most stories appeared in paperback anthologies rather than magazines. The anthologist most associated with werewolf stories during this period was Roger Elwood, who liberally scattered them about his numerous horror-story compilations.

Original to one of the earlier anthologies, *Monster Tales* (Rand McNally, 1973), was Nic Andersson's "Werewolf Boy." Set in the Middle Ages, its hero, a peasant boy called Stefan, persuades a witch to put a spell of lycanthropy upon him in order to gain revenge on a brutal baron who has wronged him; he then finds that he cannot escape from the enchantment once its purpose has been served. Steven Barnes's "Moonglow," in *Vampires, Werewolves, and Other Monsters* (Curtis Books, 1974), concerns a romantic liaison between a witch and a werewolf that ends in tragedy when the wolf is unable to control his violent rages. The same anthology also contains Robin Schaeffer's "Night of the Wolf," in which a father informs his ten-year-old son that the time has arrived when he will inherit the family curse of lycanthropy—and then takes the wise precaution of locking him in his room. Unfortunately, he neglects to fasten the bedroom window and ends up as the boy's first victim. Another of Elwood's anthologies, *The Berserkers* (Pocket, 1974), features Arthur Tofte's "The Berserks," which is based on the theory that werewolf legends from Northern Europe arose from the frenzied fighting style of the Scandinavian Berserk warriors, which was allegedly wolflike in its ferocity. Tofte describes the Berserkers' rage as a supernatural power that comes over some men like a madness and likens it to an evil force that takes over mind and body.

Solomon Kane, the swashbuckling hero of a series of stories by Karl Edward Wagner, is an indomitable fighter who vanquishes his foes with a deadly combination of brains and brawn. In "Reflections for the Winter of My Soul," in *Death Angel's Shadow* (Warner, 1973), Kane is called upon to pit his strength and cunning against a werewolf who has insinuated himself among the guests in a snowbound castle and is picking them off one by one. In typical mystery-story fashion everyone in turn falls under suspicion—including Kane—until the real culprit is finally unmasked. The plot sounds vaguely familiar because Robert E. Howard used it forty-seven years earlier for "Wolfshead."

In James Farlow's "The Demythologized Werewolf" (*Analog*, May 1977) the story's narrator, Bill, is invited by a fellow scientist, Dr. Daniel Mackerman, to his isolated laboratory, where an unusual investigation is in progress. From an observation room the visitor witnesses a young man strapped to a surgical table undergo an amazing transformation into a wolf. Bill is subsequently informed that the patient is the son of a European nobleman whose family has been periodically cursed by hereditary lycanthropy. Mackerman reveals that the werewolf's father has been pouring money into the facility's researches in the hope that modern medical technology can come up with a cure for his son's affliction. Events take an unexpected turn when the werewolf makes a bid for freedom and is killed in the ensuing melee. In a final twist, Bill becomes a recipient of the curse himself as a result of a bite he received from the werewolf and ends up taking his place as a specimen for future research.

Harlan Ellison's award-winning novelette "Adrift just off the Islets of Langerhans: Latitude 38° 54′ N, Longitude 77° 00′ 13″ W" (*The Magazine of Fantasy and Science Fiction,* October 1974) is probably the least representative story in the entire werewolf canon. Written by an author noted for his unconventional ideas, this is an absurdist fantasy in which the hero, the immortal and seemingly indestructible Lawrence Talbot, yearns for an end to his tortured existence. As a last resort he contacts a mysterious organization called Information Associates, who, at his behest, supply him with the geographical coordinates for the location of his soul—lost when he became a werewolf—which, he believes, he must regain to achieve the peace of death. He then gets in touch with his old friend Victor, a physicist, who, aided by the information Talbot has obtained, comes up with a mind-boggling solution to his problem, which involves the world-weary lycanthrope going inside his own body. To facilitate this miraculous feat, Victor creates a perfect simulacrum of Talbot, identical in every respect save that it is a million times smaller. The microscopic mite is introduced into Talbot's body—via the navel—and journeys through the vascular system until it reaches the pancreas, where the Islets of Langerhans are located. At the precise coordinates supplied by Information Associates, Talbot's miniaturized double retrieves his soul in the form of a symbol representing innocence. The plot gets increasingly surreal and metaphysical after this, but the upshot of it all is that Talbot decides that he doesn't want to die after all.

Another controversial fantasist who rose to prominence in the 1970s was Angela Carter. Included in her brilliant collection of short stories *The Bloody Chamber and Other Adult Tales* (Harper and Row, 1979) are two intellectually stimulating werewolf stories, "The Werewolf" and "The Company of Wolves." Both are based on the classic fairy tale "Little Red Riding Hood," but reinterpreted from a feminist point of view. Like most of Carter's provocative fabulations, they are full of Freudian imagery as well as being unashamedly erotic.

Carter's compatriot, the very British R. Chetwynd-Hayes, has shown a more orthodox approach to the theme in such stories as "The Werewolf" and "The Werewolf and the Vampire." "The Werewolf," from *The Fourth Monster Ghost Book* (Armada, 1978), where it was attributed to Angus Campbell, is a predictable story. A schoolboy befriends a sad-looking man living in a ruined house on the moors, then learns that he is the werewolf who has been killing a local farmer's sheep. In contrast, "The Werewolf and the Vampire," from *The Monster Club* (NEL, 1976), is an acerbic black comedy with an unexpectedly chilling finale. When the principal characters George and Carola meet it is love at first sight, but what makes them different from other young lovers is that he is a werewolf and she is a vampire. After their marriage, which is soon blessed with the birth of a baby werevamp, everything seems perfect, but their happiness is shattered when the local preacher discovers their secret. Assisted by a twelve-year-old boy who knows all about supernatural monsters from reading comics and watching horror movies, the merciless man of the cloth callously dispatches the werewolf and his spouse using traditional methods. Ironically, the authorities do not accept the clergyman's version of events, and he is confined in a mental institution, where he eventually gets his comeuppance when the werevamp and his newly reanimated parents pay a nocturnal visit on their former persecutor.

The 1970s also saw a revival of interest in the werewolf stories of H. Warner Munn following the publication of the 1976 Centaur Books paperback collection *The Werewolf of Ponkert,* which contained the title story and its sequel "The Werewolf's Daughter." Munn later reworked the other stories and produced additional entries in the series. Some of these appeared in Robert Weinberg's *Lost Fantasies* anthologies in 1977, and the entire series of thirteen stories was subsequently published in two volumes by Donald M. Grant, titled *Tales of the Werewolf Clan,* vol. 1, *In the Tomb of the Bishop* (1979), and vol. 2, *The Master Goes Home* (1980).

Other stories from the 1970s that utilized the werewolf theme were "The Thing on the Stairs" by Lee

Chater (*Coven 13*, March 1970); "Howl, Wolf, Howl" by William Cornish (*Adventures in Horror*, October 1970); "It Takes Two for Terror" by Obadiah Kemph (*Adventures in Horror*, December 1970); "One Last Death Prowl for the Man Who Howled Like a Wolf" by Michael Pretorius (*Horror Stories*, February 1971); "The Werewolf" by Dana Lamb (*In Trout Country*, edited by P. Corodimas; Little, 1971); "There's a Wolf in My Time Machine" by Larry Niven (*The Magazine of Fantasy and Science Fiction*, June 1971); "The Tempest" by Leif E. Christensen (*The Devil's Instrument and Other Danish Stories*, edited by Sven Holm; Dufour, 1971); "Who's Afraid" by Calvin Demmon (*Fantastic*, December 1972); "What Good Is a Glass Dagger?" by Larry Niven (*The Magazine of Fantasy and Science Fiction*, September 1972); "The Forges of Nainland are Cold" by Avram Davidson (*Fantastic*, August–October 1972); "Furry Night" by Joan Aiken (*Nightfrights*, edited by Peter Haining; Taplinger, 1972); "Night Beat" by Ramsey Campbell and "Loup Garou" by A. A. Attanasio (*The Haunt of Horror* no. 1, June 1973); "Cry Wolf" by Basil Copper (*Vampires, Werewolves, and Other Monsters*, edited by Roger Elwood; Curtis, 1974); "Hard Times" by Sonora Morrow (*Ellery Queen's Mystery Magazine*, December 1974); "L is for Loup-Garou" by Harlan Ellison (*The Magazine of Fantasy and Science Fiction*, October 1976); "Countess Ilona; or The Werewolf Reunion" by Roger Malisson (*Supernatural*, edited by Robert Muller; Fontana, 1977); "The Nighthawk" by Dennis Etchison (*Shadows,* edited by Charles L. Grant; Doubleday, 1978); "The Boy Who Would Be Wolf" by Richard Curtis and "Moon Change" by Ann Warren Turner (*Shape Shifters,* edited by Jane Yolen; Seabury Press, 1978); "Night Prowler" by Roger Elwood (*Spine-Chillers,* edited by Roger Elwood and Howard Goldsmith; Doubleday, 1978); "The White Beast" by Roger Zelazny (*Whispers* no. 13/14, October 1979); "The Curse" by Jonathan Baumbach (*The Return of Service;* University of Illinois Press, 1979); "The Man Who Shot the Werewolf" by Edward D. Hoch (*Ellery Queen's Mystery Magazine,* February 1979). Werewolf poems published in the same decade included "Loups-Garous" by Avram Davidson (*The Magazine of Fantasy and Science Fiction,* August 1971); "Finale" by Dale C. Donaldson (*Moonbroth* no. 2, 1971); "Cradle Song for a Baby Werewolf" by H. Warner Munn (*Whispers* no. 1, July 1973); and "Father of Werewolves" by Bill Breiding (*Moonbroth* no. 23, 1976).

Blood and Gore in the 1980s

By the 1980s, horror fiction had become big business. Book sales were at record levels and the novels of the leading writers in the field were regularly appearing on the bestseller lists. Simultaneously, horror movies were also enjoying an unprecedented boom, and their horrendous violence, strong language, and explicit sex scenes were inevitably imitated by the more commercially minded horror novelists, who vied with each other in their efforts to shock. Werewolf novels were similarly affected, and many of those published during the eighties were merely mindless gorefests with little to interest the discerning reader. Nonetheless, a few gems did sparkle among the dross, and it is to these that we turn our attention first.

One of the highlights of the decade was undoubtedly the publication, by Pocket Books, of Robert Stallman's trilogy *The Orphan* (1980), *The Captive* (1981), and *The Beast* (1982), which went on to achieve cult status after the author's untimely death shortly before the second volume's appearance. The first novel, set in the Midwestern United States during the 1930s, revolves around the adventures of a strange bearlike creature of extraterrestrial origin. Endowed with shape-shifting powers, the huge flesh-eating alien is able to assume different human forms to escape detection, and initially takes on the likeness and personality of Robert, a young orphaned boy who is adopted by an elderly farmer and his wife. The werebeast—also in the early stages of its development—finds this arrangement advantageous, since it provides it with an opportunity to experience the passage to maturity through two distinct personalities, while at the same time enabling it to prey, undetected, on the local community's livestock. Eventually the beast's real appearance is exposed, forcing it to flee and start a new life elsewhere. This time it takes the form of a teenager; but the shapechanger finds its freedom restricted after its alter ego comes into possession of an ancient stone carving that prevents the personality shift from taking place except under extreme circumstances. Once the werebeast reaches sexual maturity, it is then able to discard this unsatisfactory persona and become a handsome adult by the name of Barry Golden. The second volume sees more problems arise for the beast when it is captured after being severely injured in an accident and is put on show as a carnival exhibit. In the final volume we learn that there are more of these shapeshifting aliens in circulation, and like the main protagonist some have appropriated their human identities from the recently dead, whose souls cannot pass on as a result and are left stranded in limbo. In the end, Barry Golden's determination to live enables him to physically split away from the beast and lead a separate existence.

Chelsea Quinn Yarbro, who is best known for her series of historical vampire novels featuring Le Comte de Saint-Germain, created an equally memorable aristocratic hero in *The Godforsaken* (Warner, 1983). Set in Spain at the height of the Inquisition, this well-crafted Gothic romance chronicles the vicissitudes of Don Rolon, heir to the Spanish throne, whose position at court and his impending marriage to the beautiful Zaretta of Venezia are put in jeopardy when he succumbs to the curse of lycanthropy. Waiting to capitalize on the situation is the scheming Grand Inquisitor, Juan Murador, who would have no qualms about branding Rolon a heretic and sending him to his death—should his un godly affliction become known. As usual, Yarbro impresses with her attention to period detail; particularly noteworthy is her depiction of court intrigue, especially the bitter rivalry between the nobility and ambitious church dignitaries.

Basil Copper's *The House of the Wolf* (Arkham House, 1983) is an old-fashioned thriller that covers familiar ground. The hero, John Coleridge, an American professor, travels to the tiny village of Lugos in Hungary to attend a conference on European folklore and finds himself embroiled in a search for the perpetrator of a series of unsolved murders. The trail leads inexorably to Castle Homolky, within whose ancient walls dwell the degenerate members of the Homolky family, including the sinister count and his daughter Nadia. In the subterranean dungeon beneath the castle are the crumbling remains of a grim torture chamber, and prowling the dark, shadowy corridors and secret passages of the old edifice is a large black wolf whose real identity is revealed in the novel's thrilling climax. Harking back to an earlier period of horror writing, *The House of the Wolf* is probably intended as a homage to Bram Stoker, and movie buffs may also detect a nod in the direction of Hammer Films.

Two other British writers who made notable contributions to the werewolf canon in the 1980s were Tanith

Lee and Stephen Gallagher. The prolific Lee, whose exotic dark fantasies had already brought her many admirers on both sides of the Atlantic, further enhanced her reputation with a suspenseful mystery novel, *Lycanthia, or The Children of Wolves* (DAW, 1981). The hero here, a young French nobleman, uncovers the sinister connection between the peasants on his estate and a pack of wolves. Gallagher's equally riveting novel *Follower* (Sphere, 1984) is based on Norse mythology and features a hybrid monster, half man, half wolf, which has the ability to assume the shape of its victims.

America's undisputed master of modern horror fiction, Stephen King, has up to now used the man-into-wolf motif only sparingly. Out of all the works that have flowed from his word processor only *Cycle of the Werewolf* (Land of Enchantment, 1983; NAL/Signet, 1985) and the best-selling blockbuster *The Talisman* (Viking and Putnam, 1984; Berkley, 1985), written in collaboration with Peter Straub, have a significant werewolf element. *Cycle of the Werewolf* is told in twelve chapters, one for each month of the year, and is set in a small town in Maine. The werewolf—whose identity is not revealed until the end—turns out to be a local clergyman whose repressed desires cause him to periodically transform into a homicidal monster. In contrast, *The Talisman* is a gargantuan quest novel in which the hero, young Jack, befriends a werewolf during his search for a magic charm.

Much meatier fare is served up in S. P. Somtow's

Moon Dance (Tor, 1989), which is one of the most distinctive and controversial horror novels of recent years. Spanning two continents and over a hundred years of history—from the 1880s to the 1980s—this is an earthy, ultraviolent saga in which a group of European werewolves flee persecution in the old Austro-Hungarian Empire and settle in America. Their arrival, however, brings them into conflict with the indigenous Indians, some of whom have similar shapeshifting powers. The difference between these opposing factions is that the Native American werewolves are essentially beneficent, totemic creatures, while their European counterparts are consummately evil. Eventually the European werewolves' growing dominance is challenged by a werewolf Messiah from one of the Indian tribes, who promises to drive all the foreigners back into the ocean. The underlying theme is clearly racial conflict, with the European immigrants being portrayed as destroyers of the Native American culture.

American Indian folklore also provided the inspiration for *Sins of the Flesh* (Tor, 1989). In this impressive debut novel by brothers Don and Jay Davis, an unruly adolescent whose parents were cursed by an evil magician gradually evolves into a wendigo—a furry, shapeshifting creature with powerful talons and "orange eyes that burn with the fires of Hell." The Native American equivalent of the werewolf, this formidable monster revels in the slaughter of innocent victims and enjoys particularly the taste of human flesh.

Robert McCammon's massive blockbuster *The Wolf's Hour* (Pocket Books, 1989) is notable for the way it successfully straddles two normally incompatible genres. The central character, Michael Gallatin, is a British master spy brought out of retirement during the latter stages of World War II to undertake a vital mission in occupied Europe. Although this may sound like a familiar scenario, the catch is that Gallatin is a werewolf, which adds a supernatural flavor to the proceedings. It doesn't quite live up to its claim to be "the ultimate werewolf novel," but the ingenious twist referred to earlier and the usual thrills associated with wartime espionage stories are enough to sustain the reader's interest despite the novel's inordinate length.

The destruction of civilization on Earth is the apocalyptic vision conjured up by David Robbins in *The Wrath* (Leisure, 1988). The cause of this catastrophe, a plague that turns people into doglike monsters, is released on the world after an expedition to Egypt unearths a previously unknown tomb. All who subsequently become infected exhibit lycanthropic traits and proceed to run about on all fours, attacking everyone they encounter. An antidote is finally found, but not before mass devastation has occurred.

Many werewolf novels published in the 1980s were merely vehicles for the depiction of mass killings and gory mutilations. A prime example is Jack Woods's *Wolffile* (Pageant, 1988), a lurid, no-holds-barred account of a werewolf's frenzied rampage on a small island. Another novel that doesn't stint on the blood and gore, F. W. Armstrong's *The Changing* (Tor, 1985), takes place in the world of big business, and the werewolf's victims are all high-powered executives. Nauseating descriptions of dismemberments are the main feature of David Robbins's *The Wereling* (Leisure, 1983), in which a man masquerading as a werewolf actually becomes one when he is possessed by the Spirit of the Wolf. The multiple atrocities depicted in Robert C. Sloane's *A Nice Place to Live* (Crown, 1981; Bantam, 1982) occur when a disgruntled man changes himself into a savage creature to get revenge on his neighbors; and in Rick Hautala's *Moondeath* (Zebra, 1980) a peaceful New England town is terrorized by a serial killer after a shunned high school student is magically transformed into a wolf.

Modern-day skepticism regarding werewolves provides the rationale for Steve Vance's *The Hyde Effect* (Leisure, 1986), whose plucky heroine insists she has been attacked by a werewolf, but initially cannot find anyone who will believe her story. Similarly, in David Case's *Wolf Tracks* (Belmont Tower, 1980) a police detective's colleagues think he is going mad when he suggests that a werewolf might be responsible for a spate of brutal murders. The same sort of situation develops in Frank King's *Southpaw* (Lynx, 1988), only this time it's the ex-manager of a baseball team who has difficulty in getting the police to accept his theory that a werewolf is behind a string of atrocities at a baseball stadium.

The shapechanger in Richard Jaccoma's *The Werewolf's Tale* (Gold Medal, 1988) does his fair share of killing, but it's all for a good cause. Transformed into a werewolf after being bitten by one, he bravely accepts his lot when he finds that his newly acquired abilities stand him in good stead in his fight against Nazi tyranny. Even less like your typical werewolf is the beautiful heroine of Michael D. Weaver's trilogy, *Wolf-Dreams* (1987), *Nightreaver* (1988), and *Bloodfang* (1989), all published by Avon Books. Here, Thyri Bloodfang is a lesbian warrior with shapeshifting powers, made even more formidable by her possession of a magic sword. Another unconventional werewolf is the fourteen-year-old hero of Roger Zelazny's *A Dark Traveling* (Walker, 1987), who is part of a team guarding the transfer points between parallel worlds.

Eroticism is the key element in Alan B. Chronister's *Cry Wolf* (Zebra, 1987) and Richard Forsythe's *Fangs* (Leisure, 1985). In *Cry Wolf* a woman is seduced by a male werewolf, and in *Fangs* a sexual relationship between a young woman and a wolf results in the birth of a child with shapeshifting powers. Unnatural mating also occurs in Jeffrey Goddin's *Blood of the Wolf* (Leisure, 1987), the central character being the offspring of a werewolf and a natural wolf.

The source of the horrors depicted in Stephen R. George's *Beasts* (Zebra, 1989) is a new virus that removes people's inhibitions, thus transforming them into lycanthropic monsters; while in Mark Manley's

Throwback (Popular Library, 1987) a genetic disorder brings about a similar outcome. There is a more tangible threat to humanity in William W. Johnstone's *Wolfsbane* (Zebra, 1982), which tells of an incursion into our world by werewolves from another dimension; and, similarly, Al Sarrantonio's *Moonbane* (Bantam, 1989) revolves around an attempted invasion of Earth by extraterrestrial werewolves. Equally fanciful is Simon Hawke's *The Dracula Caper* (Ace, 1988), in which a plague of genetically engineered vampires and werewolves from the far future descends on Victorian England.

There are imaginative treatments of the theme in other 1980s novels. Edward Levy's *The Beast Within* (Berkley, 1981) portrays the Jekyll-and-Hyde struggle of a child cursed with a heritage of lycanthropy; Tim Powers's *The Anubis Gates* (Ace, 1983) features a body-switching werewolf who kills his victims to keep his identity secret; Bernard King's *Vargr-Moon* (NEL, 1986) tells of the wife of a Nordic warrior who is intent on becoming a werewolf with great magical powers; Christopher Carpenter's *The Twilight Realm* (Arrow Books, 1985) features a monastery of skull-sucking werewolves; Douglas D. Hawk's *Moonslasher* (Critic's Choice, 1987) concerns an ancient Egyptian entity who uses arcane powers to create a werewolf; Florence Stevenson's *Household* (Leisure, 1989) is about a witch whose curse turns succeeding generations of a noble family into werewolves and other creatures of the night;

and in Dean R. Koontz's *Midnight* (Putnam, 1989; Berkley, 1989) a computer genius plans to create a race of superbeings but succeeds only in turning the people involved in his experiments into violent shapechangers. The following novels from the 1980s also utilize the werewolf theme: *The Werewolf Family* (Houghton Mifflin, 1980) by Jack Gantos; *Wolfcurse* (NEL, 1981) by Guy N. Smith; *Blood Fever* (Pocket, 1982) by Shelley Hyde (pseudonym of Kit Reed); *The Hanging Stones* (Doubleday, 1982) by Manly Wade Wellman; *Quarrel with the Moon* (Tor, 1982) by J. C. Conaway; *Werewolf* (Hodder and Stoughton, 1982) by Philip McCutchan; *Isle of the Shapeshifters* (Houghton Mifflin, 1983; Bantam, 1985) by Otto Coontz; *Frontier of the Dark* (Ace, 1984) by A. Bertram Chandler; *Dark Cry of the Moon* (Donald M. Grant, 1985) by Charles L. Grant; *Werewolves of Kregen* (DAW, 1985) by Alan Burt Akers; *Love Child* (Tor, 1986) by Andrew Neiderman; *The Devouring* (Tor, 1987) by F. W. Armstrong; *Fangs of the Werewolf* (Century-Hutchinson, 1987; Barron's, 1988) by John Halkin; *Ursula's Gift* (Donald I. Fine, 1988) by Roger DiSilvestro; *Wolf Moon* (Signet, 1988) by Charles de Lint; *The Devil's Auction* (Owlswick, 1988) by Robert Weinberg; *Howling Mad* (Ace, 1989) by Peter David; and, lastly, *Wolfman* (Donald I. Fine, 1989) by Art Bourgeau.

Although novels on the werewolf theme predominated throughout the 1980s, short stories revolving around the same motif continued to appear from time to time in anthologies and magazines. Most reflected the prevailing vogue for visceral explicitness, with nauseating descriptions of discmbowclments almost obligatory. A prime example of this is Suzy McKee Charnas's "Boobs," which initially appeared in the July 1989 issue of *Isaac Asimov's Science Fiction Magazine*. The story's heroine, a teenage girl nicknamed Boobs because of her large breasts, becomes the target of school bullies, but she turns the tables on the ringleader after she miraculously acquires the power to change into a wolf. Luring her unsuspecting victim to a park at night, she pounces on him in her wolf form and proceeds to tear him to pieces, first chomping down hard on his face, then ripping out his throat, and finally tearing his belly open and feasting messily on the warm innards. The cold-blooded killer shows no remorse over the boy's death, reasoning that "there are people who just do not deserve to live."

Another story written from a provocative feminist perspective is Tanith Lee's "Bloodmantle" (in *Forests of the Night,* Unwin, 1989). Dark and quirky, it is yet another variation on the Little Red Riding-Hood fairy tale, but this time the nubile heroine willingly submits to the handsome werewolf's sexual demands so she can enfold his body in her scarlet cloak and drain all his energy. In Stephen Laws's "Guilty Party" (*Fear!* no. 2, September 1988) the bemused hero is mistaken for the son of a strange old couple living in a secluded cottage in the English countryside. The demented duo's crazed ramblings reveal that their real son is expected home that very evening, having vowed ten years earlier to return from the dead to get revenge on his parents for shooting him after they had discovered he was a werewolf. Clive Barker's "Twilight at the Towers" (*Books of Blood,* vol. 6, Sphere Books, 1985) takes place in the Cold War era, when specially programmed werewolves were used as undercover agents. No less bizarre is Barry Malzberg's "Nightshapes," which made one of its earliest appearances in *Horrors,* edited by Charles L. Grant (Playboy, 1981). In this tense, melodramatic story, an elderly professor's attempts to prevent his young wife's nightly transformation into a werewolf end tragically when the potion he has been secretly administering to her has the unforeseen effect of making her tear out her own throat. What's even more ironic is that the professor, who is a vampire, is just as devastated at being deprived of his regular blood supply as he is by his wife's gruesome demise.

One of the least effective short stories from this period is Scott Bradfield's "The Dream of the Wolf" (*Interzone* no. 10, winter 1984/85). The neurotic protagonist is so obsessed with wolves that he thinks about them all day and dreams of them at night. The tale is extremely vague and inconclusive, and ultimately leads the reader up a blind alley.

Two outstanding novellas from the 1980s are George R. R. Martin's "The Skin Trade" (*Night Visions 5,* Dark Harvest, 1988; *The Skin Trade,* Berkley, 1990) and Ray Garton's "Monsters" (*Night Visions 6,* Dark Harvest, 1988; *The Bone Yard,* Berkley, 1991). In "The Skin Trade," a female private investigator discovers that someone she has known for years is a werewolf when the skinned bodies of his victims—all of whom belong to a secret society of werewolves—start turning up all over town. Ray Garton's disturbing thriller is about a writer who returns to his hometown, from which he had been hounded years before, and is literally turned into a monster by the prejudiced attitude of the people who live there.

The list of stories from the 1980s also includes "Footsteps" by Harlan Ellison (*Gallery,* December 1980; *Horrorstory,* vol. 3, edited by Karl Edward Wagner, Underwood-Miller, 1992); "Lair of the White Wolf" by J. R. Schifino (*Fantasy Tales* no. 6, summer 1980); "Wolfland" by Tanith Lee (*The Magazine of Fantasy and Science Fiction,* October 1980; *Red as Blood, or Tales from the Sisters Grimmer,* DAW, 1983); "In the Lost Lands" by George R. R. Martin (*Amazons II,* edited by Jessica Amanda Salmonson, DAW, 1982); "Cheriton" by Peter Robins (*The Gay Touch,* Crossing Press, 1982; *Embracing the Dark,* edited by Eric Garber, Alyson, 1991); "The Day of the Wolf" by Ian Watson (*Changes,* edited by Michael Bishop and Ian Watson, Ace, 1983); "An Authentic Werewoman" by Darrell Schweitzer (*Night Voyages* no. 9, winter/spring 1983); "The Weird of Caxton" by Kelvin Jones (*Dark Horizons* no. 26, spring 1983); "Mistral" by Jon Wynne-Tyson

(*The Twilight Zone Magazine,* July/August 1983; *Horrorstory,* vol. 4, edited by Karl Edward Wagner, Underwood-Miller, 1990); "Out of Sorts" by Bernard Taylor and "Gravid Babies" by Michael Bishop (*The Dodd, Mead Gallery of Horror,* edited by Charles L. Grant, Dodd, Mead, 1983); "The Werewolf" by Tommaso Landolfi (*Words in Commotion and Other Stories,* Viking 1986); "Confession" by David Starkey (*Grue Magazine* no. 4, 1987); "Curse of the Werewolf's Wife" by Bruce Boston (*Weird Tales,* fall 1988); "The Werewolf of Hollywood" by Ron Goulart (*Pulphouse: The Hardback Magazine,* issue 3, edited by Kristine Kathryn Rusch, Pulphouse, 1989). Two poems from the same decade are "Werewolf, Manhattan" by Steve Rasnic Tem (*Eldritch Tales* no. 9, April 1983) and "Lycanthropy" by Alexander M. Phillips (*Weirdbook* no. 18, summer 1983).

A Werewolf Bonanza

In the final period covered in this survey—the 1990s—the number of werewolf novels that made it into print was quite phenomenal, eclipsing the output of any previous decade by a wide margin. Unfortunately for devotees of the form there was no corresponding improvement in the standard of writing, which was generally at a low level. Looking down the list of well over a hundred titles it is possible to pick out a few that have real merit, but the vast majority are crudely written "splatter" novels providing vicarious thrills for those readers who enjoy extreme forms of physical horror.

Possibly the best, and certainly one of the most literate, werewolf novels from the period now under review is Michael Cadnum's *Saint Peter's Wolf* (Carroll and Graf, 1991; Zebra, 1993). The hero, Benjamin Byrd, a successful psychologist and collector of rare objects, finds his whole world turned upside down after he forms an intimate relationship with a mysterious woman named Johanna Fisher. Through her he meets the renowned collector Jacob Zinser, who presents him with an extraordinary artifact—a set of wolf's fangs mounted on a silver base. Suddenly Byrd begins to experience vivid dreams in which he becomes a wolf and roams the night in search of human prey. As the story progresses it gradually becomes apparent that he has actually been transformed into a werewolf and is responsible for a string of atrocities currently under investigation by the police. The sting in the tail is that after his animal nature becomes dominant, Byrd no longer has the urge to kill wantonly and comes to regard such behavior as intrinsically evil.

The same sentiment is expressed with equally strong conviction in Whitley Strieber's *The Wild* (Wilson and Neff, 1991; Tor, 1991). In this moving novel the principal character, Bob Duke, has had dreams of becoming a wolf since early childhood, and he suddenly finds them coming true when he is miraculously transformed into a wolf in front of his wife and son. They are understandably bewildered by this alarming occurrence but resolve to stand by him in the hope that the change will be temporary. However, an incident at their apartment, in which a visitor is badly bitten, leads to the transmogrified hero being forcibly taken into custody and locked up in the municipal dog pound. During his incarceration, Duke begins to experience life from a wolf's perspective as his newly acquired animal senses open up a new world of sounds and smells. He also becomes much stronger, which is especially advantageous when an opportunity to gain his freedom arises. After escaping from the pound, Duke roams the streets of New York but soon heads north in his desire to reach the wolf's natural habitat. At length, in a snow-covered wilderness near the Canadian border, he finally encounters a pack of timber wolves and finds true fulfillment when he is eventually accepted as one of them and becomes the father of cubs. The only villainy in the novel is perpetrated by human hunters, whose warped delight in killing wolves for sport is portrayed as fundamentally evil.

Dennis Danvers's *Wilderness* (Poseidon, 1991; Pocket Star, 1992) also features a nonviolent werewolf, but of the opposite gender. Alice White, the beautiful heroine, is intelligent and artlessly sensual, yet she lives a lonely life devoid of friendship or love because of her dark secret: that one night in every month she metamorphoses into a wolf. Then, quite unexpectedly, she meets and falls madly in love with Erik, a biology professor, whom

she believes may be the one man who will truly understand her and accept her for what she is. Putting him to
the ultimate test she tells him the truth about herself,
but Erik struggles to come to terms with this incredible
revelation. Alice, fearing their love is doomed, flees to
the wilds of Canada with the intention of joining a
wolf pack. Eventually, Erik regains her trust and they
come to a mutually acceptable arrangement whereby
Alice is allowed to share her time between him and the
wolf pack. Although enthusiastically received by the
critics, this novel is hardly the "bold and extraordinary feat of imagination" it was supposed to be. On the
contrary, take away the werewolf element—which is
played down, anyway—and what is left is a run-of-the-
mill love story very much in the traditional mold.

Another novel dealing with an emotionally charged
situation, Melanie Tem's *Wilding* (Dell/Abyss, 1992), is
about an extended family of female werewolves who
have been secretly living within human society for four
generations, during which they have kept to their own
distinctive way of life and paid little heed to the outside
world. Quarrels within this close-knit group regularly
flare up, and the tension is heightened considerably by
the behavior of one of the younger werewolves, who
has failed her rite of passage and is roaming the streets,
pregnant and confused. In this unstable mental state
she is regarded as a threat to the security of the other
members of the family, forcing them to set aside their
petty squabbles and unite in an effort to silence her. As

in Danvers's *Wilderness,* this novel is primarily concerned with the emotional state of the werewolves, and their predatory activities are downplayed.

A more intellectual approach to the theme is taken by Brian Stableford in his blockbuster *The Werewolves of London* (Simon and Schuster, 1990; Carroll and Graf, 1992), which is the first in a trilogy of scientific romances noted mainly for their lengthy speculations on the nature of reality and the supernatural. The opening volume begins in the Victorian era and concerns the strangely similar predicaments of David Lydyard and Gabriel Gill, who find themselves possessed by mysterious forces and become pawns in an epic struggle between ancient powers and fallen angels, with the fate of the world hanging on the outcome. Gill, a young boy, subsequently comes under the tutelage of Mandorla Soulier, the female leader of an ancient race of werewolves, who hopes to use the youngster's visionary powers to bring about the extermination of the human race. As more is revealed about the werewolves it turns out that they were originally natural wolves who were transformed during a misguided act of creation into a new, more powerful form; not only do they have the power to change shape, they are also immortal. Completing the trilogy are *The Angel of Pain* (Simon and Schuster, 1991; Carroll and Graf, 1993) and *The Carnival of Destruction* (Simon and Schuster, 1994; Carroll and Graf, 1994). The action in these last two books becomes increasingly subservient to the metaphysical waffle, making the final volume extremely difficult to understand.

In contrast, Cheri Scotch's entertaining trilogy— *The Werewolf's Kiss, The Werewolf's Touch,* and *The Werewolf's Sin*—makes no demands on the reader's intellect whatsoever. Primarily dark romances with a strong love interest, each volume features members of the Marley family of New Orleans, who have a heritage of lycanthropy. In *The Werewolf's Kiss* (Diamond, 1992) the heroine is seventeen-year-old Sylvie Marley, a beautiful debutante whose father, an Episcopal bishop, is a former shapeshifter. Despite his warnings, Sylvie finds herself irresistibly drawn to the Louisiana bayous, where she conducts clandestine assignations with her lover, Lucien, who persuades her to become a werewolf like himself. Thereafter she regularly consorts with the Bayou Goula loups-garous, most of whom are prominent citizens in the community. Once initiated into their world she discovers that werewolves are long-lived, aging one year for every ten human years; they also possess the gift of clairvoyance and have remarkable recuperative powers if injured. To remain true to the code by which they abide they must transform into beast-form at least once a month and consume a human heart. They kill selectively, choosing their victims from among the criminal fraternity and others who, in their opinion, deserve to die.

The second volume in the sequence, *The Werewolf's Touch* (Diamond, 1993), relates, in a series of historical flashbacks, dramatic incidents in the lives of Sylvie's ancestors. We learn that the Marleys' New Orleans dynasty was founded by Stephen Marley, an English immigrant, who paid a heavy price for marrying a local voodoo queen when a curse she put on him resulted in the firstborn of each Marley generation becoming a werewolf at the proudest moment in his or her life.

The final volume, *The Werewolf's Sin* (Diamond, 1994), is something of a departure from the other two, in that it gives key roles to two well-known figures from ancient literature—Lycaon, the legendary Arcadian monarch who was transformed into a werewolf by Jupiter, and Apollonius of Tyre, the immortal magician, who was, in turn, infected with the curse of lycanthropy by Lycaon. Ever since, this formidable duo have been bitter rivals and have become the antithesis of each other. Lycaon looks upon loups-garous as pawns to be manipulated for his own ends, while Apollonius tries to instill a code of honor in them. Inevitably there is a final showdown, in which the prize for the victor is the collective soul of the shapeshifters.

A benevolent werewolf has a supporting role in *The Spiral Dance* (William Morrow, 1991; AvoNova, 1993) by R. Garcia y Robertson. Set in the sixteenth century, this above-average historical romance centers on the plight of Anne Percy, Countess of Northumberland, whose husband's doomed rebellion against Queen Elizabeth's ruthless suppression of Catholics in Tudor England forces her to flee to Scotland, where she embarks on a series of adventures in the company of the afore-mentioned werewolf.

Peaceful werewolves find themselves the target of an unknown assassin in Tanya Huff's *Blood Trail* (DAW, 1992), which is the second volume in a series of mystery adventure novels featuring a crime-fighting vampire. In Richard Jaccoma's *The Werewolf's Revenge* (Fawcett Gold Medal, 1991), a sequel to *The Werewolf's Tale,* a lone werewolf—whose intentions are far from peaceful—takes on the might of the Third Reich. This time Hitler's fiendish minions have recruited mummies and zombies to their evil cause. Nazis are also the villains in *WerewolveSS* (Pinnacle, 1990) by Jerry and Sharon Ahern. Set in the late twentieth century, this offbeat thriller is about an elite German military unit made up of supersoldiers who can change into werewolves at will. Ageless and all-but-invulnerable, they have lain low since the end of World War II but have suddenly emerged from their hideout to mount an attack on America's eastern seaboard, with the ultimate objective of world domination. Jeffrey Sackett's *Mark of the Werewolf* (Bantam, 1990) is on similar lines, but the villains in this novel are American fascists who plan to use a three-thousand-year-old werewolf to breed an invincible army of superpatriotic soldiers.

The much-utilized scenario of whole communities of people being menaced by a race or colony of werewolves who have been secretly living in their midst for years formed the basis for several novels in the 1990s.

One of the goriest was Gene Lazuta's *Vyrmin* (Diamond, 1992), the title of which refers to an ancient race of werewolf-like creatures who terrorize a small community when they suddenly emerge from their hideaway after years of concealment. Another novel in the same vein is *The Others* (Leisure, 1993) by D. M. Wind. Here, werewolves from another dimension intend to reveal themselves after years of secretly feasting on the human race. Somewhat more sociable, but no less deadly, are the ancient, godlike shapeshifters in John Skipp and Craig Spector's *Animals* (Bantam, 1993), who satisfy their insatiable lust for blood and human flesh by preying on the clientele of roadside dives.

In Pat Murphy's *Nadya* (Tor, 1996) the main motif is hereditary lycanthropy. The eponymous heroine, a young girl living on the edge of the Missouri wilderness in the early nineteenth century, senses she is different from other girls, but doesn't discover what this means until she matures and begins to exhibit the lycanthropic traits inherited from her parents. Similar problems beset the heroine of Greg Almquist's *Wolf Kill* (Pocket, 1990). A member of a proud family periodically afflicted by lycanthropy, she fears the deadly curse is about to strike again after sensing the presence of a wolflike figure on the night of the full moon. Hereditary lycanthropy also plays a significant part in Jane Toombs's historical romance *Moonrunner 1: Under the Shadow* (Roc, 1992). The daughter of a Mexican grandee falls in love with an amnesiac to whom she has given succor, but then makes the shocking discovery that he is the unfortunate victim of a hereditary curse that turns him into a werewolf when the moon is full. Toombs utilized the same type of situation in two other novels, *Moonrunner 2: Gathering Darkness* (Roc, 1993) and *The Volan Curse* (Silhouette Shadows, 1994).

The adaptability of the werewolf theme has been demonstrated in recent years by such novels as Wayne Smith's *Thor* (St. Martin's, 1992). This highly original fantasy is written from the point of view of a German shepherd dog who finds his loyalties sorely tested when "Uncle Ted" comes to stay with his owners. Unbeknown to other members of the household, the avuncular guest is a werewolf with an uncontrollable thirst for blood. In another offbeat novel, *Quantum Moon* (Ace, 1996), by Denise Vitola, a female detective prowling the dark streets of the mid-twenty-first century is aided in her hunt for a murderer by her ability to transform into a werewolf. Equally bizarre is Laurell K. Hamilton's *Guilty Pleasures* (Ace, 1993), which features a tough female private investigator working in an alternate-world America where vampires and werewolves have gained civil rights as oppressed minorities. An unusual situation also develops in *Wolf Flow* (St. Martin's, 1992) by K. W. Keter, when a drug dealer left to die in the desert by rival crooks is fortuitously rescued and left to recuperate in an abandoned health spa whose healing waters exert a strange, controlling power over him.

Other novels representative of this period are briefly summarized as follows: *Night, Winter, and Death* (Ballantine, 1990) by Lee Hawks tells of the malevolent spirit of a dead man that enters a living person and turns him into a werewolf; *Shifter* (Roc, 1990) by Judith and Garfield Reeves-Stevens features a werewolf that has crossed over from a parallel world; *Silverwolf* (Banned Books, 1990) by Roger Edmondson concerns werewolves who possess hypnotic powers; *Shapes* (Leisure, 1991) by Steve Vance focuses on a group of people obsessed with the idea of tracking down a werewolf; *Wake of the Werewolf* (Diamond, 1991) by Geoffrey Caine deals with a psychic detective's efforts to vanquish a plague of werewolves; *Wolf in the Fold* (Ace, 1991) by Simon R. Green is set in a haunted house, where one of the guests turns out to be a shapechanger; *Moon of the Werewolf* (Zebra, 1991) by Ronald Kelly focuses on the activities of a colony of European werewolves who emigrate to rural America; *Something out There* (Zebra, 1991), also by Ronald Kelly, concerns a female shapechanger under the control of an elderly man; *Tombley's Walk* (Avon, 1991) by Crosland Brown is set in a small American town plagued by a lycanthropic serial killer who attacks his victims with animal-like ferocity; *The Attic* (Zebra, 1991) by Jack Scapparo concerns an elderly witch with shapeshifting powers; *Nightlife* (Dell/Abyss, 1991) by Brian Hodge is about a new drug that turns people into werewolf-like monsters; *Bureau 13* (Ace, 1991) by Nick Pollotta is about a secret department of the FBI that deals with supernatural phenomena of various kinds, including werewolves; *Dawn of the Vampire* (Pinnacle, 1991) by William Hill is mainly concerned with vampirism, but werewolves also play a minor part in the proceedings; *Night of the Living Shark* (Ace, 1991) by David Bischoff is a comic novel whose bevy of strange characters include bald werewolves; *Kiss of Death* (Bantam, 1992) by Joseph Locke (pseudonym of Ray Garton) is an erotic story about a teenage werewolf of the female gender; *The Master of Whitestorm* (Grafton, 1992) by Janny Wurts is about were-leopards; *Blood Wolf* (Grosset and Dunlap, 1993) by John Peel concerns the bitter rivalry between claimants to an ancient throne, resulting in one of them being transformed into a werewolf; *Naked Came the Sasquatch* (TSR, 1993) by John Boston guys the hackneyed situation of a werewolf preying on the citizens of a small town; *Heart-Beast* (Dell/Abyss, 1993) by Tanith Lee revolves around a devilish gemstone, known as the "wolf diamond," that transmits the curse of lycanthropy to those who possess it; *All Things under the Moon* (Berkley, 1994) by Robert Morgan focuses on the activities of a detective specializing in supernatural cases, who is assigned to track down a werewolf; *Wild Blood* (Roc, 1994) by Nancy A. Collins utilizes a rock music setting; *The Werewolf Chronicles* (Zebra, 1994) by Traci Briery follows the attempts by the female recipient of a werewolf's bite to adjust to her new way of life as a shapechanger; *The Jaguar Princess* (Tor, 1994) by Clare Bell is about a female descendant of the ancient Olmec jaguar gods who can change, at will, into a wild jaguar; *One Foot in the Grave* (Baen, 1995) by Wm. Mark Simmons involves vampires, witches, and werewolves; *Demon Moon* (Tor, 1995) by Jack Williamson is set in a fantasy kingdom where the inhabitants ride on winged unicorns to protect their land from werewolves and other deadly menaces; *Silver Crown* (White Wolf, 1995) by William Bridges concerns a tribe of werewolves called Silver Fangs and the battle between two rival contenders for the throne; *Breathe Deeply* (White Wolf, 1995) by Don Bassingthwaite tells of the Garou, a tribe of werewolves from the San Francisco Bay area who are engaged in keeping their ancient foe the Wyrm at bay; *Hell-Storm* (Harper/Prism, 1996) by James A. Moore is another novel about the Garou, but this time the locale is Las Vegas; *Call to Battle* (White Wolf, 1996) by Doug Murray concerns the trials and tribulations of a browbeaten cadet at a military school whose problems get even worse when he discovers he is a werewolf; *Night Calls* (Harper/Prism, 1996) by Katharine Eliska Kimbriel focuses on the plight of a young woman forced to learn the Wise Arts in order to combat werewolves; *Panther in Argyll* (Mammoth, 1996) by Lisa Tuttle is about a werepanther; *Feet of Clay* (Gollancz, 1996) by Terry Pratchett is a comic novel full of oddball characters, including a female werewolf suffering from Pre-Lunar Tension; *Hair of the Dog* (Baen, 1997) by Brett Davis revolves around the efforts of a group of scientists to find a cure for lycanthropy; *The Sword of Life* (Hodder, 1997) by Dave Morris concerns a young warrior monk caught up in a terrifying attack by werewolves, which results in him being charged with a quest to prevent the return of chaos to a land full of wonder and magic; *Darker Angels* (Gollancz, 1997) by S. P. Somtow features were-leopards; and *The Changeling Prince* (Harper/Prism, 1998) by Vivian Vande Velde tells of a werewolf enslaved by a sorceress.

Among the many other novels from this period that incorporated a werewolf theme were *Cry Wolf* (Constable, 1990) by Ian Stuart Black; *Dark Reunion* (Zebra, 1990) by Stephen R. George; *Wolfwalker* (Ballantine, 1990) by Tara K. Harper; *The Werewolf and the Wormlord* (Corgi, 1991) by Hugh Cook; *The Living Dark* (Zebra, 1991) by Stephen Gresham; *Werewolf* (Longmeadow, 1991) by Peter Rubie; *Nightfeeder* (Roc, 1991) by Judith and Garfield Reeves-Stevens (sequel to *Shifter*); *Wulf* (Headline, 1991) by Steve Harris; *Watchers in the Woods* (Kensington, 1991) by William W. Johnstone; *When Darkness Falls* (Pinnacle, 1992) by Sidney Williams; *Lucifer Jones* (Warner Questar, 1992) by Mike Resnick; *Black Maria* (Mammoth, 1992) by Diana Wynne Jones; *Striper Assassin* (Signet, 1992) by Nyx Smith; *Full Moonster* (Ace, 1992) by Nick Pollotta; *Embrace of the Wolf* (Diamond, 1993) by Pat Franklin; *The St. Andrews Werewolf* (HarperCollins, 1993) by Eric Wilson; *Shadow Dance* (Pocket, 1994) by Jessica Palmer;

The Wolf and the Raven (Avon, 1994) by Diana Paxson; *The Year the Wolves Came* (Dutton, 1994) by Bebe Faas Rice; *The Laughing Corpse* (Ace, 1994) by Laurell K. Hamilton; *Walking Wolf* (Mark Ziesing, 1995) by Nancy A. Collins (prequel to *Wild Blood*); *Wyrm Wolf* (Harper/Prism, 1995) by Edo van Belkom; *Moondog* (St. Martin's, 1995) by Henry Garfield; *Conspicuous Consumption* (Harper/Prism, 1995) by Stewart von Allmen; *The Dubious Hills* (Tor, 1995) by Pamela Dean; *Cry Wolf* (Zebra, 1995) by Victoria Thompson; *Full Moon* (Players Press, 1995) by Barry P. Rumble; *The Fire Duke* (Avon, 1995) by Joel Rosenberg; *Werewolf Wars* (Commonwealth, 1996) by Randy Goldman; *Wolfsong* (Zebra, 1996) by Traci Briery; *Mark of the Wolf* (Masquerade, 1996) by Derek Adams; *Howl-o-ween* (Leisure, 1996) by Gary L. Holleman; *The Fire Rose* (Baen, 1996) by Mercedes Lackey; *Angry Moon* (Forge, 1996) by Terrill Lankford; *Cry of the Werewolf* (Xlibris Corporation, 1997) by Richard P. Haesche Sr.; *Enchanted* (Harlequin, 1997) by Claire Delacroix; *Challenging the Wolf* (Squane's Press, 1997) by Steve Harris; *Wolf Moon* (Bantam, 1997) by John R. Holt; *The Boy Who Cried Werewolf* (Berkley, 1998) by Elvira and John Paragon; *Leopard Lord* (Ace, 1998) by Alanna Morland; *Return of the Wolf Man* (Boulevard, 1998) by Jeff Rovin; *Killing Frost* (Press-Tige Press, 1998) by Dan L. Blake; *When Wolves Cry* (Picasso Publications, 1998) by Chris N. Africa; and *Only Silver Can Kill a Werewolf* (Upublish.com., 1999) by Dragan Vujic.

Love at First Bite: Romantic Werewolves

A relatively new category of popular fiction—distinct from the horror novel but similarly dealing with supernatural themes—is the paranormal romance. Aimed primarily at women readers, these novels are for the most part spicy love stories in which vampires, werewolves, and other supernatural beings play a major role in the plot. There are, however, some striking differences between the supernormal protagonists of novels in this category and their counterparts in horror fiction. Werewolves of the male gender, for instance, are generally portrayed as misunderstood outsiders who regard their ability to change into a wolf as an asset rather than a curse. Dark, brooding, and slightly dangerous to know, they embody the admirable as well as the wild and unpredictable qualities of the wolf; but, most importantly, they are magnetically attractive lovers whom the heroine is unable to resist, even after she has learned their dark secret.

Luke Gevaudan, the shapeshifting hero of Susan Krinard's *Prince of Wolves* (Bantam, 1994) is a typical example. One of the last survivors of a race of werewolves who live in a secret village cut off from the outside world, he has endured years of loneliness. His luck changes when he guides a vulnerable young woman through the rugged Canadian Rockies and realizes, as love blossoms between them, that she is his soul mate. Following this novel's success Krinard penned three similar werewolf romances, *Prince of Shadows* (Bantam, 1996), *Touch of the Wolf* (Bantam, 1999), and *Once a Wolf* (Bantam, 2000), which have also proved popular.

Another leading exponent of the paranormal romance is Connie Flynn, who has written two werewolf-themed novels to date, *Shadow on the Moon* (Topaz, 1997) and *Shadow of the Wolf* (Topaz, 1998). In the earlier novel the heroine, a biologist who specializes in wolves, heads for Arizona to investigate a series of mysterious slayings. This leads to her becoming romantically involved with a lonely, tormented man who sleeps behind iron bars and disappears at night when the moon is full. It transpires that he is a reluctant werewolf desperately trying to get the curse removed.

Matters of a slightly more complicated nature are touched on in *Wolf in Waiting* (Harlequin, 1995) by Rebecca Flanders. The novel's troubled heroine is an anthromorph—the offspring of werewolf parents but with a defect that prevents her from shapeshifting. Because of her disability, her life is blighted by the fact that she cannot give birth to any baby werewolves.

In Donna Boyd's *The Passion* (Avon, 1998), an erotic and tense saga of love and betrayal, the heroine, Tessa LeGuerre, falls under the spell of a very powerful, very sensual werewolf named Alexander Devoncroix. He belongs to a hidden werewolf society, members of which secretly hold all the positions of power in the world and claim responsibility for every major advance in the history of civilization. Tessa's willingness to

understand and experience the werewolves' lifestyle results in her being the first human introduced into their
community; but the couple's passionate and often dangerous love affair ends in tragedy when Alexander is
killed in a power struggle within the were-community.
More fascinating details about the complex political
structure of this alien society in our midst are revealed
in the sequel, *The Promise* (Avon, 1999). Here, a young
woman comes to the aid of a werewolf who has been
badly injured in a helicopter crash and learns secret information about him and his fellow werewolves from a
manuscript she finds in the wreckage.

A novel not marketed as a paranormal romance but
with all the trappings of one is Alice Borchardt's blockbuster *The Silver Wolf* (Ballantine/Del Rey, 1998),
which is set against the colorful backdrop of Rome in
the twilight of its splendor. The youthful heroine, Regeane, who is of imperial lineage, suffers from the curse
of hereditary lycanthropy, making her a target for abuse
and blackmail by those members of her politically ambitious family who know her secret. Of these the most
ruthless is Regeane's depraved uncle, who threatens to
betray her to the Church unless she assists him in his
sinister schemes. If this scenario has a familiar ring to it
that is because of the similarity it bears to the plot of
Chelsea Quinn Yarbro's *The Godforsaken*, mentioned
earlier in this survey. But despite being derivative *The
Silver Wolf* was a brilliant debut novel and well de-
served the plaudits it received.

Borchardt's second novel, *Night of the Wolf* (Ballantine/Del Rey, 1999), goes even farther back in time to the days of Julius Caesar and involves a tempestuous love affair between the shapeshifting heroine and a charismatic male werewolf. The third and final novel in the series, *The Wolf King* (Ballantine/Del Rey, 2001), returns to the same historical era as the first and offers a similar mix of passionate romance and political intrigue.

Other paranormal romances with a werewolf theme are Evelyn Vaughn's *Waiting for the Wolf Moon* (Harlequin/Silhouette Shadows, 1993); Saranne Dawson's *Heart of the Wolf* (Love Spell, 1993); Sharon Green's *Werewolf Moon* (Harlequin/Intrigue, 1993); Carla Cassidy's *Heart of the Beast* (Harlequin/Silhouette Shadows, 1993); Lori Handeland's *Full Moon Dreams* (Love Spell, 1996); Saranne Dawson's *Secrets of the Wolf* (Love Spell, 1998); and Rebecca Flanders's *Secret of the Wolf* (Harlequin/Silhouette Shadows, 1999).

Growing Up with Monsters: Werewolf Stories for Children

The late twentieth century also saw a significant rise in the number of children's books about werewolves and other scary monsters. Indeed, so all-pervading was the mania for monsters during this period that even preschool children encountered them in their storybooks. This inevitably drew howls of protest from those parents, teachers, and religious groups who regard stories about supposedly demonic creatures as unfit reading matter for young children. Nevertheless, there is little evidence to show that this moral backlash has had any real effect in stemming the flow of this material. On the contrary, the popularity of books of this type appears to have grown rather than diminished.

The most prolific author of preteen thrillers is R. L. Stine, whose popular Goosebumps series has deservedly earned him a host of fans around the world. One of the best werewolf novels in this series is *The Werewolf of Fever Swamp* (Scholastic, 1993), which heightens the suspense by concealing the identity of the werewolf until the very end. There are also some scary moments in *Night in Werewolf Woods* (Scholastic, 1996), in which a boy's vacation at Wood World is soured by rumors that it is the haunt of werewolves. Stine is also in good form in *Werewolf Skin* (Scholastic, 1997). In this cautionary tale a boy visiting his aunt and uncle in Wolf Creek is told to keep away from the creepy house next door and never to venture into the woods, but, of course, he fails to heed their warning and suffers the inevitable consequences. The same author's *The Werewolf in the Living Room* (Scholastic, 1999) has a slightly surreal feel to it. Here a father and his son think they have captured a real live werewolf and keep it a prisoner in their living room. Two other werewolf novels in the Goosebumps series are *The Werewolf of Twisted Tree Lodge* (Scholastic, 1998) and *Full Moon Fever* (Scholastic, 1999).

Bad Blood (Berkley, 1993), in which a hungry were-wolf starts picking off children at a summer camp, is the first of three werewolf novels coauthored by Debra Doyle and James D. Macdonald. The other two, *Hunter's Moon* (Berkley, 1994) and *Judgment Night* (Berkley, 1995), both feature a reluctant teenage werewolf named Valerie Sherwood. In *Hunter's Moon* she tries to protect her hometown from a group of vampires, and in *Judgment Night* she is menaced by a Wendigo, which thrives on her fear.

W. R. Philbrick's "Werewolf Chronicles" trilogy, which is made up of *Night Creature* (Scholastic, 1996), *Children of the Wolf* (Scholastic, 1996), and *The Wereing* (Scholastic, 1996), revolves around the adventures of a boy raised by wolves, who reluctantly becomes a were-wolf and ends up clashing with full-blooded werewolves bent on forcing other children to join their ranks.

While summer camps and other wooded areas tend to be the most popular locations for children's were-wolf novels, quite a few are set in the neighborhood where the principal protagonist resides, and the were-wolf is often someone they know. Pete Johnson's *My Friend's a Werewolf* (Yearling, 1997) tells of a young boy's new neighbor, who turns out to have shapeshift-ing tendencies. Similar situations arise in David Lu-bar's *The Wavering Werewolf* (Scholastic/Apple, 1997) and Nancy Garden's *My Brother, the Werewolf* (Ran-dom House, 1995). In Lubar's novel a schoolboy sud-denly starts sprouting hair on his face and body in front of his startled classmates; in Garden's book a boy metamorphoses into a wolf and attacks the livestock on his uncle's farm. The amusingly titled *Norman Newman and the Werewolf of Walnut Street* (Little Rainbow/ Troll, 1995) by Ellen Conford focuses on a youngster's growing apprehension when he hears rumors about a werewolf stalking his neighborhood. Don Whittington's *Werewolf Tonight* (William Morrow, 1995) concerns the confrontation between two brave schoolmates and a wily werewolf. Edward Packard's *Night of the Werewolf (Choose Your Own Nightmare)* (Bantam, 1995) challenges the reader to investigate rumors about a werewolf while making the decisions that will lead them to the discovery of the deadly monster's true identity. In Stephen Bowkett's *The World's Smallest Werewolf* (Macdonald Young Books, 1996) a couple arrive at a town called Glenbarra and wonder why they are treated so strangely. They subsequently find out that all the inhabitants are werewolves.

Other werewolf novels aimed primarily at children in the preteen age range are *Fifth Grade Monsters no. 12: Werewolf Come Home* (Avon Camelot, 1990) by Mel Gilden; *Werewolves Don't Go to Summer Camp* (Scholastic, 1991) by Debbie Dadey; *Weird Wolf* (Henry Holt, 1991) by Margery Cuyler; *The Runton Werewolf* (Red Fox, 1996) by Ritchie Perry; and *Curse of Werewolf Castle* (Poolbeg Press, 1996) by Gordon Snell.

Werewolves are also occasionally featured in young adult novels, which have teenagers as their target audience. Books in this category usually play on the fears and anxieties of modern teenage life, and when they utilize horror themes tend to be more explicitly violent than the children's novels previously discussed. This is certainly true of Patricia Windsor's *The Blooding* (Scholastic, 1996), which revels in gory scenes of savagery. The heroine, Maris Pelham, goes to work as a mother's help in England and is shocked to discover that the entire family she is staying with are werewolves. Nevertheless, when she is invited to become one of them she rashly agrees, but becomes emotionally disturbed when her growing delight in blood and killing conflicts with her gentle side.

The plucky heroine of John Peel's *Dances with Werewolves* (Archway, 1995) bravely thwarts a werewolf killer and is rewarded by winning the nomination for Midwinter Dance Queen; but her joy is short-lived when she discovers that a second werewolf is out to get her. In another typical young adult novel, *Heart of the Hunter* (Archway, 1997) by R. L. Stine, a love-sick teenager buys a love potion from a medicine woman and is transformed into a wolf after drinking it. Then, to his horror, he learns that if his true love sees him in his brute form the transformation will become permanent. Annette Curtis Klause's *Blood and Chocolate* (Delacorte Press, 1997) also deals with frustrated love and chronicles the longings and passions of a teenage werewolf whose pack family live quietly in a Maryland suburb. The girl's true nature is unsuspected by the other pupils at her school, but when she gets a crush on a boy in her class she is faced with the difficult choice of keeping him in the dark about her background, or telling him the truth and risking rejection.

Some of the most popular young adult novels are spin-offs from hit television series, such as *Buffy the Vampire Slayer* and *Sweet Valley High*. Although she is usually preoccupied with combating vampires, Buffy takes on a pack of were-coyotes disguised as carnival workers in John Vornholt's *Coyote Moon* (Archway, 1998); and Liz and Jess, the twins from Sweet Valley High, get dangerously involved with an aristocratic werewolf in the three-volume series comprising *Love and Death in London* (Bantam, 1994), *Date with a Werewolf* (Bantam, 1994), and *Beware the Wolfman* (Bantam, 1994), authorship of which was shared by Francine Pascal and Kate William.

7

Werewolf Anthologies

Because many of the short stories mentioned in this survey are buried in old books and magazines, the easiest way to gain access to a sizable chunk of them is through anthologies devoted exclusively to werewolf stories. Fortunately these anthologies are a relatively recent phenomenon—dating back only to the mid-1960s—and most, therefore, should still be available from used-book dealers specializing in horror material.

The first all-werewolf anthology was *Way of the Werewolf* (Panther, 1966), edited by Douglas Hill. Published in England, this well-balanced collection of stories contains "The Phantom Farmhouse" by Seabury Quinn, "Gabriel-Ernest" by Saki, "Running Wolf" by Algernon Blackwood, "Wolves Don't Cry" by Bruce Elliott, "The Gâloup" by Claude Seignolle, "The

Refugee" by Jane Rice, "The White Wolf of the Hartz Mountains" by Frederick Marryat, and "Canis Lupus Sapiens" by Alex Hamilton.

After this pioneering effort came *Book of the Werewolf* (Sphere, 1973), edited by Brian J. Frost, about which I can obviously speak with some authority. It was, I can reveal, compiled at the behest of a director of Sphere Books, who had been shown a copy of the British fanzine *Shadow* containing my first attempt at a survey of werewolf fiction. The book sold over forty thousand copies and contained an expanded version of my original survey, as well as thirteen stories, ranging from Victorian classics to contemporary pieces. Mostly personal favorites, the stories selected were "Hugues, the Wer-Wolf" by Sutherland Menzies, "The White Wolf of Kostopchin" by Sir Gilbert Campbell, "The Eyes of the Panther" by Ambrose Bierce, "The Were-Wolf" by Clemence Housman, "Mère Maxim" by Elliott O'Donnell, "The Werewolf of Ponkert" by H. Warner Munn, "The Wolf of St. Bonnot" by Seabury Quinn, "The Kill" by Peter Fleming, "Eena" by Manly Banister, "The Drone" by A. Merritt, "The Adventure of the Tottenham Werewolf" by August Derleth, "Mrs. Kaye" by Beverly Haaf, and "Pia!" by Dale C. Donaldson. The only contentious selection in the book was "The Drone," to which some people objected on the grounds that it wasn't really a werewolf story. This is a valid point, and the only reason I can offer for including this story—apart from the fact that it included a couple of references to shapeshifting in the prologue—is that I was a huge fan of the author at the time. Another interesting sidelight is that although *Book of the Werewolf* was not officially distributed in the United States, copies were imported in some quantity; and I have it on good authority that H. Warner Munn snapped up as many of these as he could find to present to friends.

The first American anthology devoted solely to this type of material was *Werewolf! A Chrestomathy of Lycanthropy* (Arbor House, 1979), which was one of a series of single-theme anthologies edited by Bill Pronzini in the late 1970s and early 1980s. Generally regarded as a model of its kind, *Werewolf!* is divided into three sections: "Classic Stories," "Contemporary Tales," and "Two Visions of the Future." Gathered together in the first section are "The Were-Wolf" by Clemence Housman, "The Wolf" by Guy de Maupassant, "The Mark of the Beast" by Rudyard Kipling, "Dracula's Guest" by Bram Stoker, and "Gabriel-Ernest" by Saki. The second section contains "There Shall Be No Darkness" by James Blish, "Nightshapes" by Barry N. Malzberg, "The Hound" by Fritz Leiber, "Wolves Don't Cry" by Bruce Elliott, and "Lila the Werewolf" by Peter S. Beagle. The final section has only two stories: "A Prophecy of Monsters" by Clark Ashton Smith, and "Full Sun" by Brian W. Aldiss. Although the stories are all excellent examples of the form, perhaps more imagination might have been shown in the choice of classic stories, since those selected had been reprinted many times.

Peter Haining, who has compiled dozens of single-theme anthologies over the past thirty years has, surprisingly, only one all-werewolf anthology to his credit, *Werewolf: Horror Stories of the Man-Beast* (Severn House, 1987). The usual mixture of vintage and modern stories, the full lineup is as follows: "The Lycanthropist" by Catherine Crowe, "The Werwolves" by Henry Beaugrand, "The Wolves of God" by Algernon Blackwood, "The Master of the House" by Oliver Onions, "The Phantom Werewolf" by Montague Summers, "The Wolf Girl" by Guy Endore, "Fortune's Fools" by Seabury Quinn, "Wolfshead" by Robert E. Howard, "Beast of the Island" by Paul Selonke, "The Refugee" by Jane Rice, "The Man Who Cried 'Wolf!'" by Robert Bloch, "I Was a Teenage Werewolf" by Ralph Thornton, "The Point of Thirty Miles" by T. H. White, "Cry Wolf" by Basil Copper, and "The Demythologised Werewolf" by James Farlow. It could be argued, I suppose, that Blackwood's "The Wolves of God" is not really a werewolf story. Admittedly there is a minor reference to shapeshifting, but the supernatural beings known as "the Wolves of God" are actually a ghostly pack of wolves who, according to Native American lore, punish malefactors. The two rarest stories are "The Werwolves" and "The Wolf Girl." According to the introduction, which provides background information about the stories, Beaugrand's yarn was the first to incorporate the American Indian origin of lycanthropy and also inspired the first motion picture on the subject, a "two-reeler" called *The Werewolf,* produced in 1913. Endore's piece purports to be based on an Alaskan legend, but anyone who has read Clemence Housman's "The Were-Wolf" will immediately recognize where the idea for the story really came from. True to form, Haining drops the odd clanger in his introductory notes. For instance, he mistakenly calls Crowe's "A Story of a Weir-Wolf" a novel when it is actually a short story; and another factual error is the allusion to a story by Greye La Spina called "The Devil's Shadow." As there is no such story by this author, one presumes he means "The Devil's Pool."

Werewolves (Harper and Row, 1988), edited by Jane Yolen and Martin H. Greenberg, is a collection of all-original short stories tailored for juvenile readers. The introduction by Yolen is intriguingly titled "How to Become a Werewolf," and the fifteen stories—mostly the work of talented young authors—comprise "Bad Blood" by Debra Doyle and J. D. Macdonald, "The Werewolf's Gift" by Ru Emerson, "The White Wolf" by Leigh Ann Hussey, "Not All Wolves" by Harry Turtledove, "Wolfskin" by Mary K. Whittington, "Night Calls" by Katharine Eliska Kimbriel, "Wolf from the Door" by Elizabeth Ann Scarborough, "Monster Mash" by Sherwood Smith, "The Passing of the Pack" by Bruce Coville, "Flesh and Blood" by Marguerite W. Davol, "Green Messiah" by Jane Yolen, "The Wolf's Flock" by Susan M. Shwartz, "Met by Moonlight" by Anne Eliot Crompton, "A Winter's Night" by Esther M. Friesner, and "One Chance" by Charles de Lint.

243

Another anthology primarily made up of original stories is *The Ultimate Werewolf* (Dell, 1991), edited by Byron Preiss, which was compiled to celebrate the fiftieth anniversary of the release of the famous werewolf movie *The Wolf Man,* starring Lon Chaney Jr. Appropriately, his character in the film, Lawrence Talbot, is featured in the opening selection, Harlan Ellison's "Adrift just off the Islets of Langerhans," which is one of the few retreads among the eighteen stories. Also included is Philip José Farmer's "Wolf, Iron, and Moth," which has a truly memorable transformation scene, even surpassing the one in Bloch's "The Man Who Cried 'Wolf'!" In this deftly constructed story, a doctor who has recently settled in a small town in Arkansas possesses a wolf skin that transforms him into a wolf when he drapes it over his shoulders in the moonlight, compelling him to attack local residents. A major drawback, however, is that in between transformations he is forced to consume large quantities of food to compensate for the dramatic loss in weight he incurs during the transformation process. These sudden changes in his appearance soon arouse the suspicion of the local sheriff; and in the ensuing battle of wits the lawman outtricks the shapeshifting doctor, who is ambushed and killed while in wolf form. The sheriff, however, makes the fatal mistake of skinning the carcass and hanging the pelt above his fireplace, where it begins to exert a malign influence over him. In a final, masterly touch, the lawman's impending doom is tellingly expressed in the following words: "The hungry wolf will try to get at the meat even if he sees the trap. An iron filing does not will not to fly to the magnet. The moth does not extinguish the flame so that it will not be incinerated." Also noteworthy is Pat Murphy's "South of Oregon City," in which a lonely trapper learns to live with the discovery that his new bride periodically transforms into a she-wolf and goes on nocturnal forays. Matters are complicated even further when she teams up with a white dog-wolf, which creates an unusual love triangle. Other bright spots in an ultimately disappointing collection are "Angels' Moon" by Kathe Koja, "Day of the Wolf" by Craig Shaw Gardner, and "The Werewolf Gambit" by Robert Silverberg. Also included are "Unleashed" by Nina Kiriki Hoffman, "The Mark of the Beast" by Kim Antieau, "At War with the Wolf Man" by Jerome Charyn, "Moonlight on the Gazebo" by Mel Gilden, "Raymond" by Nancy A. Collins, "There's a Wolf in My Time Machine" by Larry Niven, "Special Makeup" by Kevin J. Anderson, "Pure Silver" by A. C. Crispin and Kathleen O'Malley, "Close Shave" by Brad Linaweaver, "Partners" by Robert J. Randisi, "Ancient Evil" by Bill Pronzini, "And the Moon Shines Full and Bright" by Brad Strickland, "Full Moon over Moscow" by Stuart M. Kaminsky, and "Wolf Watch" by Robert Weinberg. Most of these tend to be gimmicky, relying on the concluding punch line for their effect. Sandwiching the stories are the wonderfully nostalgic introduction by Harlan Ellison—worth the price of the book alone—and a selected filmography by Leonard Wolf.

The biggest, and possibly the best, collection of werewolf stories is *The Mammoth Book of Werewolves* (Robinson, 1994), edited by Stephen Jones. A mixture of reprints and original stories, it eschews the all-too-familiar standards and places the emphasis on newer stories. The oldest selection is Manly Wade Wellman's novelette "The Hairy Ones Shall Dance," which dates from 1938; the only other work of a similar vintage is Hugh B. Cave's "The Whisperers," which originally appeared in a slightly different form in the April 1942 issue of *Spicy Mystery Stories*. One of Cave's best stories, it centers on the terrifying events that take place in an old house recently purchased by a newly married couple, who become disturbed by strange whispering noises coming from the cellar. An investigation by the husband leads to the discovery that the eerie sounds are made by demonic entities dwelling at the bottom of a cistern hidden beneath the floor of the cellar, whose malign influence on the man transforms him into a vicious werewolf. In the shocking denouement he is forced to make human sacrifices to the ravenous demons, whose incessant voices increase in volume until they sound like a pack of howling wolves.

One of the newer reprints, Karl Edward Wagner's "One Paris Night," is also above-average and has an ingenious ending. Two soldiers of fortune take refuge in a wrecked cathedral during the siege of Paris in the Franco-Prussian War of 1870. They are joined by a prostitute, who insists that a werewolf—whom she calls Bertrand—is prowling outside, preying on the corpses of those recently killed in the fighting. Concerned that he will come for them next, the soldiers hunt among the rubble for something made of silver that they can melt down and make into bullets. In an ancient crypt they find a silver chalice blackened with age, which seems ideal for this purpose. No sooner have they completed the task of making the bullets than, all of a sudden, the werewolf—who is probably meant to be Bertrand Caillet—bursts in on them. One of the men shoots him and immediately flames gush from the wounds, spectacularly reducing the screaming werewolf to a pile of ashes. Scurrying from the building, the three companions bump into an aged priest, who tells them that the very cup from which Christ had drunk at the Last Supper—the legendary Holy Grail—had been kept in the cathedral in secret throughout the centuries. The old man begs them to help him search for the priceless relic, but they haven't the heart to tell him what they have done with it.

Also among the reprint material culled from modern sources is Les Daniels's "Wereman," in which a visit to the supermarket takes on a new perspective when seen through the eyes of a wolf who periodically changes into a man but has little understanding of human ways. The only thing that grates about this tip-top story is the title, which, from an etymological standpoint, is redundant, since "were" (from Old English) and "man" both mean the same.

Of the stories original to this anthology the best is undoubtedly Roberta Lannes's "Essence of the Beast," told from the viewpoint of a vivacious female werewolf. She and three other werewolves live together in a ramshackle house and pose as a family—mother and father and their two daughters. Unsuspecting wayfarers who pay them a visit usually end up on the dinner table; but when a handsome young man turns up offering to fix up their dilapidated house for a reasonable price, the young female werewolf soon finds her carnal desires taking precedence over her carnivorous nature. Essentially a love story, this poignant tale scotches the notion that all werewolves are vicious brutes without tender feelings.

Kim Newman's novelette "Out of the Night, When the Full Moon Is Bright . . ." which was also specially written for this anthology, is only partially successful. About a Zorro-like werewolf who leaves a zigzag mark on the faces of his victims, it doesn't get off first base as a horror story but scores heavily as a history lesson.

The Mammoth Book of Werewolves also contains "Twilight at the Towers" by Clive Barker, "The Dream of the Wolf" by Scott Bradfield, "Night Beat" by Ramsey Campbell, "The Werewolf" by R. Chetwynd-Hayes, "Rain Falls" by Michael Marshall Smith,

"Guilty Party" by Stephen Laws, "Immortal" by Mark Morris, "Cry Wolf" by Basil Copper, "Rug" by Graham Masterton, "And I Shall Go in the Devil's Name" by David Sutton, "The Foxes of Fascoum" by Peter Tremayne, "Soul of the Wolf" by Brian Mooney, "Heart of the Beast" by Adrian Cole, "Anything But Your Kind" by Nicholas Royle, "The Nighthawk" by Dennis Etchison, "The Cell" by David Case, and "Boobs" by Suzy McKee Charnas.

Werewolves (DAW, 1995), edited by Martin H. Greenberg—not to be confused with his earlier anthology bearing the same title—is devoted solely to contemporary stories, all of which are original to this collection. Making up the contents are "Extinctions in Paradise" by Brian Hodge, "Bindlestiff" by Peter Crowther, "Never Moon a Werewolf" by Barbara Paul, "Dumpster Diving" by Nina Kiriki Hoffman, "Woofman" by Brenda Crank and Scott Nickell, "Nick of Time" by Matthew J. Costello, "The Nighttime Is the Right Time" by Bill Crider, "Double Identity" by Wendi Lee and Terry Beatty, "Little Boy Riding Hood" by Lawrence Schimel, "Wolf" by Max Allan Collins, "Children of the Night" by Cheri Scotch, "Bark at the Moon" by Mike Baker, "Nights in the Mountains of Haiti" by Hugh B. Cave, "The Last Link between Life and Death" by J. N. Williamson, "Asleep in the Mist" by Billie Sue Mosiman, "The Pack" by Norman Partridge, "Waiting for Moonlight" by Roman A. Ranieri, "A Taste of Blood and Roses" by David Niall Wilson,

"Sand Boils" by Tracy Knight, "Only the Strong Survive" by Richard T. Chizmar and Barry Hoffman, "The Night of Howling" by Mickey Zucker Reichert, and "Some Touch of Pity" by Gary A. Braunbeck.

The stories in *Werewolves* utilize the theme in a variety of different ways, presenting images as diverse as South American street urchins transforming into wolf-like animals in order to survive, and a self-help group for lycanthropes that discusses the finer points of transformation and predation. The stories also display a variety of moods: some are uncompromisingly bleak, some poignant, and others humorous. All in all, there is something to suit every taste, but don't expect to find anything of lasting appeal.

Recommended to those with a liking for stories with a shared background is *When Will You Rage?* (White Wolf, 1994), edited by Stewart Wieck. Another all-original collection, it contains "The Waters of Lethe" by Bill Bridges, "Coyote Full Moon" by Sam Chupp, "A Sheep in Wolf's Clothing" by Vincent Courtney, "Transitions" by Nigel D. Findley, "Fang of the Wolf" by Owl Goingback, "Hunter's Blues" by Scott Ciencin, "The Bye-Bye Club" by Ray Winninger, "Wolf Trap" Richard Lee Byers, "Predator and Prey" by David Chart, "Lone Werewolf" by Lois Tilton, "Shards" by Phil Brucato, "A Day Off" by Thomas Kane, "Little Flea" by Scott Urban, "A Wolf in Shepherd's Clothing" by Edo van Belkom, "For Auld Lang Syne" by James A. Moore, "A Third World" by Graham Watkins, "A Useless Death" by Don Bassingthwaite, "Calley's Story" by Alara Rogers, and "Trickster Moon" by J. S. Banks.

When Will You Rage? is different from other werewolf anthologies because all the stories feature members of a race of werewolves called the Garou, who are located in the San Francisco Bay Area and are made up of different tribes, each with its own customs and rituals. Undetectable in their human form except by others of their kind, the Garou have infiltrated human society and hold posts in all walks of life. They are of either wolf or human ancestry, although the latter predominate; and, being extremely adaptable, are able to adopt several guises, including Crinos (half-wolf, half-human form), Hispos (near-wolf form), and Lupus (complete wolf form). The Garou also have their own peculiar language and culture and can communicate with natural wolves. Highly religious, they meet regularly at sacred places called caerns, where contact with the spirit world takes place. A group of Garous who live near and tend an individual caern are called a sept and are bound by similar totems and lifestyles. Normally the Garou are more than a match for human adversaries but are not totally invulnerable—silver bullets can pierce their mystic defenses. Nevertheless, they have remarkable recuperative powers and can survive even the most serious wounds. Their ancient enemy is the Wyrm, which is the manifestation and symbol of evil, entropy, and decay in the world. Vampires are manifestations of the Wyrm, as is the corrupting, destroying ecological ruin humans wreak upon the environment. In fighting this insidious menace the Garou see themselves as doomed warriors protecting a dying world.

The sex life of the Garou is unusual. It is forbidden for them to mate with their own kind; they must either choose a human or a wolf as a partner. Sexual intercourse between two werewolves is regarded as unnatural as incest between a human brother and sister. Any offspring from such a union is called a metis and is reviled and treated as an outcast. They are easily recognizable as they all have some physical deformity. In "Lone Werewolf," for instance, the metis around whom the story revolves has a misshapen foot and is cruelly nicknamed "Chester" (after the lame character in the old TV series) by young members of his tribe. Generally, however, these outcasts are portrayed in a sympathetic light and are invariably the heroes in the stories in which they appear.

A personal favorite among the nineteen stories in *When Will You Rage?* is "A Sheep in Wolf's Clothing," which is not only chock full of exciting action but also has a powerful message. The principal character, Klaus Hurst, is the leader of a group of werewolves called the Sword of Heimdall, which was originally formed in Germany in the 1930s. At that time Garous held important positions in the Nazi party and were instrumental in promoting the policy of annihilating the Jewish community, whom they regarded as agents of the Wyrm. During the war, Klaus's father, Dieter, a commandant of a concentration camp, had forced himself upon a beautiful Jewess, who bore him two sons, Klaus and Max. Max, who was not a werewolf like his father and brother, was thought to have died after his father callously shot him and his mother during a massacre of the camp's inmates. However, the boy miraculously survived and he was rescued and brought up in America by a GI. Half a century later Max learns of his father and brother's arrival in San Francisco and plots his revenge. Dieter deservedly gets his comeuppance, but the two brothers are dramatically reconciled after Klaus finally learns the truth about the shameful circumstances surrounding his birth.

The Garou are also featured in seven out of the twenty-two stories in *Dark Destiny* (White Wolf, 1995), edited by Edward E. Kramer. All the stories in this anthology are set in White Wolf's imaginary World of Darkness, and those with a werewolf motif focus on the challenges faced by individual members of the Garou, in particular their battles with vampires and other agents of the Wyrm. One of the most enjoyable stories among this septet is C. Dean Andersson's "Small Brown Bags of Blood," which is set in the eighth century at the time of the Viking raids on northern Britain. The hero, a Garou named Egil, is the leader of a band of seafaring Viking warriors. Forced to make land after a storm, he and his crew are made captive by the evil priests of Lindisfarne, who are in league with vampires. These hideous fiends—shaped like small wriggling bags—burrow into the flesh of their victims and drain all the blood from their bodies, after which they reanimate the corpses and drive them to commit similar acts of vampirism. Egil, enraged by these abominations, metamorphoses into a Berserking Man-Wolf and furiously attacks the diminutive monsters, killing all but one. On a return trip to look for the escaped blood-drinker, Egil and his men find other vampires of the same loathsome kind hiding in the crypts of churches all over Britain. After further investigation, it is discovered that they have infested holy places throughout Christendom.

The other werewolf stories in this excellent anthology are "Leaders of the Pack" by Nancy Holder, "Go Hungry" by Wayne Allen Sallee, "Winter Queen" by Rick Hautala, "Lone Wolf" by Edo van Belkom, "Night Games" by Richard Lee Byers, and "The Love of Monsters" by Nancy A. Collins. The last-named revolves around an elderly vampire's doomed love affair with a rebellious young female werewolf and is ultimately quite moving.

Sexually explicit stories about female werewolves (who bare more than just their fangs) make up the contents of *The Beast Within: Erotic Tales of Werewolves* (Circlet Press, 1994), edited by Cecelia Tan. Lycanthropic ladies also dominate in *Women Who Run with the Werewolves* (Cleis Press, 1996), edited by Pam Keesey, which contains "A Model of Transformation" by Renee M. Charles, "Teamwork" by Paul Allen, "Sisters of the Weird" by Thomas S. Roche, "Euphorbia Helioscopia" by Jeremy E. Johnson, and "Wilding" by Melanie Tem.

Providing a disturbing glimpse of the future, *Tomorrow Bites* (Baen, 1995), edited by Greg Cox and T. K. F. Weisskopf, presents fictional works that treat lycanthropy as a scientific phenomenon. There are eleven stories altogether: "Werehouse" by Michael Flynn, "Operation Afreet" by Poul Anderson, "There Shall Be No Darkness" by James Blish, "There's a Wolf in My Time Machine" by Larry Niven, "Wolf Enough" by Jane Mailander, "A Prophecy of Monsters" by C. A. Smith, "A Midwinter's Tale" by Michael Swanwick, "The Hero as Werewolf" by Gene Wolfe, "FlowereW" by John J. Ordover, "Frontier of the Dark" by A. Bertram Chandler, and "Werewolves of Luna" by R. Garcia y Robertson. While some of the older stories may be familiar, only the most avid reader of contemporary science fiction magazines will have previously encountered the six newer stories.

All the stories in *Isaac Asimov's Werewolves* (Ace, 1999), edited by Gardner Dozois and Sheila Williams, have been culled from the pages of *Asimov's Science Fiction Magazine*. They include "What Seen But the Wolf" by Gregg Keizer, "Boobs" by Suzy McKee Charnas, "Two Bad Dogs" by R. A. Cross, "Madonna of the Wolves" by S. P. Somtow, "Red" by Sarah Clemens, and "An American Childhood" by Pat Murphy.

Clusters of werewolf stories have also appeared in

anthologies devoted to more than one theme. *Rod Serling's Triple W: Witches, Warlocks and Werewolves* (Bantam, 1963), edited by Rod Serling, includes "The Mark of the Beast" by Rudyard Kipling, "Wolves Don't Cry" by Bruce Elliott, and "The Black Retriever" by Charles G. Finney, *Monsters Galore* (Fawcett Gold Medal, 1965), edited by Bernhardt J. Hurwood, includes "The Eyes of the Panther" by Ambrose Bierce, "The Werewolf" by Captain Marryat, "The Wer-Bear" by Sir Walter Scott, "The Mark of the Beast" by Rudyard Kipling, and "The Were-Tiger" by Sir Hugh Clifford; *The Dark Dominion: Eight Terrifying Tales of Vampires and Werewolves* (Paperback Library, 1970), anonymously edited, includes "The Kill" by Peter Fleming, "The Refugee" by Jane Rice, "The Werewolf" by Frederick Marryat, "A Case of Irish Lycanthropy" by Giraldus Cambrensis, and "Stubbe Peeter" by Anon., adapted by Bernhardt J. Hurwood; *Beware the Beasts* (MacFadden-Bartell, 1970), edited by Roger Elwood and Vic Ghidalia, includes "The Hound" by Fritz Leiber and "The Mark of the Beast" by Rudyard Kipling; *Spine-Chillers* (Doubleday, 1978), edited by Roger Elwood and Howard Goldsmith, includes "Dracula's Guest" by Bram Stoker, "Running Wolf" by Algernon Blackwood, "Moonglow" by Steven Barnes, and "Night Prowler" by Roger Elwood; *Vampires, Werewolves, and Other Monsters* (Curtis Books, 1974), edited by Roger Elwood, includes "Moonglow" by Steven Barnes, "Diary of a Werewolf" by Joseph Payne Brennan,

"Night of the Wolf" by Robin Schaeffer, and "Cry Wolf" by Basil Copper; *Shape Shifters* (Seabury Press, 1978), edited by Jane Yolen, includes "The Boy Who Would Be Wolf" by Richard Curtis, "Gabriel-Ernest" by Saki, "The Wonderful Dog Suit" by Donald Hall, and "Moon Change" by Ann Warren Turner; and *Vampire and Werewolf Stories* (Kingfisher, 1998), edited by Alan Durant, includes "Terror in the Tatras" by Winifred Finlay, "Howl" by Alan Durant, and "Freeze-up" by Anthony Masters.

Finally, two anthologies that fail to live up to the promise of their titles are *The Dark Shadows Book of Vampires and Werewolves* (Paperback Library, 1970), nominally edited by "Barnabas and Quentin Collins," and *Monster Tales: Vampires, Werewolves, and Things* (Rand McNally, 1973), edited by Roger Elwood. Both contain several vampire stories but have only one genuine werewolf story apiece—Bruce Elliott's "Wolves Don't Cry" in *The Dark Shadows Book of Vampires and Werewolves* and Nic Andersson's "Werewolf Boy" in *Monster Tales.*

Bibliography

Nonfiction

Ahmed, Rollo. *The Black Art*. London: John Long, 1936. Reprint, London: Arrow Books, 1966. Chapter 8, "Witchcraft, Vampirism and Werewolves in Europe."

Ashley, Leonard N. *The Complete Book of Werewolves*. Fort Lee, N.J.: Barricade Books, 2001.

Ashton, John. *Curious Creatures in Zoology*. London, 1890. Includes a section on werewolves.

Aylesworth, Thomas G. *Werewolves and Other Monsters*. Reading, Mass.: Addison-Wesley, 1971.

———. *The Story of Werewolves*. New York: McGraw-Hill, 1978.

Baring-Gould, Sabine. *The Book of Were-Wolves: Being an Account of a Terrible Superstition*. London: Smith, Elder, 1865. New York: Causeway Books, 1973. Detroit: Gale Research, 1973.

Beauvoys de Chauvincourt, Le Sieur de. *Discours de la Lycanthropie*. Paris, 1599.

Black, George F. *A List of Works Relating to Lycanthropy*. New York: New York Public Library, 1920.

259

Bleiler, Everett F. *The Guide to Supernatural Fiction*. Kent, Ohio: Kent State University Press, 1983.

Bloom, Clive, ed. *Creepers: British Horror and Fantasy in the Twentieth Century*. London: Pluto Press, 1993. Chapter 12, "At Home All Was Blood and Feathers: The Werewolf in the Kitchen—Angela Carter and Horror."

Bodin, Jean. *De la Démonomanie des Sorciers*. Paris, 1580.

Boguet, Henri. *Discours des Sorciers*. Lyons, 1590. Translated by E. Allen Ashwin as *An Examen of Witches*. London: John Rodker, 1929.

Cohen, Daniel. *A Natural History of Unnatural Things*. New York: E. P. Dutton, 1971.

———. *Super-Monsters*. New York: Pocket Books, 1978.

———. *Werewolves*. New York: Cobblehill, 1996.

Copper, Basil. *The Werewolf in Legend, Fact and Art*. London: Robert Hale, 1977; New York: St. Martin's Press, 1977.

Crowe, Catherine. *Light and Darkness; or, Mysteries of Life*. London: Routledge, 1850. Case histories of human villainy, including a chapter called "The Lycanthropist," which is a dramatized account of the crimes and subsequent trial of Sergeant Bertrand.

Davidson, H. R. Ellis. "Shape-changing in the Old Norse Sagas." In *Animals in Folklore*, edited by J. R. Porter and W. M. S. Russell. London: D. S. Brewer, 1978.

Davis, Richard, ed. *The Octopus Encyclopedia of Horror*. London: Octopus Books, 1981. Includes a section on vampires and werewolves, written by Basil Copper.

Douglas, Adam. *The Beast Within: A History of the Werewolf*. London: Chapmans, 1992. Reprinted as *The Beast Within: Man, Myths and Werewolves*. London: Orion, 1993.

Douglas, Drake. *Horror!* New York: Macmillan, 1966. British edn. retitled *Horrors!* London: John Baker, 1967. Includes a chapter on the werewolf.

Eisler, Robert. *Man into Wolf: An Anthropological Interpretation of Sadism, Masochism and Lycanthropy.* London: Spring Books, 1950. London: Routledge and Kegan Paul, 1951. Reprint, New York: Greenwood Press, 1969.

Enright, D. J., ed. *The Oxford Book of the Supernatural.* London: Oxford University Press, 1996. Includes a chapter titled "Vampires, Werewolves, Zombies, and Other Monsters."

Farson, Daniel. *Vampires, Zombies, and Monster Men.* London: Aldus Books, 1975; New York: Doubleday, 1976.

Finné, Jacques. *La Bibliographie de Dracula.* Lausanne: L'Age d'Homme, 1986. Includes an extensive bibliography of vampire, werewolf, and ghoul stories.

Frank, Frederick S., ed. *Gothic Fiction: A Master List of Twentieth Century Criticism and Research.* Westport, Conn.: Meckler/Greenwood Publishing Group, 1988.

Frost, Brian J. "The Werewolf Theme in Weird Fiction." In *Book of the Werewolf,* edited by Brian J. Frost. London: Sphere Books, 1973.

Garden, Nancy. *Werewolves.* Philadelphia: Lippincott, 1973.

Golden, Christopher, et al. *Buffy the Vampire Slayer: The Monster Book.* New York: Pocket Books, 2000. Includes a section on werewolves and other were-creatures.

Grant, Kenneth. *Cults of the Shadow.* London: Frederick Muller, 1975.

———. *Nightside of Eden.* London: Frederick Muller, 1977.

Hamel, Frank. *Human Animals.* London: William Rider and Son, 1915. Reprint, New York: University Books, 1969.

Haskins, Jim. *Werewolves.* New York: Franklin Watts, 1981.

Hertz, Wilhelm. *Der Werwolf.* Stuttgart: Kröner, 1862.

Hicks, Jim, ed. *Mysteries of the Unknown: Transformations.* New York: Time-Life Books, 1989.

Hill, Douglas. *Return from the Dead*. London: Macdonald, 1970. American edition retitled *The History of Ghosts, Vampires, and Werewolves*. New York: Harrow Books, 1973.

Hill, Douglas, and Pat Williams. *The Supernatural*. London: Aldus Books, 1965. New York: NAL/Signet, 1967. Chapter 8, "Here Be Monsters."

Howe, Cliff. *Scoundrels, Fiends, and Human Monsters*. New York: Ace Books, 1968.

Hurwood, Bernhardt J. *Vampires, Werewolves, and Ghouls*. New York: Ace Books, 1968.

———. *Vampires, Werewolves, and Other Demons*. New York: Scholastic, 1972.

Jackson, Nigel. *Compleat Vampyre: The Vampyre, Shaman, Werewolves, in Witchery and the Dark Mythology of the Undead*. Chieveley, England: Capall Bann Publishing, 1995. Many references to werewolves, especially chapter 1 "The Chronicle of the Wolfcoats," chapter 2 "Between the Quick and the Dead," and chapter 9 "Lycanthropy without Tears."

James I, King (of England). *Daemonologie*. Edinburgh, 1597.

Jones, Ernest. *On the Nightmare*. London: Hogarth, 1931, 1949; New York: Liveright, 1951, 1971. Chapter 5, "The Werewolf."

Katzeff, Paul. *Moon Madness*. London: Robert Hale, 1990.

Kelly, Walter K. *Curiosities of Indo-European Tradition and Folk-lore*. London, 1863. Includes a chapter on the werewolf.

Kies, Cosette. *Presenting Young Adult Horror Fiction*. New York: Twayne Publishers, 1992. Contains a reference to contemporary werewolf fiction in a chapter titled "Monsters, Vampires and Werewolves: The Sympathetic Beasts of Anne Rice and Chelsea Quinn Yarbro."

King, Stephen. *Danse Macabre.* New York: Everest House, 1981. London: Macdonald, 1981. New York: Berkley, 1982.

Kriss, Marika. *Werewolves, Shapeshifters, and Skinwalkers.* Los Angeles: Shelbourne Press, 1972.

Leadbeater, C. W. *The Astral Plane: Its Scenery, Inhabitants, and Phenomena.* London: Theosophical Publishing Society, 1895.

Lévi, Eliphas. *Mysteries of Magic.* London, 1897. Originally published in France, c. 1862.

———. *Transcendental Magic: Its Doctrine and Ritual.* London: Rider, 1962. Originally published in France, 1856.

McHargue, Georgess. *Meet the Werewolf.* Philadelphia: Lippincott, 1976.

McNally, Raymond T. *Dracula Was a Woman: In Search of the Blood Countess of Transylvania.* New York: McGraw-Hill, 1983. London: Robert Hale, 1984. London: Hamlyn, 1985. Chapter 9, "The Werewolf: Mirror, Mirror on the Wall . . ."

Myring, Lynn. *Vampires, Werewolves, and Demons.* London: Usborne, 1979.

Noll, Richard. *Vampires, Werewolves, and Demons: Twentieth Century Reports in the Psychiatric Literature.* New York: Brunner/Mazel, 1992.

Nynauld, Jean de. *De la Lycanthropie, Transformation, et Extase des Sorciers.* Paris, 1615.

O'Donnell, Elliott. *Werwolves.* London: Methuen, 1912. Reprint, New York: Longvue Press, 1965.

———. "Vampires, Were-wolves, Fox-women, etc." In *Satanism and Witches,* edited by Dennis Wheatley. London: Sphere Books, 1974.

Otten, Charlotte F., ed. *A Lycanthropy Reader: Werewolves in Western Culture.* Syracuse, N.Y.: Syracuse University Press, 1986. Reprint, New York: Dorset Press, 1989.

Pass, Geoff. *Lycanthropes*. Skokie, Ill.: Mayfair Games, Inc., 1991. Sourcebook revealing the folklore behind the "wolfman."

Pollard, John. *Wolves and Werewolves*. London: Robert Hale, 1964. Comprehensive history of the wolf's role in folklore.

Price, Vincent, and V. B. Price. *Monsters*. New York: Grosset and Dunlap, 1981. Suggests the reason people are intrigued by werewolves is because they are figures symbolizing human anxiety and are related to the seemingly universal need humans have to distinguish themselves from nature and other animals.

Prieur, Claude. *Dialogue de la Lycanthropie*. Louvain, 1596.

Rottensteiner, Franz. *The Fantasy Book: An Illustrated History from Dracula to Tolkien*. New York: Collier, 1978. London: Thames and Hudson, 1978.

Rovin, Jeff. *The Encyclopedia of Monsters*. New York: Facts on File, 1989.

Rudorff, Raymond. *Monsters: Studies in Ferocity*. London: Neville Spearman, 1968.

Russell, W. M. S., and Claire Russell. "The Social Biology of Werewolves." In *Animals in Folklore*, edited by J. R. Porter and W. M. S. Russell. London: D. S. Brewer, 1978.

Scot, Reginald. *The Discoverie of Witchcraft*. London, 1584. Reprint, London: Montague Summers, 1930.

Seabrook, William. *Witchcraft: Its Power in the World Today*. New York: Harcourt Brace, 1940. Reprint, New York: Lancer, 1968. Allegedly true instances of lycanthropy are recounted in two chapters, "The Caged White Werewolf of the Saraban" and "Werewolf in Washington Square."

Senn, Harry A. *Were-Wolf and Vampire in Romania*. Boulder,

Colo.: Eastern European Monographs, 1982; New York: Columbia University Press, 1982.

Smith, Kirby Flower. "An Historical Study of the Werewolf in Literature." *Publications of the Modern Languages Association of America*, 9, 1 (n.s. 2, 1), 1894.

Smith, Warren. *Strange Monsters and Madmen*. New York: Popular Library, 1969.

South, Malcolm, ed. *Mythical and Fabulous Creatures: A Source Book and Research Guide*. Westport, Conn.: Greenwood Press, 1987. Includes a section tracing the history of the werewolf.

Sprenger, James, and Heinrich Kramer. *Malleus Maleficarum*. Nuremberg, 1486–1487. English translation by Montague Summers. London, 1928.

Steiger, Brad. *Demon Lovers: Cases of Possession, Vampires, and Werewolves*. New Brunswick, N.J.: Inner Light, 1987.

———. *The Werewolf Book: The Encyclopedia of Shapeshifting Beings*. Farmington Hills, Mich.: Visible Ink Press, 1999. Contains nearly 250 descriptive entries arranged alphabetically. Also has a "werewolf resources" section, which provides a listing of werewolf-related material. This includes a filmography and a guide to werewolf sites on the World Wide Web.

Stewart, Caroline Taylor. "The Origins of the Werewolf Superstition." The University of Missouri Studies, vol. 2, no. 3. Social Science Series, April 1909.

Sullivan, Jack, ed. *The Penguin Encyclopedia of Horror and the Supernatural*. New York: Viking Penguin, 1986. Includes an entry on werewolves, written by Colin Wilson.

Summers, Montague. *The Werewolf*. London: Kegan Paul, Trench, Trubner, 1933. Reprint, New York: University Books, 1966.

Tannahill, Reay. *Flesh and Blood: A History of the Cannibal*

Complex. New York: Stein and Day, 1973. London: Hamish Hamilton, 1975.

Twitchell, James B. *Dreadful Pleasures: An Anatomy of Modern Horror.* New York: Oxford University Press, 1985. Looks at the way the werewolf is portrayed in horror fiction and films in a chapter titled "Dr. Jekyll and Mr. Wolfman."

Villeneuve, Roland. *Loups-garous et Vampires.* Paris: La Palatine, 1963.

Warren, Ed, and Lorraine Warren. *Werewolf: A True Story of Demonic Possession.* New York: St. Martin's, 1991.

Weyer (Weir), Johann. *De Praestigiis Daemonum.* Basle, 1563.

Wolfeshusius, Joannes Fridericus. *De Lycanthropis.* Lipsiae, 1591.

Woodward, Ian. *The Werewolf Delusion.* London: Paddington Press, 1979.

Zinck, Charles K., and Myra Zinck. *Psychological Studies on the Increase of Lycanthropy and Vampirism in America: 1930–1941.* New Orleans: Zachary Ken, 1952.

Zipes, Jack. *The Trials and Tribulations of Little Red Riding Hood.* London: Heinemann, 1983.

Fiction

Adams, Derek. *Mark of the Wolf.* New York: Masquerade, 1996.

Africa, Chris N. *When Wolves Cry.* Edmonton, Alta.: Picasso Publications, 1998.

Ahern, Jerry, and Sharon Ahern. *WerewolveSS.* New York: Pinnacle Books, 1990.

Aiken, Joan. "Furry Night." *Argosy* (UK), November 1958. Reprinted in *Nightfrights,* edited by Peter Haining. New York: Taplinger, 1972.

Akers, Alan Burt. *Werewolves of Kregen.* New York: DAW Books, 1985.

Aldiss, Brian W. "The Flowers of the Forest." *Science Fantasy,* August 1957. Reprinted in *Tropical Chills,* edited by Tim Sullivan. New York: Avon, 1988.

———. "Full Sun." In *Orbit 2,* edited by Damon Knight. New York: Putnam, 1967; New York: Berkley Medallion, 1967. Reprinted in *Werewolf! A Chrestomathy of Lycanthropy,* edited by Bill Pronzini. New York: Arbor House, 1979.

Alexander, Jan. *The Wolves of Craywood.* New York: Lancer Books, 1970.

Allen, J. B. "Wash and Were." *Amazing Stories,* March 1986.

Allen, Mark. *Wolf Den.* Philadelphia: Xlibris Corporation, 2001.

Allen, Paul. "Teamwork." In *Women Who Run with the Werewolves,* edited by Pam Keesey. Pittsburgh, Penn.: Cleis Press, 1996.

Almquist, Greg. *Wolf Kill.* New York: Pocket Books, 1990.

Anderson, Kevin J. "Special Makeup." In *The Ultimate Werewolf,* edited by Byron Preiss. New York: Dell, 1991.

Anderson, Poul. "Operation Afreet." *The Magazine of Fantasy and Science Fiction,* September 1956. Reprinted in *Tomorrow Bites,* edited by Greg Cox and T. K. F. Weisskopf. New York: Baen Books, 1995.

———. *Three Hearts and Three Lions.* Garden City, N.Y.: Doubleday, 1961. A werewolf has a cameo role.

———. *Operation Chaos.* Garden City, N.Y.: Doubleday, 1971.

———. *Operation Luna.* New York: Tom Doherty, 2000.

Andersson, C. Dean. "Small Brown Bags of Blood." In *Dark Destiny,* edited by Edward E. Kramer. Clarkston, Ga.: White Wolf, 1995.

Andersson, Nic. "Werewolf Boy." In *Monster Tales: Vampires, Werewolves and Things,* edited by Roger Elwood. Chicago: Rand McNally, 1973.

Andrews, Val. *Sherlock Holmes and the Foulhaven Werewolf.* Ottawa, Ont.: Magico, 1983.

Anon. "The Rabbi Who Was Turned into a Werewolf." In *The Mayse-Book* (1602). Reprinted in *Great Tales of Jewish Fantasy and the Occult,* edited by Joachim Neugroschell. New York: The Overlook Press, 1987.

Anon. "The Severed Arm; or, The Wehr-Wolf of Limousin." In *Tales of Superstition.* London: Dean and Mundy, c. 1820. Reprinted in *The Shilling Shockers,* edited by Peter Haining. London: Victor Gollancz, 1978.

Anon. "The Wehr Wolf." *The Story-teller, or Journal of Fiction,* 1833.

Anon, ed. *The Dark Dominion: Eight Terrifying Tales of Vampires and Werewolves.* New York: Paperback Library, 1970.

Antieau, Kim. "The Mark of the Beast." In *The Ultimate Werewolf,* edited by Byron Preiss. New York: Dell, 1991.

Apel, Johann August. "The Boarwolf." In *Tales of Terror; or, The Mysteries of Magic,* edited by Henry St. Clair. Boston: C. Gaylord, 1835. Also published under the alternative title "The Demon's Victim" in *Tales of All Nations.* London: T. Allman, 1848.

Armstrong, F. W. *The Changing.* New York: Tor, 1985.

———. *The Devouring.* New York: Tor, 1987.

Armstrong, Kelley. *Bitten.* New York: Viking Penguin, 2001.

"Arthur and Gorlagon." (late 13th century). A modern prose version by Frank A. Milne is included in *A Lycanthropy Reader: Werewolves in Western Culture,* edited by Charlotte F. Otten. New York: Dorset Press, 1989.

Ascher, Eugene. "The Man Who Howled." In *Uncanny Adventures*. London: Everybody's Books, n.d. (*c.* 1944).

Attanasio, A. A. "Loup Garou." *The Haunt of Horror* no. 1, June 1973.

Avallone, Michael. *The Werewolf Walks Tonight*. New York: Warner, 1974.

Bagot, Richard. *A Roman Mystery*. London: John Lane, 1902.

Bailey, Harry. "The Wolf of the Campagna." *Weird Tales*, February 1925.

Baker, Charles L. "Excerpt from an Autobiography of a Werewolf." *Eldritch Tales* no. 10, 1984.

Baker, Mike. "Bark at the Moon." In *Werewolves*, edited by Martin H. Greenberg. New York: DAW Books, 1995.

Ball, Clifford. "The Werewolf Howls." *Weird Tales*, November 1941. Reprinted in *100 Creepy Little Creature Stories*, edited by Stefan R. Dziemianowicz, Robert Weinberg, and Martin H. Greenberg. New York: Barnes and Noble, 1994.

Banister, Manly. "Satan's Bondage." *Weird Tales*, September 1942.

———. "Devil Dog." *Weird Tales*, July 1945.

———. "Loup-Garou." *Weird Tales*, May 1947.

———. "Eena." *Weird Tales*, September 1947. Reprinted in *Book of the Werewolf*, edited by Brian J. Frost. London: Sphere Books, 1973.

———. "Cry Wolf!" *The Nekromantikon*, spring 1950.

Banks, J. S. "Trickster Moon." In *When Will You Rage?*, edited by Stewart Wieck. Clarkston, Ga.: White Wolf, 1994.

Barker, Clive. "Twilight at the Towers." In *Clive Barker's Books of Blood*. Vol. 6. London: Sphere Books, 1985. Reprinted in *The Mammoth Book of Werewolves*, edited by

Stephen Jones. New York: Carroll and Graf, 1994; London: Robinson Books, 1994.

Barnes, Steven. "Moonglow." In *Vampires, Werewolves and Other Monsters,* edited by Roger Elwood. New York: Curtis Books, 1974. Also included in *Spine-Chillers,* edited by Roger Elwood and Howard Goldsmith. Garden City, N.Y.. Doubleday, 1978.

Bassingthwaite, Don. *Breathe Deeply.* Clarkston, Ga.: White Wolf, 1995.

―――. "A Useless Death." In *When Will You Rage?,* edited by Stewart Wieck. Clarkston, Ga.: White Wolf, 1994.

Baumbach, Jonathan. "The Curse." In *The Return of Service.* Urbana, Ill.: University of Illinois Press, 1979.

Beagle, Peter S. "Farrell and Lila the Werewolf." *Guabi,* 1969. Reprinted (as "Lila the Werewolf") in *Werewolf! A Chrestomathy of Lycanthropy,* edited by Bill Pronzini. New York: Arbor House, 1979.

Beaugrand, H. "The Werwolves." *The Century,* August 1898. Reprinted in *Werewolf: Horror Stories of the Man-Beast,* edited by Peter Haining. London: Severn House, 1987.

Bell, Clare. *The Jaguar Princess.* New York: Tor, 1994.

Bellem, Robert Leslie. "Wooed by a Werewolf." *Uncanny Tales,* November 1939.

Benedict, Steve. "Come, My Sweet." *The Nekromantikon,* midyear 1951.

Benson, Claude E. "In the Full of the Moon." *The London Magazine,* vol. 21, September 1908.

Benson, R. H. "Father Meuron's Tale." In *A Mirror of Shalott.* London: Pitman, 1907.

Bierce, Ambrose. "The Eyes of the Panther." In *In the Midst of Life.* New York: Putnam, 1898; London: Chatto and Windus, 1898. Also included in *Monsters Galore,* edited by Bernhardt J. Hurwood. New York: Fawcett Gold Medal, 1965. *Book of the Werewolf,* edited by Brian J. Frost. London: Sphere Books, 1973.

Bill, Alfred H. *The Wolf in the Garden.* New York: Longmans, Green, 1931. New York: Centaur Books, 1972.

Bischoff, David. *Nightworld.* New York: Ballantine, 1979.

———. *Night of the Living Shark.* New York: Ace Books, 1991. Werewolves have cameo role.

Bishop, Michael. "Gravid Babies." In *The Dodd, Mead Gallery of Horror,* edited by Charles L. Grant. New York: Dodd, Mead, 1983.

Biss, Gerald. *The Door of the Unreal.* London: Eveleigh Nash, 1919.

Bixby, Jerome. "The Young One." *Fantastic,* April 1954. Reprinted in *Asimov's Ghosts and Monsters,* edited by Isaac Asimov, Martin H. Greenberg, and Charles G. Waugh. London: Armada, 1988.

Black, Ian Stuart. *Cry Wolf.* London: Constable, 1990.

Black, J. R. *Guess Who's Dating a Werewolf.* New York: Random House, 1993. Young adult novel.

Black, Robert [pseud. of Robert Holdstock]. *Legend of the Werewolf.* London: Sphere Books, 1976.

Blackburn, John. *A Beastly Business.* London: Robert Hale, 1982.

Blackburn, Thomas. *The Feast of the Wolf.* London: MacGibbon and Kee, 1971.

Blackwood, Algernon. "The Camp of the Dog." In *John Silence, Physician Extraordinary.* London: Eveleigh Nash, 1908. London: John Baker, 1969.

———. "The Empty Sleeve." *The London Magazine,* January 1911. Reprinted in *The Wolves of God and Other Fey Stories.* London: Cassell, 1921.

———. "Running Wolf." *The Century,* August 1920. Reprinted in *The Wolves of God and Other Fey Stories.* London: Cassell, 1921. Also included in *Way of the Werewolf,* edited by Douglas Hill. London: Panther, 1966. *Spine-Chillers,* edited by Roger Elwood and Howard Goldsmith. Garden City, N.Y.: Doubleday, 1978.

———. "The Wolves of God." In *The Wolves of God and Other Fey Stories.* London: Cassell, 1921. Reprinted in *Werewolf: Horror Stories of the Man-Beast,* edited by Peter Haining. London: Severn House, 1987.

Blake, Dan L. *Killing Frost.* New York: Press-Tige Press, 1998.

Blish, James. "There Shall Be No Darkness." *Thrilling Wonder Stories,* April 1950. Also included in *Magazine of Horror,* January 1969. *Werewolf! A Chrestomathy of Lycanthropy,* edited by Bill Pronzini. New York: Arbor House, 1979. *Masters of Fantasy,* edited by Terry Carr and Martin H. Greenberg. New York: Galahad Books, 1992. *Tomorrow Bites,* edited by Greg Cox and T. K. F. Weisskopf. New York: Baen Books, 1995.

Bloch, Robert. "The Hound of Pedro." *Weird Tales,* November 1938. Reprinted in *The Hounds of Hell,* edited by Michel Parry. London: Gollancz, 1974.

———. "Nursemaid to Nightmares." *Weird Tales,* November 1942. Reprinted in *Dragons and Nightmares.* Baltimore: Mirage Press, 1969.

———. "The Man Who Cried 'Wolf'!" *Weird Tales,* May 1945. Also included in *Werewolf: Horror Stories of the Man-Beast,* edited by Peter Haining. London: Severn House, 1987. *The Ultimate Werewolf,* edited by Byron Preiss. New York: Dell, 1991.

———. "The Bogey Man Will Get You." *Weird Tales,* March 1946. Reprinted in *Nursery Crimes,* edited by

Stefan R. Dziemianowicz, Robert Weinberg, and Martin H. Greenberg. New York: Barnes and Noble, 1993.

Bloxham, Frederick. *Lycanthropia.* San Francisco, Calif.: Robert D. Reed, 2000.

Bolen, C. Edgar. "Lycanthropus." *Weird Tales,* August/September 1936. Poem.

Bond, Evelyn. *Doomway.* New York: Beagle Books, 1971.

Borchardt, Alice. *The Silver Wolf.* New York: Ballantine/Del Rey, 1998.

———. *Night of the Wolf.* New York: Ballantine/Del Rey, 1999.

———. *The Wolf King.* New York: Ballantine/Del Rey, 2001.

Boston, Bruce. "Curse of the Werewolf's Wife." *Weird Tales,* fall 1988.

Boston, John. *Naked Came the Sasquatch.* Lake Geneva, Wis.: TSR, 1993.

Boucher, Anthony [pseud. of William A. P. White]. "The Compleat Werewolf." *Unknown Worlds,* April 1942. Reprinted in *The Compleat Werewolf and Other Tales of Fantasy and Science Fiction.* New York: Simon and Schuster, 1969.

———. "The Ambassadors." *Startling Stories,* June 1952. Reprinted in *Galaxy of Ghouls,* edited by Judith Merril. New York: Lion Library Edition, 1955.

Bourgeau, Art. *Wolfman.* New York: Donald I. Fine, 1989.

Bowkett, Stephen. *The World's Smallest Werewolf.* New York: Macdonald Young Books, 1996. For preteens.

Boyd, Donna. *The Passion.* New York: Avon, 1998.

———. *The Promise.* New York: Avon, 1999.

Bradfield, Scott. "The Dream of the Wolf." *Interzone* no. 10, winter 1984/85. Reprinted in *The Mammoth Book of Werewolves,* edited by Stephen Jones. New York: Carroll and Graf, 1994; London: Robinson Books, 1994.

Brand, Max [pseud. of Frederick Faust]. "The Werewolf." *Western Story Magazine,* December 1926.

Brandner, Gary. *The Howling.* New York: Fawcett Gold Medal, 1977.

———. *The Howling II: The Return.* New York: Fawcett Gold Medal, 1978.

———. *Cat People.* New York: Fawcett Gold Medal, 1982. Features were-panthers.

———. *The Howling III: Echoes.* New York: Fawcett Gold Medal, 1985.

Braunbeck, Gary A. "Some Touch of Pity." In *Werewolves,* edited by Martin H. Greenberg. New York: DAW Books, 1995.

Breiding, Bill. "Father of Werewolves." *Moonbroth* no. 23, 1976. Poem.

Breiding, G. Sutton. "Werewolf Manqué." *Grue* no. 11, 1990. Poem.

Brennan, Herbie. *Emily and the Werewolf.* New York: Simon and Schuster, 1993. For preteens.

Brennan, Joseph Payne. "Diary of a Werewolf." *Macabre,* winter 1960. Reprinted in *Vampires, Werewolves and Other Monsters,* edited by Roger Elwood. New York: Curtis Books, 1974.

Brett, Leo [pseud. of R. Lionel Fanthorpe]. "White Wolf." *Supernatural Stories,* July 1959.

Bridges, Bill. "The Waters of Lethe." In *When Will You Rage?,* edited by Stewart Wieck. Clarkston, Ga.: White Wolf, 1994.

Bridges, William. *Silver Crown.* Clarkston, Ga.: White Wolf, 1995.

Briery, Traci. *The Werewolf Chronicles.* New York: Zebra Books, 1994.

———. *Wolfsong.* New York: Zebra Books, 1996.

Briscoe, Pat A. *The Other People*. Reseda, Calif.: Powell, 1970.

Brodie-Innes, J. W. *For the Soul of a Witch*. London: Rebman, 1910.

Brown, Crosland. *Tombley's Walk*. New York: Avon, 1991.

Brucato, Phil. "Shards." In *When Will You Rage?*, edited by Stewart Wieck. Clarkston, Ga.: White Wolf, 1994.

Buchanan, Paul. *Dances with Werewolves*. Nashville, Tenn.: Broadman and Holman, 2000. For preteens.

Butcher, Jim. *Full Moon*. New York: Roc, 2001.

Byers, Richard Lee. "Wolf Trap." In *When Will You Rage?*, edited by Stewart Wieck. Clarkston, Ga.: White Wolf, 1994.

———. "Night Games." In *Dark Destiny*, edited by Edward E. Kramer. Clarkston, Ga.: White Wolf, 1995.

Byrne, Brooke. "The Werewolf's Howl." *Weird Tales*, December 1934. Reprinted in *100 Creepy Little Creature Stories*, edited by Stefan R. Dziemianowicz, Robert Weinberg, and Martin H. Greenberg. New York: Barnes and Noble, 1994.

Cabell, James Branch. *The White Robe: A Saint's Summary*. New York: McBride, 1928.

Cacek, P. D. *Canyons*. New York: Tor, 2000.

Cadnum, Michael. *Saint Peter's Wolf*. New York: Carroll and Graf, 1991; New York: Zebra Books, 1993.

Caine, Geoffrey. *Wake of the Werewolf*. New York: Diamond Books, 1991.

Callahan, Jay. *Night of the Wolf*. New York: Leisure Books, 1979.

Calmus, Bernard L. "The Howl of the Werewolf." *Phantom*, April 1957.

Cambrensis, Giraldus [literary name of Girald de Barri]. "A Case of Irish Lycanthropy." Originally appeared in *Topographia Hibernica* (1158). Reprinted in *The Dark*

Dominion: Eight Terrifying Tales of Vampires and Werewolves. New York: Paperback Library, 1970.

Campbell, Angus [pseud. of R. Chetwynd-Hayes]. "The Werewolf." In *The Fourth Monster Ghost Book.* London: Armada, 1978.

Campbell, Sir Gilbert. "The White Wolf of Kostopchin." In *Wild and Weird; or, Remarkable Stories of Russian Life.* London: Ward, Lock, 1889. Reprinted in *Book of the Werewolf,* edited by Brian J. Frost. London: Sphere Books, 1973.

Campbell, Grace M. "The Law of the Hills." *Weird Tales,* August 1930.

Campbell, Ramsey. "Night Beat." *The Haunt of Horror* no. 1, June 1973. Reprinted in *The Mammoth Book of Werewolves,* edited by Stephen Jones. New York: Carroll and Graf, 1994; London: Robinson Books, 1994.

Capes, Bernard. "The Thing in the Forest." In *The Fabulists.* London: Mills and Boon, 1915. Reprinted in *100 Hair-Raising Little Horror Stories,* edited by Al Sarrantonio and Martin H. Greenberg. New York: Barnes and Noble, 1993.

Carleton, S. "The Lame Priest." *Atlantic Monthly,* 1901. Also included in *Beware After Dark!,* edited by T. Everett Harré. New York: Macauley, 1929. *Incredible Adventures* no. 2, edited by Gene Marshall and Carl F. Waedt. Chicago: Weinberg, 1977.

Carney, Lance. "Antidote for a Lycanthrope." *Into the Darkness* no. 4, 1995.

Carolin, E. O. *The Soul of the Wolf.* London: John Long, 1923.

Carpenter, Christopher. *The Twilight Realm.* London: Arrow Books, 1985.

Carr, John Dickson. *It Walks by Night.* London: Harper, 1930.

Carroll, Jonathan. "My Zoondel." In *The Panic Hand*. New York: St. Martin's Press, 1996.

Carroll, Lucy E. "Crystal Lycanthrope." *Marion Zimmer Bradley Fantasy Magazine*, no. 7, winter 1990.

Carter, Angela. "The Company of Wolves." *Bananas*, 1979. Reprinted in *The Bloody Chamber and Other Adult Tales*. New York: Harper and Row, 1979.

———. "The Werewolf." In *The Bloody Chamber and Other Adult Tales*. New York: Harper and Row, 1979.

Carter, Margaret L. *Shadow of the Beast*. Darien, Ill.: The Design Image Group, 1998.

Casanova, Mary. *Curse of a Winter Moon*. New York: Hyperion Books for Children, 2000.

Case, David. "The Cell." In *The Cell, and Other Tales of Horror*. London: Macdonald, 1969. Reprinted in *The Mammoth Book of Werewolves*, edited by Stephen Jones. New York: Carroll and Graf, 1994; London: Robinson Books, 1994.

———. "The Hunter." In *The Cell, and Other Tales of Horror*. London: Macdonald, 1969.

———. "A Cross to Bear." In *Fengriffen and Other Stories*. London: Macdonald, 1971.

———. "Strange Roots." In *Fengriffen and Other Stories*. London: Macdonald, 1971.

———. *Wolf Tracks*. New York: Belmont Tower Books, 1980.

Cassidy, Carla. *Heart of the Beast*. New York: Harlequin/Silhouette Shadows, 1993.

Castletown, Lord. "Once Upon a Time." In *A Bundle of Lies*. London: H. J. Drane, n.d. (*c.* 1925).

Cave, Hugh B. "The Whisperers." *Spicy Mystery Stories*, April 1942. A slightly revised version is included in *The Mammoth Book of Werewolves*, edited by Stephen Jones.

New York: Carroll and Graf, 1994; London: Robinson Books, 1994.

———. "Nights in the Mountains of Haiti." In *Werewolves,* edited by Martin H. Greenberg. New York: DAW Books, 1995.

Cawein, Madison. "The Werewolf." In *The Poems of Madison Cawein.* Vol. 4, *Poems of Mystery and of Myth and Romance.* Boston: Small, Maynard, 1908.

Chandler, A Bertram. "Frontier of the Dark." *Astounding Science-Fiction,* September 1952. Reprinted in *Tomorrow Bites,* edited by Greg Cox and T. K. F. Weisskopf. New York: Baen Books, 1995.

Charles, Renee M. "A Model of Transformation." In *Women Who Run with the Werewolves,* edited by Pam Keesey. Pittsburgh, Penn.: Cleis Press, 1996.

Charnas, Suzy McKee. "Boobs." *Isaac Asimov's Science Fiction Magazine,* July 1989. Also included in *The Mammoth Book of Werewolves,* edited by Stephen Jones. New York: Carroll and Graf, 1994; London: Robinson Books, 1994. *Isaac Asimov's Werewolves,* edited by Gardner Dozois and Sheila Williams. New York: Ace Books, 1999.

Chart, David. "Predator and Prey." In *When Will You Rage?,* edited by Stewart Wieck. Clarkston, Ga.: White Wolf, 1994.

Charyn, Jerome. "At War with the Wolf Man." In *The Ultimate Werewolf,* edited by Byron Preiss. New York: Dell, 1991.

Chater, Lee. "The Thing on the Stairs." *Coven 13,* March 1970.

Chetwynd-Hayes, R. "The Werewolf and the Vampire." In *The Monster Club.* London: New English Library, 1976. Reprinted in *Vampires: Two Centuries of Great Vampire*

Stories, edited by Alan Ryan. Garden City, N.Y.: Doubleday, 1987.

———. "The Werewolf." In *The Mammoth Book of Werewolves,* edited by Stephen Jones. New York: Carroll and Graf, 1994; London: Robinson Books, 1994.

Chizmar, Richard T., and Barry Hoffman. "Only the Strong Survive." In *Werewolves,* edited by Martin H. Greenberg. New York: DAW Books, 1995.

Christensen, Leif E. "The Tempest." In *The Devil's Instrument and Other Danish Stories,* edited by Sven Holm. Chester Springs, Penn.: Dufour, 1971.

Chronister, Alan B. *Cry Wolf.* New York: Zebra Books, 1987.

Chupp, Sam. "Coyote Full Moon." In *When Will You Rage?,* edited by Stewart Wieck. Clarkston, Ga.: White Wolf, 1994.

Ciencin, Scott. "Hunter's Blues." In *When Will You Rage?,* edited by Stewart Wieck. Clarkston, Ga.: White Wolf, 1994.

Clark, Glenn Slade, Jr. *Cry Wolf.* Philadelphia: Xlibris Corporation, 1999.

Clark, Simon. "The Last Barnsley Werewolf." *Strange Attractor* no. 1, 1992.

Clemens, Sarah. "Red." *Asimov's Science Fiction Magazine,* June 1998. Reprinted in *Isaac Asimov's Werewolves,* edited by Gardner Dozois and Sheila Williams. New York: Ace Books, 1999.

Clifford, Sir Hugh. "The Were-Tiger." In *In Court and Kampong.* Privately published in 1927. Reprinted in *Monsters Galore,* edited by Bernhardt J. Hurwood. New York: Fawcett Gold Medal, 1965.

Cogswell, Theodore. "Wolfie." *Beyond Fantasy Fiction,* January 1954.

Cole, Adrian. "Heart of the Beast." In *The Mammoth Book*

of Werewolves, edited by Stephen Jones. New York: Carroll and Graf, 1994; London: Robinson Books, 1994.

Collins, Barnabas and Quentin, eds. *The Dark Shadows Book of Vampires and Werewolves.* New York: Paperback Library, 1970. Barnabas and Quentin Collins are, of course, fictional characters, and the actual editing was done by Bernhardt J. Hurwood.

Collins, Max Allan. "Wolf." In *Werewolves,* edited by Martin H. Greenberg. New York: DAW Books, 1995.

Collins, Nancy A. "Raymond." In *The Ultimate Werewolf,* edited by Byron Preiss. New York: Dell, 1991.

———. *Wild Blood.* New York: Roc, 1994.

———. "The Love of Monsters." In *Dark Destiny,* edited by Edward E. Kramer. Clarkston, Ga.: White Wolf, 1995.

———. *Walking Wolf.* Shingletown, Calif.: Mark V. Ziesing, 1995.

Colvin, James [pseud. of Michael Moorcock]. "Wolf." In *The Deep Fix.* London: Compact, 1966.

Conaway, J. C. *Quarrel with the Moon.* New York: Tor, 1982.

Coney, Michael G. "Werewolves in Sheep's Clothing." *The Magazine of Fantasy and Science Fiction,* September 1996.

Conford, Ellen. *Norman Newman and the Werewolf of Walnut Street.* Mahwah, N.J.: Little Rainbow/Troll Associates, 1995. For preteens.

Cook, Hugh. *The Werewolf and the Wormlord.* London: Corgi, 1991.

Coontz, Otto. *Isle of the Shapeshifters.* Boston: Houghton Mifflin, 1983. New York: Bantam Books, 1985.

Copper, Basil. "Cry Wolf." In *Vampires, Werewolves and Other Monsters,* edited by Roger Elwood. New York: Curtis Books, 1974. *Werewolf: Horror Stories of the Man-Beast,* edited by Peter Haining. London: Severn House, 1987. *The Mammoth Book of Werewolves,* edited by Stephen

Jones. New York: Carroll and Graf, 1994; London: Robinson Books, 1994.

———. *The House of the Wolf.* Sauk City, Wis.: Arkham House, 1983.

Cornish, William. "Howl, Wolf, Howl." *Adventures in Horror,* October 1970.

Cosmic, Ray [pseud. of John S. Glasby]. "Lycanthrope." *Supernatural Stories,* May 1954.

Costello, Dudley. "Lycanthropy in London; or, The Wehr-Wolf of Wilton Crescent." *Bentley's Miscellany,* 1855.

Costello, Matthew J. "Nick of Time." In *Werewolves,* edited by Martin H. Greenberg. New York: DAW Books, 1995.

Courtney, Vincent. "A Sheep in Wolf's Clothing." In *When Will You Rage?,* edited by Stewart Wieck. Clarkston, Ga.: White Wolf, 1994.

Coville, Bruce. "The Passing of the Pack." In *Werewolves,* edited by Jane Yolen and Martin H. Greenberg. New York: Harper and Row, 1988.

Cox, Greg, and T. K. F. Weisskopf, eds. *Tomorrow Bites.* New York: Baen Books, 1995.

Crank, Brenda, and Scott Nickell. "Woofman." In *Werewolves,* edited by Martin H. Greenberg. New York: DAW Books, 1995.

Crawford, Terry. *The Werewolf Miracles.* Ottawa, Ont.: Oberon Press, 1976.

Crider, Bill. "Wolf Night." In *Westeryear,* edited by Ed Gorman. New York: Evans, 1988.

———. "The Nighttime Is the Right Time." In *Werewolves,* edited by Martin H. Greenberg. New York: DAW Books, 1995.

Crispin, A. C., and Kathleen O'Malley. "Pure Silver." In *The Ultimate Werewolf,* edited by Byron Preiss. New York: Dell, 1991.

Crockett, S. R. *The Black Douglas*. London: Smith, Elder, 1899. New York: Doubleday, McClure, 1899.

Crompton, Anne Eliot. "Met by Moonlight." In *Werewolves*, edited by Jane Yolen and Martin H. Greenberg. New York: Harper and Row, 1988.

Cross, Ronald Anthony. "Two Bad Dogs." *Isaac Asimov's Science Fiction Magazine*, September 1990. Reprinted in *Isaac Asimov's Werewolves*, edited by Gardner Dozois and Sheila Williams. New York: Ace Books, 1999.

Crowe, Catherine. "A Story of a Weir-Wolf." *Hogg's Weekly Instructor*, May 16, 1846.

———. "The Lycanthropist." In *Light and Darkness; or, Mysteries of Life*. London: Routledge, 1850. Reprinted in *Werewolf: Horror Stories of the Man-Beast*, edited by Peter Haining. London: Severn House, 1987.

Crowther, Peter. "Bindlestiff." In *Werewolves*, edited by Martin H. Greenberg. New York: DAW Books, 1995.

Curtis, Richard. "The Boy Who Would Be Wolf." In *Shape Shifters*, edited by Jane Yolen. New York: Seabury Press, 1978.

Cuyler, Margery. *Weird Wolf*. New York: Henry Holt, 1991. For preteens.

Dadey, Debbie. *Werewolves Don't Go to Summer Camp*. New York: Scholastic, 1991. For preteens.

———. *Wolfmen Don't Hula Dance*. New York: Scholastic, 1999. For preteens.

Daniels, Keith Allen. "Fragments of a Shattered Glass Werewolf Poem." *Dreams and Nightmares* no. 39, 1992. Poem.

Daniels, Les. "Wereman." In *Borderlands*, edited by Thomas F. Monteleone. New York: Avon, 1990. Reprinted in *The Mammoth Book of Werewolves*, edited by Stephen Jones. New York: Carroll and Graf, 1994; London: Robinson Books, 1994.

Danvers, Dennis. *Wilderness*. New York: Poseidon Press, 1991; New York: Pocket Star, 1992.

David, Peter. *Howling Mad*. New York: Ace Books, 1989.

Davidson, Avram. "Loups-Garous." *The Magazine of Fantasy and Science Fiction*, August 1971. Poem.

———. "The Forges of Nainland Are Cold." *Fantastic*, August–October 1972.

Davidson, Mary Janice. "Love's Prisoner." In *Secrets*. Vol. 6. Seminole, Fla.: Red Sage Publishing, Inc., 2000.

Davis, Brett. *Hair of the Dog*. New York: Baen Books, 1997.

Davis, Don, and Jay Davis. *Sins of the Flesh*. New York: Tor, 1989.

Davis, R. L. "Once Upon a Werewolf." *Coven 13*, November 1969.

Davol, Marguerite W. "Flesh and Blood." In *Werewolves*, edited by Jane Yolen and Martin H. Greenberg. New York: Harper and Row, 1988.

Dawson, Saranne. *Heart of the Wolf*. New York: Leisure Books/Love Spell, 1993.

———. *Secrets of the Wolf*. New York: Leisure Books/Love Spell, 1998.

Day, J. Wentworth. "The Dog-Man Horror of the Valley." In *50 Great Horror Stories*, edited by John Canning. New York: Taplinger, 1969; London: Hamlyn/Odhams, 1969.

Dean, Pamela. *The Dubious Hills*. New York: Tor, 1995.

DeAndrea, William L. *The Werewolf Murders*. Garden City, N.Y.: Doubleday, 1992.

de Camp, L. Sprague, and Fletcher Pratt. *The Castle of Iron*. *Unknown*, April 1941. Expanded book versions: New York: Gnome Press, 1950. New York: Pyramid, 1962.

Delacroix, Claire. *Enchanted*. New York: Harlequin Historical, 1997.

de Lint, Charles. "One Chance." In *Werewolves*, edited by

Jane Yolen and Martin H. Greenberg. New York: Harper and Row, 1988.

———. *Wolf Moon*. New York: Signet, 1988.

Demmon, Calvin. "Who's Afraid." *Fantastic,* December 1972.

Derleth, August. "The Adventure of the Tottenham Werewolf." In *The Memoirs of Solar Pons*. Sauk City, Wis.: Mycroft and Moran, 1951. Reprinted in *Book of the Werewolf,* edited by Brian J. Frost. London: Sphere Books, 1973.

Derleth, August, and Mark Schorer. "The Woman at Loon Point." *Weird Tales,* December 1936. Reprinted in *Colonel Markesan and Less Pleasant People*. Sauk City, Wis.: Arkham House, 1966.

DeWeese, Gene. *The Adventures of a Two-Minute Werewolf.* Garden City, N.Y.: Doubleday, 1983. Young adult novel.

Dickson, Gordon. "The Girl Who Played Wolf." *Fantastic,* August 1958. Reprinted in *Strange Fantasy,* fall 1969.

Diffin, Charles Willard. "The Dog That Laughed." *Strange Tales of Mystery and Terror,* September 1931.

DiSilvestro, Roger. *Ursula's Gift*. New York: Donald I. Fine, 1988.

Dixon, Franklin W. *The Night of the Werewolf* (Hardy Boys' Mystery Stories, no. 59). New York: Pocket Books, 1979. For preteens.

Donaldson, Dale C. "Pia!" *Coven 13,* November 1969. Reprinted in *Book of the Werewolf,* edited by Brian J. Frost. London: Sphere Books, 1973.

———. "Finale." *Moonbroth* no. 2, 1971. Poem.

Doyle, Arthur Conan. "A Pastoral Horror." *People,* December 21, 1890. Reprinted in *The Unknown Conan Doyle*. Garden City, N.Y.: Doubleday, 1984.

Doyle, Debra, and James D. Macdonald. "Bad Blood." In *Werewolves,* edited by Jane Yolen and Martin H. Greenberg. New York: Harper and Row, 1988.

———. *Bad Blood.* New York: Berkley Books, 1993. Young adult novel.

———. *Hunter's Moon.* New York: Berkley Books, 1994. Young adult novel.

———. *Judgment Night.* New York: Berkley Books, 1995. Young adult novel.

Dozois, Gardner, and Sheila Williams, eds. *Isaac Asimov's Werewolves.* New York: Ace Books, 1999.

Drake, Leah Bodine. "They Run Again." *Weird Tales,* June/July 1939. Poem.

Dreadstone, Carl [House pseud.]. Written by Ramsey Campbell. *The Wolfman.* New York: Berkley Books, 1977.

———. Written by Walter Harris. *The Werewolf of London.* New York: Berkley Books, 1977.

Driver, Lee. *Full Moon—Bloody Moon.* Schererville, Ind.: Full Moon Publishing, 2000.

Dumas, Alexandre. *The Wolf-Leader.* Paris: Cadot, 1857 (as *Le Meneur des Loups*). London: Methuen, 1904. Philadelphia: Prime Press, 1950.

Dunne, Colin. *The Werewolf.* London: Madcap Books, 1999. Young adult novel.

Durant, Alan. "Howl." In *Vampire and Werewolf Stories,* edited by Alan Durant. London: Kingfisher, 1998. New York: Kingfisher US, 1998.

Durant, Alan, ed. *Vampire and Werewolf Stories.* London: Kingfisher, 1998. New York: Kingfisher US, 1998.

Eadie, Arlton [pseud. of Leopold Eady]. "The Wolf-Girl of Josselin." *Weird Tales,* August 1938. Reprinted in *Kurt*

Singer's Ghost Omnibus, edited by Kurt Singer. London: W. H. Allen, 1965.

Eddy, C. M., Jr. "The Ghost-Eater." *Weird Tales,* April 1924. Ghost-written by H. P. Lovecraft. Reprinted in *The Horror in the Museum and Other Revisions,* edited by August Derleth. Sauk City, Wis.: Arkham House, 1970.

Edmondson, Roger. *Silverwolf.* Banned Books, 1990.

Eggar, Arthur. *The Hatanee: A Tale of Burman Superstition.* London: John Murray, 1906. Were-tiger yarn.

Elflandsson, Galad. *The Black Wolf.* West Kingston, R.I.: Donald M. Grant, 1979.

Elliott, Bruce. "Wolves Don't Cry." *The Magazine of Fantasy and Science Fiction,* April 1954. Also included in *Way of the Werewolf,* edited by Douglas Hill. London: Panther, 1966. *Rod Serling's Triple W: Witches, Warlocks, and Werewolves,* edited by Rod Serling. New York: Bantam Books, 1963. *The Dark Shadows Book of Vampires and Werewolves,* edited by Barnabas and Quentin Collins. New York: Paperback Library, 1970. *Werewolf! A Chrestomathy of Lycanthropy,* edited by Bill Pronzini. New York: Arbor House, 1979.

Ellis, Jeremy. "Silver Bullets." *Weird Tales,* April 1930.

Ellison, Harlan. "Adrift just off the Islets of Langerhans: Latitude 38°54' N, Longitude 77° 00' 13" W." *The Magazine of Fantasy and Science Fiction,* October 1974. Reprinted in *The Ultimate Werewolf,* edited by Byron Preiss. New York: Dell, 1991.

———. "L is for Loup-Garou." *The Magazine of Fantasy and Science Fiction,* October 1976. Reprinted in *100 Great Fantasy Short Short Stories,* edited by Isaac Asimov, Terry Carr, and Martin H. Greenberg. Garden City, N.Y.: Doubleday, 1984.

———. "Footsteps." *Gallery,* December 1980. Reprinted in *Horrorstory.* Vol. 3, edited by Karl Edward Wagner. Lancaster, Penn.: Underwood-Miller, 1992.

Elvira, and John Paragon. *The Boy Who Cried Werewolf.* New York: Berkley Books, 1998.

Elwood, Roger. "Night Prowler." In *Spine-Chillers,* edited by Roger Elwood and Howard Goldsmith. Garden City, N.Y.: Doubleday, 1978.

Elwood, Roger, ed. *Monster Tales: Vampires, Werewolves and Things.* Chicago: Rand McNally, 1973.

———. *Vampires, Werewolves and Other Monsters.* New York: Curtis Books, 1974.

Elwood, Roger, and Vic Ghidalia, eds. *Beware the Beasts.* New York: MacFadden-Bartell, 1970.

Elwood, Roger, and Howard Goldsmith, eds. *Spine-Chillers.* Garden City, N.Y.: Doubleday, 1978.

Emerson, Ru. "The Werewolf's Gift." In *Werewolves,* edited by Jane Yolen and Martin H. Greenberg. New York: Harper and Row, 1988.

Endore, Guy. "The Wolf Girl." *Argosy,* December 1920. Reprinted in *Werewolf: Horror Stories of the Man-Beast,* edited by Peter Haining. London: Severn House, 1987.

———. *The Werewolf of Paris.* New York: Farrar and Rinehart, 1933. New York: Ace Books, 1962. London: Sphere Books, 1974. New York: Pocket Books, 1993.

Erckmann-Chatrian [combined pen-name of Emile Erckmann and Alexandre Chatrian]. "The Man-Wolf." First book appearance in *Contes de la Montagne.* Paris: Levy, 1860 (as "Hugues-le-Loup"). Translated into English for *The Man-Wolf and Other Tales.* London: Ward, Lock and Tyler, 1876; Rpt. New York: Arno Press, 1976. Also included in *The Man-Wolf and Other Horrors,* edited by

Hugh Lamb. London: W. H. Allen, 1978. *The Best Tales of Terror of Erckmann-Chatrian,* edited by Hugh Lamb. London: Millington, 1981.

Etchison, Dennis. "The Nighthawk." In *Shadows,* edited by Charles L. Grant. Garden City, N.Y.: Doubleday, 1978. Reprinted in *The Mammoth Book of Werewolves,* edited by Stephen Jones. New York: Carroll and Graf, 1994; London: Robinson Books, 1994.

Evans, Ada Louvie. "Between Two Worlds." *The Thrill Book,* October 1919.

Fanthorpe, R. Lionel. "Call of the Werewolf." *Out of This World,* August 1958.

———. "Werewolf at Large." *Supernatural Stories,* November 1960.

———. "Moon Wolf." *Supernatural Stories,* June 1963.

Farlow, James. "The Demythologized Werewolf." *Analog,* May 1977. Reprinted in *Werewolf: Horror Stories of the Man-Beast,* edited by Peter Haining. London: Severn House, 1987.

Farmer, Philip José. "Wolf, Iron, and Moth." In *The Ultimate Werewolf,* edited by Byron Preiss. New York: Dell, 1991.

Field, Eugene. "The Werewolf." In *The Second Book of Tales.* New York: Charles Scribner's Sons, 1896.

Findley, Nigel D. "Transitions." In *When Will You Rage?,* edited by Stewart Wieck. Clarkston, Ga.: White Wolf, 1994.

Finlay, Winifred. "Terror in the Tatras." In *Vampire and Werewolf Stories,* edited by Alan Durant. London: Kingfisher, 1998; New York: Kingfisher US, 1998.

Finney, Charles G. *The Circus of Dr. Lao.* New York: Viking Press, 1935. A werewolf is one of the exhibits in a strange circus.

———. "The Black Retriever." *The Magazine of Fantasy and Science Fiction,* October 1958. Reprinted in *Rod Serling's Triple W: Witches, Warlocks and Werewolves,* edited by Rod Serling. New York: Bantam Books, 1963.

Fiske, Tarleton [pseud. of Robert Bloch]. "Flowers from the Moon." *Strange Stories,* August 1939.

Flanders, Rebecca. *Wolf in Waiting.* New York: Harlequin/ Silhouette Shadows, 1995.

———. *Secret of the Wolf.* New York: Harlequin/Silhouette Shadows, 1999.

Fleming, Peter. "The Kill." In *Creeps by Night,* edited by Dashiell Hammett. New York: John Day, 1931. Also included in *The Dark Dominion: Eight Terrifying Tales of Vampires and Werewolves.* New York: Paperback Library, 1970. *Book of the Werewolf,* edited by Brian J. Frost. London: Sphere Books, 1973.

Fletcher, Jo. "Bright of Moon." In *The Mammoth Book of Werewolves,* edited by Stephen Jones. New York: Carroll and Graf, 1994; London: Robinson Books, 1994. Poem.

Flynn, Connie. *Shadow on the Moon.* New York: Topaz, 1997.

———. *Shadow of the Wolf.* New York: Topaz, 1998.

Flynn, Michael. "Werehouse." In *Tomorrow Bites,* edited by Greg Cox and T. K. F. Weisskopf. New York: Baen Books, 1995.

Forest, Salambo. *Night of the Wolf.* New York: Ophelia Press, 1969.

Forester, E. Lascelles. *"Ware Wolf!"* London: Cassell, 1928.

Forsythe, Richard. *Fangs.* New York: Leisure Books, 1985.

Franklin, Pat. *Embrace of the Wolf.* New York: Diamond Books, 1993.

Fraser, Mrs. Hugh. *Further Reminiscences of a Diplomatist's Wife.* London: Hutchinson, 1912. Contains an allegedly true anecdote titled "A Were-Wolf of the Campagna."

This was included as an additional item in Tartarus Press's 1999 reprint of F. Marion Crawford's classic collection *Uncanny Tales.* Crawford was Mrs. Fraser's brother.

French, Allen. "Sir Marrok the Wolf." In *The Mammoth Book of Arthurian Legends,* edited by Mike Ashley. London: Robinson Books, 1998. Extracted from *Sir Marrok* (1902).

Friesner, Esther M. "A Winter's Night." In *Werewolves,* edited by Jane Yolen and Martin H. Greenberg. New York: Harper and Row, 1988.

Frost, Brian J., ed. *Book of the Werewolf.* London: Sphere Books, 1973.

Fry, Gordon. "Seven Curses of Lust." *Monster Parade,* November 1958.

Gallagher, Stephen. *Follower.* London: Sphere Books, 1984.

Gantos, Jack. *The Werewolf Family.* Boston: Houghton Mifflin, 1980.

Garcia y Robertson, R. *The Spiral Dance.* New York: William Morrow, 1991. New York: Morrow AvoNova, 1993.

———. "Werewolves of Luna." In *Tomorrow Bites,* edited by Greg Cox and T. K. F. Weisskopf. New York: Baen Books, 1995.

Garden, Nancy. *My Brother, the Werewolf.* New York: Random House, 1995. For preteens.

Gardner, Craig Shaw. "Day of the Wolf." In *The Ultimate Werewolf,* edited by Byron Preiss. New York: Dell, 1991.

Gardner, John. *The Werewolf Trace.* London: Hodder and Stoughton, 1977. Garden City, N.Y.: Doubleday, 1977.

Gardner, John C. "Julius Caesar and the Werewolf." *Playboy,* September 1984. Reprinted in *Playboy Stories: The Best of Forty Years of Short Fiction,* edited by Alice K. Turner. New York: Penguin/Dutton, 1994.

Garfield, Henry. *Moondog*. New York: St. Martin's Press, 1995.

———. *Room 13*. New York: St. Martin's Press, 1997.

Garmon, Larry Mike. *The Wolf Man: Blood Moon Rising*. New York: Scholastic, 2001. For preteens.

Garnett, David. *Lady into Fox*. London: Chatto and Windus, 1922; New York: Alfred A. Knopf, 1924.

Garton, Ray. "Monsters." In *Night Visions 6*, edited by Anon. Arlington Heights, Ill: Dark Harvest, 1988; *The Bone Yard*. New York: Berkley Books, 1991.

George, Stephen R. *Beasts*. New York: Zebra Books, 1989.

———. *Dark Reunion*. New York: Zebra Books, 1990.

Gilden, Mel. *Fifth Grade Monsters no. 12: Werewolf Come Home*. New York: Avon Camelot, 1990. For preteens.

———. "Moonlight on the Gazebo." In *The Ultimate Werewolf*, edited by Byron Preiss. New York: Dell, 1991.

Goddin, Jeffrey. *Blood of the Wolf*. New York: Leisure Books, 1987.

Goingback, Owl. "Fang of the Wolf." In *When Will You Rage?*, edited by Stewart Wieck. Clarkston, Ga.: White Wolf, 1994.

———. "Shaman Moon." In *The Essential World of Darkness*, edited by Stewart Wieck and Anna Branscombe. Clarkston, Ga.: White Wolf, 1997.

Golden, Christopher. *Prowlers*. New York: Pocket Books, 2000.

Goldman, Ken. "Cry of the Red Wolf." *Shapeshifter!*, 1995.

Goldman, Randy. *Werewolf Wars*. Edmonton, Alta.: Commonwealth Publications, Inc., 1996.

Gorman, Brice Patrick. "The Werewolf." *The Thirteenth Moon*, March 1994. Poem.

Gorman, Ed. *I, Werewolf*. Boston: Little, Brown, 1992.

———. *Wolf Moon*. New York: Fawcett, 1993.

Gorska, Halina. "Prince Godfrey Frees Mountain Dwellers and Little Shepherds from a Savage Werewolf and from Witches." In *Prince Godfrey.* New York: Roy, 1946. Reprinted in *The First Armada Ghost Book,* edited by Christine Bernard. London: Armada, 1967.

Goulart, Ron. *Hawkshaw.* Garden City, N.Y.: Doubleday, 1972.

————. "The Werewolf of Hollywood." In *Pulphouse: The Hardback Magazine,* issue 3, edited by Kristine Kathryn Rusch. Eugene, Ore.: Pulphouse, 1989.

Graham, Felix [pseud. of Fredric Brown]. "Heil, Werewolf!" *Dime Mystery Magazine,* November 1942.

Grant, Charles L. *The Dark Cry of the Moon.* West Kingston, R.I.: Donald M. Grant, 1985.

Graves, Emerson. "When the Werewolf Howls." *Horror Stories,* May 1940.

Gray, Sir Arthur. "The Necromancer." In *Tedious Brief Tales of Granta and Granmarye.* W. Heffer and Sons, 1919. Reprinted in *100 Creepy Little Creature Stories,* edited by Stefan R. Dziemianowicz, Robert Weinberg, and Martin H. Greenberg. New York: Barnes and Noble, 1994.

Green, Sharon. *Werewolf Moon.* New York: Harlequin/Intrigue, 1993.

Green, Simon R. *Wolf in the Fold.* New York: Ace Books, 1991.

Greenberg, Gary, and Jerome Tuccile. *War of the Werewolf.* Philadelphia: Xlibris Corporation, 2000.

Greenberg, Martin H., ed. *Werewolves.* New York: DAW Books, 1995.

Greene, The Hon. Mrs. *Bound by a Spell; or, The Hunted Witch of the Forest.* London: Cassell, 1885.

Greenough, Mrs. Richard S. "Monare." In *Arabesques: Monare, Apollyona, Domitia, Ombra*. Boston: Roberts Brothers, 1872.

Gregory, Franklin. *The White Wolf.* New York: Random House, 1941.

Gresham, Stephen. *The Living Dark*. New York: Zebra Books, 1991.

Grew, David. *The Werewolf of Edmonton*. London: Hutchinson, 1934.

Grey, John. "Werewolf Instructions." *Shapeshifter!* 1995. Poem.

———. "The Clown Who Is a Werewolf." *Weird Tales,* summer 1999. Poem.

Griffin, Peni R. "The Wolf Man's Wife." *Realms of Fantasy,* October 1997.

Grosser, E. A. "The Psychomorph." *Unknown,* February 1940. Reprinted in *Unknown Worlds* (British edn.), spring 1948.

Guillaume de Palerne. Medieval French romance, translated into Middle English about 1350. Also known as *William and the Werewolf.* The best modern version is *William of Palerne,* edited by W. W. Skeat. Early English Text Society. London, 1867.

Haaf, Beverly. "Mrs. Kaye." *Startling Mystery Stories,* winter 1968/69. Reprinted in *Book of the Werewolf,* edited by Brian J. Frost. London: Sphere Books, 1973.

Haesche, Richard P., Sr. *Cry of the Werewolf.* Philadelphia: Xlibris Corporation, 1997.

Haining, Peter, ed. *Werewolf: Horror Stories of the Man-Beast.* London: Severn House, 1987.

Halkin, John. *Fangs of the Werewolf.* London: Century-Hutchinson, 1987. New York: Barron's 1988.

Hall, Donald. "The Wonderful Dog Suit." In *Shape Shifters,* edited by Jane Yolen. New York: Seabury Press, 1978.

Hamilton, Alex. "Canis Lupus Sapiens." In *Way of the Werewolf,* edited by Douglas Hill. London: Panther, 1966.

Hamilton, Laurell K. *Guilty Pleasures.* New York: Ace Books, 1993.

———. *The Laughing Corpse.* New York: Ace Books, 1994.

Hammer, Charles D. "The Man Who Believed in Werewolves." *Monster Parade,* November 1958.

Handeland, Lori. *Full Moon Dreams.* New York: Leisure Books/Love Spell, 1996.

Harper, Tara K. *Wolfwalker.* New York: Ballantine, 1990.

Harris, Steve. *Wulf.* London: Headline Books, 1991.

———. *Challenging the Wolf.* Chatham, England: Squane's Press, 1997.

Hautala, Rick. *Moondeath.* New York: Zebra Books, 1980.

———. "Winter Queen." In *Dark Destiny,* edited by Edward E. Kramer. Clarkston, Ga.: White Wolf, 1995.

Hawk, Douglas D. *Moonslasher.* New York: Critic's Choice Paperback/Lorevan Publishing, Inc., 1987.

Hawke, Simon. *The Dracula Caper.* New York: Ace Books, 1988.

Hawks, Lee. *Night, Winter, and Death.* New York: Ballantine, 1990.

Henderson, B. S. "Wer' Wolf—The Mystery of Chateau Fontmarcelle." *Mystery Stories,* no. 10 (c. 1937).

Herron, Vennette. "Toean Matjan." *Weird Tales,* January 1938.

Hesse, Hermann. *Steppenwolf.* London: Secker and Warburg, 1929. Translation by Basil Creighton of *Der Steppenwolf* (1927).

Hill, Douglas, ed. *Way of the Werewolf.* London: Panther, 1966.

Hill, Elizabeth Starr. *Fangs Aren't Everything.* New York: Dutton/Plume, 1985. For preteens.

Hill, William. *Dawn of the Vampire*. New York: Pinnacle, 1991.

Hindin, Nathan. "Fangs of Vengeance." *Weird Tales,* April 1937.

Hoch, Edward D. "The Man Who Shot the Werewolf." *Ellery Queen's Mystery Magazine,* February 1979.

Hodge, Brian. *Nightlife*. New York: Dell/Abyss, 1991.

———. "Extinctions in Paradise." In *Werewolves,* edited by Martin H. Greenberg. New York: DAW Books, 1995.

Hodgell, P. C. *Dark of the Moon*. New York: Berkley Books, 1987.

Hoff, Robert M. *Crackers for a Lycanthrope*. Lycanthrocorp Literature, 1996.

Hoffman, Nina Kiriki. "Unleashed." In *The Ultimate Werewolf,* edited by Byron Preiss. New York: Dell, 1991.

———. "Dumpster Diving." In *Werewolves,* edited by Martin H. Greenberg. New York: DAW Books, 1995.

———. *The Silent Strength of Stones*. New York: Avon, 1995.

Holder, Nancy. "Leaders of the Pack." In *Dark Destiny,* edited by Edward E. Kramer. Clarkston, Ga.: White Wolf, 1995.

Holland, David. *Murcheston: The Wolf's Tale*. New York: St. Martin's Press, 2000.

Holleman, Gary L. *Howl-o-ween*. New York: Leisure Books, 1996.

Holt, John R. *Wolf Moon*. New York: Bantam Books, 1997.

Holton, Leonard. *Deliver Us From Wolves*. New York: Dell, 1963.

Household, Geoffrey. "Taboo." In *The Salvation of Pisco Gabar and Other Stories*. London: Jonathan Cape, 1939. Reprinted in *Realms of Darkness*. New York: Chartwell Books, 1988.

Housman, Clemence. "The Were-Wolf." *Atalanta,* October 1890 to September 1891. Book version: *The Were-Wolf.*

London: John Lane, 1896. Also included in *Masters of Horror,* edited by Alden H. Norton. New York: Berkley Books, 1968. *Book of the Werewolf,* edited by Brian J. Frost. London: Sphere Books, 1973. *Werewolf! A Chrestomathy of Lycanthropy,* edited by Bill Pronzini. New York: Arbor House, 1979. *Barbarians,* edited by Robert Adams, Martin H. Greenberg, and Charles G. Waugh. New York: NAL/Signet, 1986.

Howard, Robert E. "In the Forest of Villefere." *Weird Tales,* August 1925. Reprinted in *The Dark Man and Others.* Sauk City, Wis.: Arkham House, 1963.

———. "Wolfshead." *Weird Tales,* April 1926. Reprinted in *Werewolf: Horror Stories of the Man-Beast,* edited by Peter Haining. London: Severn House, 1987.

———. "The Lost Race." *Weird Tales,* January 1927. Reprinted in *Bran Mak Morn.* New York: Dell, 1969.

———. "The Hyena." *Weird Tales,* March 1928. Reprinted in *The Dark Man and Others.* Sauk City, Wis.: Arkham House, 1963.

———. "Black Hound of Death." *Weird Tales,* November 1936. Reprinted in *Weird Tales,* edited by Peter Haining. London: Neville Spearman, 1976.

Huff, Tanya. *Blood Trail.* New York: DAW Books, 1992.

Hurst, Mont. "The Wolf Man." *Ghost Stories,* July 1928.

Hurwood, Bernhardt J., ed. *Monsters Galore.* New York: Fawcett Gold Medal, 1965.

Hussey, Leigh Ann. "The White Wolf." In *Werewolves,* edited by Jane Yolen and Martin H. Greenberg. New York: Harper and Row, 1988.

Hyde, Shelley [pseud. of Kit Reed]. *Blood Fever.* New York: Pocket Books, 1982.

Iverson, Eric [pseud. of Harry Turtledove]. *Wereblood.* New York: Belmont Tower Books, 1979.

———. *Werenight.* New York: Belmont Tower Books, 1979.

———. "Blue Fox and Werewolf." *Amazing Stories,* September 1983.

Ivery, Martha. *Camp Werewolf.* New York: Press-Tige Press, 1999. Young adult novel.

Jaccoma, Richard. *The Werewolf's Tale.* New York: Fawcett Gold Medal, 1988.

———. *The Werewolf's Revenge.* New York: Fawcett Gold Medal, 1991.

Jacobi, Carl. "The Phantom Pistol." *Weird Tales,* May 1941.

Jacobson, Edith and Ejler. "The Werewolf of Wall Street." *Dime Mystery Magazine,* July 1938.

Jenkins, Will F. "Night Drive." *Today's Woman,* March 1950. Reprinted in *Twisted,* edited by Groff Conklin. New York: Belmont Books, 1962.

John, Anthony. *The Predator.* New York: Ballantine, 1983.

Johnson, Jeremy E. "Euphorbia Helioscopia." In *Women Who Run with the Werewolves,* edited by Pam Keesey. Pittsburgh, Penn.: Cleis Press, 1996.

Johnson, Morgan. "The Panthers of Shevgaon." *Hutchinson's Adventure-Story Magazine,* October 1926. Reprinted in *By Daylight Only,* edited by Christine Campbell Thomson. London: Selwyn and Blount, 1929. Werepanther story.

Johnson, Pete. *My Friend's a Werewolf.* New York: Dell Yearling, 1997. For preteens.

Johnson, S. S. "The House by the Crab Apple Tree." *The Magazine of Fantasy and Science Fiction,* February 1964. Reprinted in *The Best from Fantasy and Science Fiction: 14,* edited by Avram Davidson. Garden City, N.Y.: Doubleday, 1965.

Johnstone, William W. *Wolfsbane.* New York: Zebra Books, 1982.

———. *Watchers in the Woods*. New York: Kensington Books, 1991.

Jones, Diana Wynne. *Black Maria*. London: Mammoth, 1992.

Jones, Kelvin. "The Weird of Caxton." *Dark Horizons* no. 26, spring 1983.

Jones, Stephen, ed. *The Mammoth Book of Werewolves*. New York: Carroll and Graf, 1994; London: Robinson Books, 1994.

Kallas, Aino. *The Wolf's Bride: A Tale from Estonia*. London: Jonathan Cape, 1930.

Kaminsky, Stuart M. "Full Moon over Moscow." In *The Ultimate Werewolf,* edited by Byron Preiss. New York: Dell, 1991.

Kane, Thomas. "A Day Off." In *When Will You Rage?,* edited by Stewart Wieck. Clarkston, Ga.: White Wolf, 1994.

Kaveney, Roz. "A Wolf to Man." In *The Weerde: Book 1,* edited by Mary Gentle and Roz Kaveney. London: Roc Books, 1992.

Keesey, Pam, ed. *Women Who Run with the Werewolves*. Pittsburgh: Cleis Press, 1996.

Keizer, Gregg. "What Seen But the Wolf." *Isaac Asimov's Science Fiction Magazine,* February 1984. Reprinted in *Isaac Asimov's Werewolves,* edited by Gardner Dozois and Sheila Williams. New York: Ace Books, 1999.

Kelleam, Joseph E. "Revenge of the Were-Thing." *Monsters and Things,* January 1959.

Keller, David A. "Heredity." *The Vortex* no. 2, 1947. First book publication in *Life Everlasting and Other Tales of Science, Fantasy and Horror*. Newark, N.J.: Avalon, 1947. Also included in *Vamps,* edited by Martin H. Greenberg and Charles G. Waugh. New York: DAW Books, 1987.

Kelly, Ronald. *Moon of the Werewolf.* New York: Zebra Books, 1991.

———. *Something out There.* New York: Zebra Books, 1991.

Kemph, Obadiah. "It Takes Two for Terror." *Adventures in Horror,* December 1970.

Kenyon, Theda. "The House of the Golden Eyes." *Weird Tales,* September 1930.

Kerruish, Jessie Douglas. *The Undying Monster: A Tale of the Fifth Dimension.* London: Heath, Cranton, 1922. Reprint, London: Tandem Books, 1975.

Keter, K. W. *Wolf Flow.* New York: St. Martin's Press, 1992.

Kimbriel, Katharine Eliska. "Night Calls." In *Werewolves,* edited by Jane Yolen and Martin H. Greenberg. New York: Harper and Row, 1988.

———. *Night Calls.* New York: Harper/Prism, 1996.

Kincaid, C. A. "The Werewolf." In *The Penguin Book of Indian Ghost Stories.* New Delhi, India: Penguin Books, India, 1993.

King, Bernard. *Vargr-Moon.* London: New English Library, 1986.

King, Frank. *Southpaw.* New York: Lynx, 1988.

King, Robert J. *Heart of Midnight.* Lake Geneva, Wis.: TSR, 1992.

King, Stephen. "The Night of the Tiger." *The Magazine of Fantasy and Science Fiction,* February 1978. Reprinted in *The Best Horror Stories from The Magazine of Fantasy and Science Fiction.* Vol. 1, edited by Edward L. Ferman and Anne Devereaux Jordan. New York: St. Martin's Press, 1989. Were-tiger story.

———. *Cycle of the Werewolf.* New York: NAL/Signet, 1985. Originally published as *Cycle of the Werewolf Portfolio.* Westland, Mich.: Land of Enchantment, 1983.

King, Stephen, and Peter Straub. *The Talisman*. New York: Viking and Putnam, 1984. London: Viking, 1984. New York: Berkley Books, 1985.

Kipling, Rudyard. "The Mark of the Beast." In *Life's Handicap*. London: Macmillan, 1891. Also included in *Monsters Galore*, edited by Bernhardt J. Hurwood. New York: Fawcett Gold Medal, 1965. *Rod Serling's Triple W: Witches, Warlocks and Werewolves*, edited by Rod Serling. New York: Bantam Books, 1963. *Beware the Beasts*, edited by Roger Elwood and Vic Ghidalia. New York: MacFadden-Bartell, 1970. *Werewolf! A Chrestomathy of Lycanthropy*, edited by Bill Pronzini. New York: Arbor House, 1979.

Kitchin, C. H. B. "Beauty and the Beast." In *When Churchyards Yawn*, edited by Cynthia Asquith. London: Hutchinson, 1931. Reprinted in *A Century of Creepy Stories*. London: Hutchinson, 1934.

Klause, Annette Curtis. *Blood and Chocolate*. New York: Delacorte Press, 1997. Young adult novel.

Knight, Tracy. "Sand Boils." In *Werewolves*, edited by Martin H. Greenberg. New York: DAW Books, 1995.

Knox, John H. "Nightmare!" *Dime Mystery Magazine*, May 1934.

Koja, Kathe. "Angels' Moon." In *The Ultimate Werewolf*, edited by Byron Preiss. New York: Dell, 1991.

Koontz, Dean R. *A Werewolf among Us*. New York: Ballantine, 1973.

———. *Midnight*. New York: Putnam, 1989. New York: Berkley Books, 1989.

Kramer, Edward E., ed. *Dark Destiny*. Clarkston, Ga.: White Wolf, 1995.

Kreuger, Terry. *Night Cries*. New York: Dell, 1985.

Krinard, Susan. *Prince of Wolves*. New York: Bantam Books, 1994.

———. *Prince of Shadows.* New York: Bantam Books, 1996.

———. *Touch of the Wolf.* New York: Bantam Books, 1999.

———. *Once a Wolf.* New York: Bantam Books, 2000.

Kuttner, Henry. "Ballad of the Wolf." *Weird Tales,* June 1936. Poem.

———. "The Seal of Sin." *Strange Stories,* August 1940.

———. *The Dark World. Startling Stories,* summer 1946. Book version, New York: Ace Books, 1965.

Lackey, Mercedes. *The Fire Rose.* New York: Baen Books, 1996.

———. "Werehunter." In *Werehunter.* New York: Baen Books, 1998.

Lamb, Dana. "The Werewolf." In *In Trout Country,* edited by P. Corodimas. Boston: Little, Brown, 1971.

Landolfi, Tommaso. "The Werewolf." In *Words in Commotion and Other Stories.* New York: Viking, 1986.

Lang, Ralph Allen. "The Silver Knife." *Weird Tales,* January 1932. Reprinted in *100 Creepy Little Creature Stories,* edited by Stefan R. Dziemianowicz, Robert Weinberg, and Martin H. Greenberg. New York: Barnes and Noble, 1994.

Lankford, Terrill. *Angry Moon.* New York: Forge, 1996.

Lannes, Roberta. "Essence of the Beast." In *The Mammoth Book of Werewolves,* edited by Stephen Jones. New York: Carroll and Graf, 1994; London: Robinson Books, 1994.

Larson, Aaron B., and Keith Stayer. "Dances with Werewolves." *Outer Darkness* no. 11, 1997. Poem.

La Spina, Greye. "Wolf of the Steppes." *The Thrill Book,* March 1919.

———. "Invaders from the Dark." *Weird Tales,* April–June 1925. Book version: *Invaders from the Dark.* Sauk City, Wis.: Arkham House, 1960. Retitled: *Shadow of Evil.* New York: Paperback Library, 1966.

———. "The Devil's Pool." *Weird Tales,* June 1932. Reprinted in *Magazine of Horror,* November 1965.

Lauria, Frank. *Lady Sativa.* New York: Curtis Books, 1973.

Laws, Stephen. "Guilty Party." *Fear!* no. 2, September/October 1988. Reprinted in *The Mammoth Book of Werewolves,* edited by Stephen Jones. New York: Carroll and Graf, 1994; London: Robinson Books, 1994.

Layland-Barratt, F. *Lycanthia.* London: Ward, Lock, 1935.

The Lay of the Host of Igor. 13th-century Russian hero-epic. Part of the narrative recounts the story of Prince Vseslav, who turns into a bloodthirsty werewolf at night. An abridged version was included in *Medieval Myths* by Norma Lorre Goodrich. New York: NAL/Mentor, 1961.

Lazuta, Gene. *Vyrmin.* New York: Diamond Books, 1992.

Lecale, Errol. *The Tigerman of Terrahpur.* London: New English Library, 1974. Low-level were-tiger yarn.

Lee, Tanith. "Wolfland." *The Magazine of Fantasy and Science Fiction,* October 1980. Reprinted in *Red as Blood, or Tales from the Sisters Grimmer.* New York: DAW Books, 1983.

———. *Lycanthia, or The Children of Wolves.* New York: DAW Books, 1981.

———. "Bloodmantle." In *Forests of the Night.* London: Unwin, 1989.

———. *Heart-Beast.* New York: Dell/Abyss, 1993.

Lee, Wendi, and Terry Beatty. "The Black Wolf." In *Dracula: Prince of Darkness,* edited by Martin H. Greenberg. New York: DAW Books, 1992.

———. "Double Identity." In *Werewolves,* edited by Martin H. Greenberg. New York: DAW Books, 1995.

Leiber, Fritz. "The Hound." *Weird Tales,* November 1942. Also included in *Beware the Beasts,* edited by Roger

Elwood and Vic Ghidalia. New York: MacFadden-Bartell, 1970. *Werewolf! A Chrestomathy of Lycanthropy*, edited by Bill Pronzini. New York: Arbor House, 1979.

Levy, Edward. *The Beast Within*. New York: Berkley Books, 1981.

Lewis, Deborah [pseud. of Charles L. Grant]. *The Eve of the Hound*. New York: Zebra Books, 1977.

Lewton, Val. "The Bagheeta." *Weird Tales*, July 1930. Reprinted in *Weird Tales: The Magazine That Never Dies*, edited by Marvin Kaye. New York: SFBC, 1988.

Linaweaver, Brad. "Close Shave." In *The Ultimate Werewolf*, edited by Byron Preiss. New York: Dell, 1991.

Lindsay, Dan. "The Beatnik Werewolf." *The Magazine of Fantasy and Science Fiction*, April 1961.

Littke, Lael J., and Lori Littke Silfen. "The Electronic Werewolf." In *Bruce Coville's Shapeshifters*, edited by Bruce Coville. New York: Avon Camelot, 1999.

Locke, Joseph [pseud. of Ray Garton]. *Kiss of Death*. New York: Bantam Books, 1992.

Long, Frank B. *The Night of the Wolf*. New York: Popular Library, 1972.

Long, John Luther. *The Fox-Woman*. London: J. MacQueen, 1900.

Loring, F. G. "The Tomb of Sarah." *Pall Mall Magazine*, December 1900. Reprinted in *Victorian Ghost Stories*, edited by Michael Cox and R. A. Gilbert. Oxford: Oxford University Press, 1991.

Lory, Robert. *The Curse of Leo*. New York: Pinnacle, 1974.

Lovecraft, H. P. "Psychopompos." *Weird Tales*, September 1937. Poem.

Lowery, Bruce. *The Werewolf*. New York: Vanguard, 1972.

Lowitt, E. L. "The Were Wolf." *Weird Story Magazine*, no. 1, August 1940. Poem.

Lubar, David. *The Wavering Werewolf.* New York: Scholastic/Apple, 1997. For preteens.

Lukens, Adam [pseud. of Diane Detzer]. *Sons of the Wolf.* New York: Avalon, 1961. London: Consul, 1963.

Lupoff, Richard. *Lisa Kane.* Indianapolis, Ind.: Bobbs-Merrill, 1976.

Maberry, John Earl. "The Werewolf, Two Years Later." *Midnight Zoo,* 1, 5, 1991.

MacDonald, George. "The Gray Wolf." In *Works of Fantasy and Imagination.* London: Strahan, 1871. Reprinted in *100 Creepy Little Creature Stories,* edited by Stefan R. Dziemianowicz, Robert Weinberg, and Martin H. Greenberg. New York: Barnes and Noble, 1994.

Machard, Alfred. *The Wolf Man (The Were-Wolf).* New York: Edward J. Clode, 1925.

MacLaury, Cassie H. "Werewolf." *Ghost Stories,* March 1927.

Magistrale, Anthony S. "Ode for a Dead Werewolf." *Obsessions,* 1990. Poem.

Mailander, Jane. "Wolf Enough." In *Tomorrow Bites,* edited by Greg Cox and T. K. F. Weisskopf. New York: Baen Books, 1995.

Malisson, Roger [pseud. of Catherine Gleason]. "Countess Ilona; or The Werewolf Reunion." In *Supernatural,* edited by Robert Muller. London: Fontana, 1977. London: Severn House, 1977.

Malory, Sir Thomas. *Le Morte D'Arthur.* (*c.* 1470). Famous Arthurian romance in which mention is made of "Sir Marrok, the good knyghte that was bitrayed with his wyf for she made hym seuen yere a werewolf."

Malzberg, Barry N. "Nightshapes." In *Werewolf! A Chrestomathy of Lycanthropy,* edited by Bill Pronzini. New York: Arbor House, 1979.

Manley, Mark. *Throwback*. New York: Popular Library, 1987.

Mann, Jack [pseud. of E. Charles Vivian]. *Grey Shapes*. London: Wright and Brown, 1938. New York: Bookfinger, 1970.

Mansfield, Charlotte. *Trample the Lilies*. London: Stanley Paul and Co., 1927. Reputed to have a sequence involving lycanthropy.

Marie de France. "Lay of the Bisclavaret." (c. 1170). A modern prose version, titled "The Lay of the Were-Wolf," is included in *A Lycanthropy Reader: Werewolves in Western Culture*, edited by Charlotte F. Otten. New York: Dorset Press, 1989.

Marryat, [Captain] Frederick. "The Werewolf." Originally "Krantz's Narrative," chapter 39 of *The Phantom Ship*. First separate appearance in *The New Monthly Magazine*, July 1839. Reprinted in *Monsters Galore*, edited by Bernhardt J. Hurwood. New York: Fawcett Gold Medal, 1965. *The Dark Dominion: Eight Terrifying Tales of Vampires and Werewolves*, edited Anon. New York: Paperback Library, 1970. Has also appeared under the variant title "The White Wolf of the Hartz Mountains" in *The Supernatural Omnibus*, edited by Montague Summers. London: Gollancz, 1931. *Way of the Werewolf*, edited by Douglas Hill. London: Panther, 1966.

Martin, George R. R. "In the Lost Lands." In *Amazons II*, edited by Jessica Amanda Salmonson. New York: DAW Books, 1982.

———. "The Skin Trade." In *Night Visions 5*, edited by Douglas E. Winter. Arlington Heights, Ill.: Dark Harvest, 1988. *The Skin Trade*. New York: Berkley Books, 1990.

Martin, Les. *Return of the Werewolf*. New York: Random House, 1993. For preteens.

Mashburn, Kirk. "Placide's Wife." *Weird Tales,* November 1931. Reprinted in *Magazine of Horror,* August 1965. *Weird Vampire Tales,* edited by Robert Weinberg, Stefan R. Dziemianowicz, and Martin H. Greenberg. New York: Gramercy, 1992.

———. "The Last of Placide's Wife." *Weird Tales,* September 1932. Reprinted in *Magazine of Horror,* January 1968.

Masters, Anthony. "Freeze-Up." In *Vampire and Werewolf Stories,* edited by Alan Durant. London: Kingfisher, 1998. New York: Kingfisher US, 1998.

Masterton, Graham. "Rug." In *The Mammoth Book of Werewolves,* edited by Stephen Jones. New York: Carroll and Graf, 1994; London: Robinson Books, 1994.

Maturin, Charles. *The Albigenses: A Romance.* London: Hurst and Robinson, 1824. Philadelphia: S. F. Bradford and J. Laval, 1824. Reprint, New York: Arno Press, 1974.

Maupassant, Guy de. "Le Loup." Originally published in France, c. 1884. Is included, under its English title "The Wolf," in *Werewolf! A Chrestomathy of Lycanthropy,* edited by Bill Pronzini. New York: Arbor House, 1979.

McCammon, Robert. *The Wolf's Hour.* New York: Pocket Books, 1989.

McCord, Joseph. "The Girdle." *Weird Tales,* February 1927. Reprinted in *You'll Need a Night Light,* edited by Christine Campbell Thomson. London: Selwyn and Blount, 1927.

McCullough, Kelly. "Cry Werewolf." *Weird Tales,* spring 2001. Poem.

McCutchan, Philip. *Werewolf.* London: Hodder and Stoughton, 1982.

McElroy, Wendy. "Werewolf." *Amazing Stories,* September 1984. Poem.

Medcalf, Robert Randolph, Jr. "Werewolfgirl." *Eldritch Tales* no. 13, 1987. Poem.

Meek, Captain S. P. "The Curse of the Valedi." *Weird Tales,* July 1935.

Menzies, Sutherland. "Hugues, the Wer-Wolf." *The Court Magazine and Monthly Critic,* September 1838. Reprinted in *Book of the Werewolf,* edited by Brian J. Frost. London: Sphere Books, 1973.

Merak, A. J. [pseud. of John S. Glasby]. "Howl at the Moon." *Supernatural Stories,* July 1963.

Meredith, Larry Eugene. "The Last Letter from Norman Underwood." *Magazine of Horror,* January 1968.

Merritt, A. "The Drone." *Fantasy Magazine,* September 1934. Reprinted in *Book of the Werewolf,* edited by Brian J. Frost. London: Sphere Books, 1973.

———. "The Fox Woman." In *The Fox Woman and Other Stories.* New York: Avon, 1949.

Merritt, A., and Hannes Bok. *The Fox Woman and the Blue Pagoda.* New York: New Collectors Group, 1946.

Michaels, Barbara [pseud. of Barbara Gross Mertz]. *Sons of the Wolf.* London: Herbert Jenkins, 1968.

Miller, Bobbi. "Wolf Hunt." In *Sword and Sorceress VI,* edited by Marion Zimmer Bradley. New York: DAW Books, 1990.

Monet, Lireve [pseud. of Everil Worrell Murphy]. "Norn." *Weird Tales,* February 1936. Reprinted in *The Eighth Green Man and Other Strange Folk,* edited by Robert Weinberg. Mercer Island, Wash.: Starmont House, 1989.

Montgomery, Bucky. "Werewolf Saratogan." *The Scream Factory* no. 6, 1991.

Mooney, Brian. "Soul of the Wolf." In *The Mammoth Book of Werewolves,* edited by Stephen Jones. New York: Carroll and Graf, 1994; London: Robinson Books, 1994.

Moorcock, Michael. "Esbern Snare, Tale of the Northern Werewolf." In *The Revenge of the Rose: A Tale of the Albino Prince in the Years of His Wandering.* London: Grafton, 1991. New York: Ace Books, 1991.

Moore, C. L. "Werewoman." *Leaves* no. 2, fall 1938. Reprinted in *Horrors Unknown,* edited by Sam Moskowitz. New York: Walker, 1971.

Moore, James A. "For Auld Lang Syne." In *When Will You Rage?,* edited by Stewart Wieck. Clarkston, Ga.: White Wolf, 1994.

———. *Hell-Storm.* New York: Harper/Prism, 1996.

Morgan, Bassett [pseud. of Grace Jones]. "Tiger." *Strange Tales of Mystery and Terror,* March 1932. Reprinted in *Startling Mystery Stories,* spring 1969.

———. "Tiger Dust." *Weird Tales,* April 1933; Rpt. January 1954. Also included in *Keep on the Light,* edited by Christine Campbell Thomson. London: Selwyn and Blount, 1933.

Morgan, Robert. *All Things Under the Moon.* New York: Berkley Books, 1994.

Morland, Alanna. *Leopard Lord.* New York: Ace Books, 1998.

Morris, Dave. *The Sword of Life.* London: Hodder and Stoughton, 1997.

Morris, Mark. "Immortal." In *The Mammoth Book of Werewolves,* edited by Stephen Jones. New York: Carroll and Graf, 1994; London: Robinson Books, 1994.

Morrow, Sonora. "Hard Times." *Ellery Queen's Mystery Magazine,* December 1974.

Mosiman, Billie Sue. "Asleep in the Mist." In *Werewolves,* edited by Martin H. Greenberg. New York: DAW Books, 1995.

Muller, John E. *Mark of the Beast.* London: Badger Books, 1964.

Munn, H. Warner. "The Werewolf of Ponkert." *Weird Tales,* July 1925. Reprinted in *Book of the Werewolf,* edited by Brian J. Frost. London: Sphere Books, 1973.

———. "The Return of the Master." *Weird Tales,* July 1927.

———. "The Werewolf's Daughter." *Weird Tales,* October–December, 1928.

———. "The Master Strikes." *Weird Tales,* November 1930.

———. "The Master Fights." *Weird Tales,* December 1930.

———. "The Master Has a Narrow Escape." *Weird Tales,* January 1931.

———. "Cradle Song for a Baby Werewolf." *Whispers* no. 1, July 1973. Poem.

———. *The Werewolf of Ponkert.* New York: Centaur Books, 1976. Contains "The Werewolf of Ponkert" and "The Werewolf's Daughter."

———. *Tales of the Werewolf Clan.* Vol. 1, *In the Tomb of the Bishop.* West Kingston, R.I.: Donald M. Grant, 1979. Seven tales centering on the Master's revenge on the descendants of Wladislaw Brenryk.

———. *Tales of the Werewolf Clan.* Vol. 2, *The Master Goes Home.* West Kingston, R.I.: Donald M. Grant, 1980. Six tales completing the werewolf saga.

Murphy, Pat. "South of Oregon City." In *The Ultimate Werewolf,* edited by Byron Preiss. New York: Dell, 1991.

———. "An American Childhood." *Asimov's Science Fiction Magazine,* April 1993. Reprinted in *Isaac Asimov's Werewolves,* edited by Gardner Dozois and Sheila Williams. New York: Ace Books, 1999.

———. *Nadya.* New York: Tor, 1996.

Murray, Doug. *Call to Battle.* Clarkston, Ga.: White Wolf, 1996.

Neiderman, Andrew. *Love Child.* New York: Tor, 1986.

Newman, Kim. "Out of the Night, When the Full Moon Is

Bright . . ." In *The Mammoth Book of Werewolves,* edited by Stephen Jones. New York: Carroll and Graf, 1994; London: Robinson Books, 1994.

Nicolson, J. U. *Fingers of Fear.* New York: Covici-Friede, 1937. New York: Popular Library, 1966. Seattle, Wash.: Midnight House, 2002.

Niven, Larry. "There's a Wolf in My Time Machine." *The Magazine of Fantasy and Science Fiction,* June 1971. Also included in *The Ultimate Werewolf,* edited by Byron Preiss. New York: Dell, 1991. *Tomorrow Bites,* edited by Greg Cox and T. K. F. Weisskopf. New York: Baen Books, 1995.

———. "What Good is a Glass Dagger?" *The Magazine of Fantasy and Science Fiction,* September 1972. Reprinted in *Isaac Asimov's Magical Worlds of Fantasy no. 1: Wizards,* edited by Isaac Asimov, Martin H. Greenberg, and Charles G. Waugh. New York: Signet, 1983.

Norris, Frank. *Vandover and the Brute.* London: William Heinemann, 1914.

Norton, Andre. *Moon of Three Rings.* New York: Viking, 1966.

———. *The Jargoon Pard.* New York: Fawcett Crest, 1974. Features a were-leopard.

O'Donnell, Elliott, "Mère Maxim." In *Book of the Werewolf,* edited by Brian J. Frost. London: Sphere Books, 1973. Extracted from *Werwolves.* London: Rider, 1912.

———. "The Sign of the Werewolf." In *Elliott O'Donnell's Great Ghost Story Omnibus,* edited by Harry Ludlam. London: W. Foulsham, 1983.

Onions, Oliver. "The Master of the House." In *The Painted Face.* London: Heinemann, 1929. Reprinted in *Werewolf: Horror Stories of the Man-Beast,* edited by Peter Haining. London: Severn House, 1987.

Ordover, John J. "FlowereW." In *Tomorrow Bites,* edited by Greg Cox and T. K. F. Weisskopf. New York: Baen Books, 1995.

Otten, Charlotte F., ed. *Classic Werewolf Stories.* Boston: Lowell House, 1997. Young adult anthology containing eight well-known stories.

Packard, Edward. *Night of the Werewolf (Choose Your Own Nightmare).* New York: Bantam Books, 1995. For preteens.

Page, Norvell W. "The Death Beast." *Dime Mystery Magazine,* December 1933.

———. "Accursed Thirst." *Terror Tales,* September 1935.

Pain, Barry. "The Undying Thing." In *Stories in the Dark.* London: Grant Richards, 1901. Reprinted in *Gaslit Nightmares,* edited by Hugh Lamb. London: Futura, 1988.

Palmer, Jessica. *Shadow Dance.* New York: Pocket Books, 1994.

Partridge, Norman. "The Pack." In *Werewolves,* edited by Martin H. Greenberg. New York: DAW Books, 1995.

Pascal, Francine (with Kate William). *Beware the Wolfman.* New York: Bantam Books, 1994. Young adult novel.

———. *Date with a Werewolf.* New York: Bantam Books, 1994. Young adult novel.

———. *Love and Death in London.* New York: Bantam Books, 1994. Young adult novel.

Paul, Barbara. "Never Moon a Werewolf." In *Werewolves,* edited by Martin H. Greenberg. New York: DAW Books, 1995.

Paxson, Diana. *The Wolf and the Raven.* New York: Avon, 1994.

Peel, John. *Blood Wolf.* New York: Grosset and Dunlap, 1993. For preteens.

————. *Dances with Werewolves.* New York: Archway, 1995. Young adult novel.

Pei, Mario. *The Sparrows of Paris.* New York: Philosophical Library, 1958.

Pendarves, G. G. [pseud. of Gladys Gordon Trenery]. "Werewolf of the Sahara." *Weird Tales,* August/September 1936.

Perry, Ritchie. *The Runton Werewolf.* Red Fox, 1996. For preteens.

Philbin, K. *Summer of the Werewolf.* Cheltenham, England: Stanley Thornes, 1990.

Philbrick, W. R. *Children of the Wolf.* New York: Scholastic, 1996. For preteens.

————. *Night Creature.* New York: Scholastic, 1996. For preteens.

————. *The Wereing.* New York: Scholastic, 1996. For preteens.

Phillips, Alexander M. "Lycanthropy." *Weirdbook* no. 18, summer 1983.

Phillpotts, Eden. "Loup Garou!" In *Loup Garou and Other Tales.* London: Sands and Co., 1899.

————. *Lycanthrope: The Mystery of Sir William Wolf.* London: T. Butterworth, 1937.

Picard, Barbara Leonie. "The Werewolf." In *German Hero-Sagas and Folk Tales.* New York: Oxford University Press, 1958.

Pinkwater, Daniel M. *I Was a Second Grade Werewolf.* New York: Dutton, 1983. New York: NAL, 1987. For preteens.

Pocock, Roger S. *The Wolf Trail.* Oxford: B. Blackwell, 1923.

Pollotta, Nick. *Bureau 13.* New York: Ace Books, 1991.

————. *Full Moonster.* New York: Ace Books, 1992.

Powers, Tim. *The Anubis Gates.* New York: Ace Books, 1983. London: Chatto and Windus, 1985.

Pratchett, Terry. *Feet of Clay*. London: Victor Gollancz, 1996.

Preiss, Byron, ed. *The Ultimate Werewolf*. New York: Dell, 1991.

Pretorius, Michael. "One Last Death Prowl for the Man Who Howled Like a Wolf." *Horror Stories,* February 1971.

Pronzini, Bill. "Ancient Evil." In *The Ultimate Werewolf,* edited by Byron Preiss. New York: Dell, 1991.

Pronzini, Bill, ed. *Werewolf! A Chrestomathy of Lycanthropy*. New York: Arbor House, 1979.

Quinn, Seabury. "The Phantom Farmhouse." *Weird Tales,* October 1923. Also included in *Magazine of Horror,* January 1965. *Way of the Werewolf,* edited by Douglas Hill. London: Panther, 1966.

———. "The Blood Flower." *Weird Tales,* March 1927. Also included in *Startling Mystery Stories,* winter 1966/67. *The Compleat Adventures of Jules de Grandin*. Vol. 1. Shelburne, Ont.: Battered Silicon Dispatch Box, 2001.

———. "The Wolf of St. Bonnot." *Weird Tales,* December 1930. Also included in *Book of the Werewolf,* edited by Brian J. Frost. London: Sphere Books, 1973. *The Compleat Adventures of Jules de Grandin*. Vol. 2. Shelburne, Ont.: Battered Silicon Dispatch Box, 2001.

———. "The Thing in the Fog." *Weird Tales,* March 1933. Reprinted in *The Compleat Adventures of Jules de Grandin*. Vol. 2. Shelburne, Ont.: Battered Silicon Dispatch Box, 2001.

———. "Fortune's Fools." *Weird Tales,* July 1938. Reprinted in *Werewolf: Horror Stories of the Man-Beast,* edited by Peter Haining. London: Severn House, 1987.

———. "Uncanonized." *Weird Tales,* November 1939. Reprinted in *Is the Devil a Gentleman?*. Baltimore: Mirage Press, 1970.

———. "The Gentle Werewolf." *Weird Tales,* July 1940. Reprinted in *Is the Devil a Gentleman?* Baltimore: Mirage Press, 1970.

———. "Bon Voyage, Michele." *Weird Tales,* January 1944. Reprinted in *Is the Devil a Gentleman?.* Baltimore: Mirage Press, 1970.

Randisi, Robert J. "Partners." In *The Ultimate Werewolf,* edited by Byron Preiss. New York: Dell, 1991.

Ranieri, Roman A. "Waiting for Moonlight." In *Werewolves,* edited by Martin H. Greenberg. New York: DAW Books, 1995.

Ransey, Shawn. "Lycanthrope." *Deathrealm,* summer 1989. Poem.

Raspe, Rudolph Erich. *Koenigsmark the Robber.* Cassel, 1790. First English translation by J. Williams, 1801. A pirated version of 1808 was erroneously attributed to Matthew "Monk" Lewis. Gothic romance in which werewolves make a cameo appearance.

Reeves-Stevens, Judith and Garfield. *Shifter.* New York: Roc, 1990.

———. *Nightfeeder.* New York: Roc, 1991.

Reichert, Mickey Zucker. "The Night of Howling." In *Werewolves,* edited by Martin H. Greenberg. New York: DAW Books, 1995.

Resnick, Mike. *Lucifer Jones.* New York: Warner Questar, 1992. The eponymous hero crosses paths with many weird creatures, including werewolves.

Reynolds, George W. M. *Wagner, the Wehr-Wolf.* Serialized in *Reynolds's Miscellany,* November 6, 1846 to July 24, 1847. Book versions: London: Dick's English Novels, n.d. (c. 1857). New York: Dover Press, 1975.

Reynolds, Mrs. L. Baillie. "The Terrible Baron." In *The*

Terrible Baron and Other Stories. London: Wright and Brown, 1933.

Rice, Bebe Faas. *The Year the Wolves Came.* New York: E. P. Dutton, 1994. For preteens.

Rice, Jane. "The Refugee." *Unknown Worlds,* October 1943. Also included in *Way of the Werewolf,* edited by Douglas Hill. London: Panther, 1966. *The Dark Dominion: Eight Terrifying Tales of Vampires and Werewolves,* edited Anon. New York: Paperback Library, 1970. *Werewolf: Horror Stories of the Man-Beast,* edited by Peter Haining. London: Severn House, 1987.

Richardson, Flavia [pseud. of Christine Campbell Thomson]. "Brood of the Beast." *Hutchinson's Mystery-Story Magazine,* no. 28, May 1925.

Robbins, David. *The Wereling.* New York: Leisure Books, 1983.

———. *The Wrath.* New York: Leisure Books, 1988.

Robertson, William P. "Werewolf Month." *Shapeshifter!,* 1995. Poem.

Robeson, Kenneth [pseud. of Lester Dent]. *Brand of the Werewolf. Doc Savage Magazine,* January 1934. New York: Bantam Books, 1965.

Robins, Peter. "Cheriton." In *The Gay Touch.* Crossing Press, 1982. Reprinted in *Embracing the Dark,* edited by Eric Garber. Boston: Alyson, 1991.

Robinson, Frank M. "The Night Shift." *Fantasy Magazine,* no. 1, February/March 1953. Reprinted in *Fantastic Chicago,* edited by Martin H. Greenberg. Chicon V, 1991.

Roche, Thomas S. "Sisters of the Weird." In *Women Who Run with the Werewolves,* edited by Pam Keesey. Pittsburgh, Penn.: Cleis Press, 1996.

Rogers, Alara. "Calley's Story." In *When Will You Rage?,*

edited by Stewart Wieck. Clarkston, Ga.: White Wolf, 1994.

Rogers, Wayne. "Hell's Brew." *Thrilling Mystery,* January 1936.

———. "Beast-Women Stalk at Night." *Horror Stories,* August/September 1937.

Rosenberg, Joel. *The Fire Duke.* New York. Avon, 1995.

Ross, Marilyn [pseud. of Dan Ross]. *Barnabas Collins and Quentin's Demon.* New York: Paperback Library, 1969.

———. *Barnabas, Quentin, and the Mummy's Curse.* New York: Paperback Library, 1970.

———. *Barnabas, Quentin, and the Avenging Ghost.* New York: Paperback Library, 1970.

———. *Barnabas, Quentin, and the Nightmare Assassin.* New York: Paperback Library, 1970.

———. *Barnabas, Quentin, and the Crystal Coffin.* New York: Paperback Library, 1970.

———. *Barnabas, Quentin, and the Witch's Curse.* New York: Paperback Library, 1970.

———. *Barnabas, Quentin, and the Haunted Cave.* New York: Paperback Library, 1970.

———. *Barnabas, Quentin, and the Frightened Bride.* New York: Paperback Library, 1970.

———. *Barnabas, Quentin, and the Scorpio Curse.* New York: Paperback Library, 1970.

———. *Barnabas, Quentin, and the Serpent.* New York: Paperback Library, 1970.

———. *Barnabas, Quentin, and the Magic Potion.* New York: Paperback Library, 1970.

———. *Barnabas, Quentin, and the Body Snatchers.* New York: Paperback Library, 1970.

———. *Barnabas, Quentin, and Dr. Jekyll's Son.* New York: Paperback Library, 1970.

———. *Barnabas, Quentin, and the Grave Robbers*. New York: Paperback Library, 1971.

———. *Barnabas, Quentin, and the Sea Ghost*. New York: Paperback Library, 1971.

———. *Barnabas, Quentin, and the Mad Magician*. New York: Paperback Library, 1971.

———. *Barnabas, Quentin, and the Hidden Tomb*. New York: Paperback Library, 1971.

———. *Barnabas, Quentin, and the Vampire Beauty*. New York: Paperback Library, 1972.

Rovin, Jeff. *Return of the Wolf Man*. New York: Boulevard Books, 1998.

Roxbury, Kyle. *Cry Wolf!*. San Diego, Calif.: Darkroom Reader, 1970.

Royle, Nicholas. "Anything But Your Kind." In *The Mammoth Book of Werewolves,* edited by Stephen Jones. New York: Carroll and Graf, 1994; London: Robinson Books, 1994.

Rozanski, Joette M. "The Werewolf's Final Lesson." In *Sword and Sorceress XIII,* edited by Marion Zimmer Bradley. New York: DAW Books, 1996.

Rubie, Peter. *Werewolf.* Stamford, Conn.: Longmeadow Press, 1991.

Rumble, Barry P. *Full Moon*. Studio City, Calif.: Players Press, 1995.

Saberhagen, Fred. *Dominion*. New York: Pinnacle, 1982. Lycanthropes have cameo role.

Sackett, Jeffrey. *Mark of the Werewolf.* New York: Bantam Books, 1990.

Saki [pseud. of H. H. Munro]. "Gabriel-Ernest." *The Westminster Gazette,* May 29, 1909. First book publication in *Reginald in Russia*. London: Methuen, 1910. Also included in *Way of the Werewolf,* edited by Douglas Hill.

London: Panther, 1966. *Shape Shifters*, edited by Jane Yolen. New York: Seabury Press, 1978. *Werewolf! A Chrestomathy of Lycanthropy*, edited by Bill Pronzini. New York: Arbor House, 1979. *Young Monsters*, edited by Isaac Asimov, Martin H. Greenberg, and Charles G. Waugh. New York: Harper and Row, 1985. *Asimov's Ghosts and Monsters*, edited by Isaac Asimov, Martin H. Greenberg, and Charles G. Waugh. London: Armada, 1988.

Sale, Richard B. "Rescued by Satan." *Mystery Adventures*, May 1936.

Sallee, Wayne Allen. "Go Hungry." In *Dark Destiny*, edited by Edward E. Kramer. Clarkston, Ga.: White Wolf, 1995.

Salmon, Arthur L. "The Were-Wolf." In *The Ferry of Souls*. London: G. T. Foulis, 1927.

Sandemose, Aksel. *The Werewolf*. Translated from the Norwegian by Gustaf Lannesstock. Madison, Wis.: University of Wisconsin Press, 1966.

San Souci, Robert D. "The Loup-Garou." In *Short and Shivery*. Garden City, N.Y.: Doubleday, 1987. Based on a French Canadian legend.

Sarrantonio, Al. *Moonbane*. New York: Bantam Books, 1989.

Sauter, Eric. *Predators*. New York: Pocket Books, 1987.

Saxon, Peter. *The Disorientated Man*. London: Mayflower, 1966.

Scapparo, Jack. *The Attic*. New York: Zebra Books, 1991.

Scarborough, Elizabeth Ann. "Wolf from the Door." In *Werewolves*, edited by Jane Yolen and Martin H. Greenberg. New York: Harper and Row, 1988.

Scarm, Arthur N. *The Werewolf vs. the Vampire Woman*. Beverly Hills, Calif.: Guild-Hartford, 1972.

Schaeffer, Robin. "Night of the Wolf." In *Vampires, Werewolves and Other Monsters,* edited by Roger Elwood. New York: Curtis Books, 1974.

Schifino, J. R. "Lair of the White Wolf." *Fantasy Tales* no. 6, summer 1980.

Schimel, Lawrence. "Little Boy Riding Hood." In *Werewolves,* edited by Martin H. Greenberg. New York: DAW Books, 1995.

Schweitzer, Darrell. "An Authentic Werewoman." *Night Voyages* no. 9, winter/spring 1983.

Scotch, Cheri. *The Werewolf's Kiss.* New York: Diamond Books, 1992.

———. *The Werewolf's Touch.* New York: Diamond Books, 1993.

———. *The Werewolf's Sin.* New York: Diamond Books, 1994.

———. "Children of the Night." In *Werewolves,* edited by Martin H. Greenberg. New York: DAW Books, 1995.

Scott, Duncan Campbell. "The Witching Hour." In *The Witching of Elspie: A Book of Stories.* New York: Doran, 1923.

Scott, Sir Walter. "The Wer-Bear." In *Monsters Galore,* edited by Bernhardt J. Hurwood. New York: Fawcett Gold Medal, 1965. Originally published in 1827.

Seignolle, Claude. "The Gâloup." In *Way of the Werewolf,* edited by Douglas Hill. London: Panther, 1966.

———. *The Accursed.* London: Allen and Unwin, 1967. Contains two short novels, one of which, *Marie, the Wolf,* has a werewolf theme.

Selonke, Paul. "Beast of the Island." *Strange Stories,* October 1940. Reprinted in *Werewolf: Horror Stories of the Man-Beast,* edited by Peter Haining. London: Severn House, 1987.

Serling, Rod, ed. *Rod Serling's Triple W: Witches, Warlocks, and Werewolves.* New York: Bantam Books, 1963.

Service, Robert W. *The House of Fear.* New York: Dodd, Mead, 1927; London: T. Fisher Unwin, 1927.

Seth, Ronald. "The Werewolf of St. Claude." In *50 Great Horror Stories,* edited by John Canning. New York: Taplinger, 1969; London: Hamlyn/Odhams, 1969

Sheffield, Charles. *Erasmus Magister.* New York: Ace Books, 1982.

Shetterly, Will. *Elsewhere.* New York: Tor, 1991.

———. *Nevernever.* New York: Tor, 1995.

Shwartz, Susan M. "The Wolf's Flock." In *Werewolves,* edited by Jane Yolen and Martin H. Greenberg. New York: Harper and Row, 1988.

Silverberg, Robert. "The Werewolf Gambit." In *The Ultimate Werewolf,* edited by Byron Preiss. New York: Dell, 1991.

Simak, Clifford. *The Werewolf Principle.* New York: Putnam, 1967. New York: Berkley Books, 1968. London: Gollancz, 1991.

Simmons, Wm. Mark. *One Foot in the Grave.* New York: Baen Books, 1995.

Skipp, John, and Craig Spector. *Animals.* New York: Bantam Books, 1993.

Skurzynski, Gloria. *Manwolf.* New York: Clarion Books, 1981.

Sloane, Robert C. *A Nice Place to Live.* New York: Crown, 1981. New York: Bantam Books, 1982.

Smith, Chris. "Lone Lycanthrope." *SPWAO Showcase* no. 5, 1985. Poem.

Smith, Clark Ashton. "The Enchantress of Sylaire." *Weird Tales,* July 1941. Reprinted in *The Abominations of Yondo.* Sauk City, Wis.: Arkham House, 1960.

———. "A Prophecy of Monsters." *The Magazine of Fantasy*

and Science Fiction, October 1954. Also included in *Werewolf! A Chrestomathy of Lycanthropy,* edited by Bill Pronzini. New York: Arbor House, 1979. *Tomorrow Bites,* edited by Greg Cox and T. K. F. Weisskopf. New York: Baen Books, 1995. Retitled "Monsters in the Night" for its appearance in *Other Dimensions.* Sauk City, Wis.: Arkham House, 1970.

Smith, Guy N. *Werewolf by Moonlight.* London: New English Library, 1974.

————. *The Return of the Werewolf.* London: New English Library, 1977.

————. *The Son of the Werewolf.* London: New English Library, 1978.

————. *Wolfcurse.* London: New English Library, 1981.

Smith, Margaret M. "Werewolves Hate Snow." *The End* no. 3, 1995. Poem.

Smith, Michael Marshall. "Rain Falls." In *The Mammoth Book of Werewolves,* edited by Stephen Jones. New York: Carroll and Graf, 1994; London: Robinson Books, 1994.

Smith, Nyx. *Striper Assassin.* New York: Signet, 1992.

Smith, Robert Arthur. *The Werewolf's Prey.* New York: Fawcett, 1977.

Smith, Sherwood. "Monster Mash." In *Werewolves,* edited by Jane Yolen and Martin H. Greenberg. New York: Harper and Row, 1988.

Smith, Wayne. *Thor.* New York: St. Martin's Press, 1992.

Snell, Gordon. *Curse of Werewolf Castle.* Dublin: Poolbeg Press, 1996. For preteens.

Sologub, Fedor. "The White Dog." In *The Sweet-Scented Name and Other Fairy-tales, Fables and Stories.* New York: Putnam's Sons, 1915; London: Constable, 1915. Reprinted in *Weird Tales,* February 1926.

Somtow, S. P. [pseud. of Somtow Sucharitkul]. "Madonna

of the Wolves." *Isaac Asimov's Science Fiction Magazine,* November 1988. Reprinted in *Isaac Asimov's Werewolves,* edited by Gardner Dozois and Sheila Williams. New York: Ace Books, 1999.

———. *Moon Dance.* New York: Tor, 1989. London: Gollancz, 1991.

———. *Darker Angels.* London: Gollancz, 1997.

Sonnenschein, Dana. "Wolfman in the Wax Museum." *Amazing,* January 1991. Poem.

Spence, Lewis. "Enchantment on the Unicorn." In *The Archer in the Arras and Other Tales of Mystery.* London: Grant and Murray, 1932.

———. "The Temple of the Jaguars." In *The Archer in the Arras and Other Tales of Mystery.* London: Grant and Murray, 1932.

St. Clair, Margaret. "Graveyard Shift." In *Change the Sky and Other Stories.* New York: Ace Books, 1974.

St. Luz, Berthe [pseud. of Alice A. Robertson]. *Tamar Curze.* New York: R. F. Fenno, 1908.

Stableford, Brian. *The Werewolves of London.* London: Simon and Schuster, 1990. New York: Carroll and Graf, 1992.

———. *The Angel of Pain.* London: Simon and Schuster, 1991. New York: Carroll and Graf, 1993.

———. *The Carnival of Destruction.* London: Simon and Schuster, 1994. New York: Carroll and Graf, 1994.

Stallman, Robert. *The Orphan.* New York: Pocket Books, 1980.

———. *The Captive.* New York: Pocket Books, 1981.

———. *The Beast.* New York: Pocket Books, 1982.

Starkey, David. "Confession." *Grue Magazine* no. 4, 1987.

Starr, Elizabeth. *Pardon My Fangs.* New York: Holt, Rinehart, Winston, 1969. For preteens.

Stenbock, Count Eric. "The Other Side." *The Spirit Lamp,*

June 6, 1893. Reprinted in *A Lycanthropy Reader: Were-wolves in Western Culture,* edited by Charlotte F. Otten. New York: Dorset Press, 1989.

Stevenson, Drew. *The Case of the Wandering Werewolf.* New York: Penguin Putnam, 1988. New York: Pocket, 1991. For preteens.

Stevenson, Florence. *The Curse of the Concullens.* Cleveland, Ohio: World Publishing, 1970. New York: Signet, 1972.

———. *Household.* New York: Leisure Books, 1989.

Stevenson, Robert Louis. "Olalla." *Court and Society Review,* Christmas 1885. Reprinted in *The Merry Men and Other Tales and Fables.* London: Chatto and Windus, 1887.

———. *The Strange Case of Dr. Jekyll and Mr. Hyde.* London: Longmans, Green, 1886. New York: Scribner, 1888.

Stewart, Mary. *A Walk in Wolf Wood.* London: Hodder and Stoughton, 1980; New York: Fawcett, 1981. Young adult novel.

Stewart, W. Gregory. "Nocturne for the Urban Werewolf." *Dreams and Nightmares* no. 49, 1997. Poem.

Stine, R. L. *The Werewolf of Fever Swamp.* New York: Scholastic, 1993. For preteens.

———. *Night in Werewolf Woods.* New York: Scholastic, 1996. For preteens.

———. *Heart of the Hunter.* New York: Archway, 1997. Young adult novel.

———. *Werewolf Skin.* New York: Scholastic, 1997. For preteens.

———. *The Werewolf of Twisted Tree Lodge.* New York: Scholastic, 1998. For preteens.

———. *Full Moon Fever.* New York: Scholastic, 1999. For preteens.

———. *The Werewolf in the Living Room.* New York: Scholastic, 1999. For preteens.

Stoker, Bram. "Dracula's Guest." In *Dracula's Guest and Other Weird Stories*. London: Routledge, 1914. Also included in *Spine-Chillers*, edited by Roger Elwood and Howard Goldsmith. Garden City, N.Y.: Doubleday, 1978. *Werewolf! A Chrestomathy of Lycanthropy*, edited by Bill Pronzini. New York: Arbor House, 1979.

Stone, Tom B. *Little Pet Werewolf.* New York: Bantam, 1994. For preteens.

Strickland, Brad. "And the Moon Shines Full and Bright." In *The Ultimate Werewolf,* edited by Byron Preiss. New York: Dell, 1991.

Strickland, Margaret. "The Case of Sir Alister Moeran." *The Novel Magazine,* July 1913. Reprinted in *Ghost Stories and Other Queer Tales*. London: Pearson, 1931. Weretiger story.

Strieber, Whitley. *The Wolfen.* New York: Morrow, 1978. New York: Bantam Books, 1979.

———. *The Wild*. New York: Wilson and Neff, 1991; New York: Tor, 1991.

Sullivan, Alan. "Loup Garou." *Windsor Magazine,* July 1905.

———. "The Eyes of Sebastian." *The Popular Magazine,* January 1, 1925. First book publication in *Under the Northern Lights*. New York: E. P. Dutton, 1926. Reprinted in *Crime Where the Night is Six Months Long,* edited by David Skene-Melvin. Toronto: Simon and Pierre, 1999.

Summers, Montague. "The Phantom Werewolf." In *Werewolf: Horror Stories of the Man-Beast,* edited by Peter Haining. London: Severn House, 1987. Extracted from *The Werewolf*. London: Kegan Paul, Trench, Trubner, 1933.

Suter, J. Paul. "The Wolf in the Dark." *Ghost Stories,* February 1931.

Sutton, David. "And I Shall Go in the Devil's Name." In *The Mammoth Book of Werewolves*, edited by Stephen Jones. New York: Carroll and Graf, 1994; London: Robinson Books, 1994.

Swanwick, Michael. "A Midwinter's Tale." *Isaac Asimov's Science Fiction Magazine*, December 1988. Reprinted in *Tomorrow Bites*, edited by Greg Cox and T. K. F. Weisskopf. New York: Baen Books, 1995.

Swem, Charles Lee. *Werewolf.* New York: Doubleday and Doran, 1928.

Szabo, Sandor. "Werewolves are Furry." *Thriller,* July 1962.

Tan, Cecelia, ed. *The Beast Within: Erotic Tales of Werewolves.* Cambridge, Mass.: Circlet Press, 1994.

Taylor, Bernard. "Out of Sorts." In *The Dodd, Mead Gallery of Horror,* edited by Charles L. Grant. New York: Dodd, Mead, 1983.

Tem, Melanie. *Wilding.* New York: Dell/Abyss, 1992.

———. "Wilding." In *Women Who Run with the Werewolves,* edited by Pam Keesey. Pittsburgh, Penn.: Cleis Press, 1996.

Tem, Steve Rasnic. "Werewolf, Manhattan." *Eldritch Tales* no. 9, April 1983. Poem.

Tessier, Thomas. *The Nightwalker.* London: Macmillan, 1979. New York: Atheneum, 1980. New York: Berkley Books, 1981.

Thompson, Rhonda. "Midnight Serenade." In *After Twilight.* New York: Leisure Books, 2001.

Thompson, Victoria. *Cry Wolf.* New York: Zebra Books, 1995.

Thomson, Richard. "The Wehr Wolf: A Legend of the Limousin." In *Tales of an Antiquary.* Vol. 1. London: Colburn, 1828. 3 vols.

Thornton, Ralph. "I Was a Teenage Werewolf." *Screen Chills and Macabre Stories* no. 1, November 1957. Reprinted in *Werewolf: Horror Stories of the Man-Beast,* edited by Peter Haining. London: Severn House, 1987.

Tilton, Lois. "Lone Werewolf." In *When Will You Rage?,* edited by Stewart Wieck. Clarkston, Ga.: White Wolf, 1994.

Tofte, Arthur. "The Berserks." In *The Berserkers,* edited by Roger Elwood. New York: Pocket Books, 1974.

Tolkien, J. R. R. *The Lord of the Rings.* 3 vols. London: Allen and Unwin, 1954–1955. Reprinted many times since.

Tomson, Graham R. "A Ballad of the Were-wolf." *Macmillan's Magazine,* September 1890. Reprinted in *Demon Lovers,* edited by Lucy Berman. London: Tandem Books, 1970. Poem.

Toombs, Jane. *Moonrunner 1: Under the Shadow.* New York: Roc, 1992.

———. *Moonrunner 2: Gathering Darkness.* New York: Roc, 1993.

———. *The Volan Curse.* New York: Harlequin/Silhouette Shadows, 1994.

Torro, Pel [pseud. of R. L. Fanthorpe]. "Wolf Man's Vengeance." *Supernatural Stories,* February 1961.

Tremayne, Peter [pseud. of Peter Beresford Ellis]. "The Foxes of Fascoum." In *The Mammoth Book of Werewolves,* edited by Stephen Jones. New York: Carroll and Graf, 1994; London: Robinson Books, 1994.

Tubb, E. C. "Fresh Guy." *Science Fantasy,* no. 29, 1958. Reprinted in *The Vampire,* edited by Ornella Volta and Valeria Riva. London: Neville Spearman, 1963.

Turner, Ann Warren. "Moon Change." In *Shape Shifters,* edited by Jane Yolen. New York: Seabury Press, 1978.

Turtledove, Harry. "Not All Wolves." In *Werewolves,* edited by Jane Yolen and Martin H. Greenberg. New York: Harper and Row, 1988.

Tuttle, Lisa. *Panther in Argyll*. London: Mammoth, 1996.

Urban, Scott H. "Little Flea." In *When Will You Rage?*, edited by Stewart Wieck. Clarkston, Ga.: White Wolf, 1994.

van Belkom, Edo. "A Wolf in Shepherd's Clothing." In *When Will You Rage?*, edited by Stewart Wieck. Clarkston, Ga.: White Wolf, 1994.

———. "Lone Wolf." In *Dark Destiny*, edited by Edward E. Kramer. Clarkston, Ga.: White Wolf, 1995.

———. *Wyrm Wolf*. New York: HarperCollins, 1995.

Vance, Steve. *The Hyde Effect*. New York: Leisure Books, 1986.

———. *Shapes*. New York: Leisure Books, 1991.

Vande Velde, Vivian. *The Changeling Prince*. New York: Harper/Prism, 1998.

Van Loan, Geoffrey, Jr. "The Werewolf Lover." *Thriller*, February 1962.

Vaughn, Evelyn. *Waiting for the Wolf Moon*. New York: Harlequin/Silhouette Shadows, 1993.

Vercors [pseud. of Jean Bruller]. *Sylva*. New York: Putnam, 1962. Allegorical fantasy in which a vixen is transformed into a young woman.

Vinicoff, Eric. *The Weighter*. New York: Baen Books, 1992.

Visiak, E. H. [pseud. of Edward Harold Physick]. "In the Mangrove Hall." In *Masterpiece of Thrills*, edited by John Gawsworth. London: *Daily Express*, 1936.

Vitola, Denise. *Quantum Moon*. New York: Ace Books, 1996.

Volsunga Saga: The Story of the Volsungs and Niblungs. Translated from the Icelandic by Eirikir Magnusson and William Morris. London, 1888. Chapter 8 includes a famous lycanthropic episode in which two Norse warriors become spellbound shapechangers after donning wolf-shirts.

von Allmen, Stewart. *Conspicuous Consumption.* New York: Harper/Prism, 1995.

Vornholt, John. *Coyote Moon.* New York: Archway, 1998. Young adult novel.

Voxfire, Thomas. "Werewolf." *Gaslight,* August 1992. Poem

Vujic, Dragan. *Only Silver Can Kill a Werewolf.* Upublish .com, 1999.

———. *Death Hunt for the Last Werewolf.* Lincoln, Nebr.: iUniverse.com, 2000.

———. *Crimson Tears of a Werewolf.* Lincoln, Nebr.: iUniverse.com, 2001.

———. *Dark Shadow of the Werewolf.* San Jose, Calif.: Writers' Club Press, 2002.

———. *Final Harvest of the Werewolf.* San Jose, Calif.: Writers' Club Press, 2002.

———. *Tender Kiss of a Russian Werewolf.* San Jose, Calif.: Writers' Club Press, 2002.

Wagner, Karl Edward. "Reflections for the Winter of My Soul." In *Death Angel's Shadow.* New York: Warner, 1973.

———. "One Paris Night." In *Grails: Quests, Visitations and Other Occurrences,* edited by Richard Gilliam, Martin H. Greenberg and Edward E. Kramer. Atlanta, Ga.: Unnameable Press, 1992. Reprinted in *The Mammoth Book of Werewolves,* edited by Stephen Jones. New York: Carroll and Graf, 1994; London: Robinson Books, 1994.

Wakefield, H. Russell. "Death of a Poacher." In *A Ghostly Company.* London: J. Cape, 1935.

Wallace, A. B. *The Mark of the Werewolf.* Frederick, Md.: AmErica House, 2001.

Walpole, Hugh. "Tarnhelm: or, The Death of My Uncle Robert." *Liberty Magazine,* December 28, 1929. First book publication in *All Souls' Night*. London: Macmillan, 1933. Reprinted in *Horrors for Christmas,* edited by Richard Dalby. London: Michael O'Mara, 1992.

Walsh, Anne C. "Werewolf." *Midnight Zoo* 2, 4, 1992. Poem.

Wandrei, Howard. "In The Triangle." *Weird Tales,* January 1934.

———. "The Hand of the O'Mecca." *Weird Tales,* April 1935. Reprinted in *Sleep No More,* edited by August Derleth. New York: Farrar and Rinehart, 1944.

Watkins, Graham. "A Third World." In *When Will You Rage?,* edited by Stewart Wieck. Clarkston, Ga.: White Wolf, 1994.

Watson, Ian. "The Day of the Wolf." In *Changes,* edited by Michael Bishop and Ian Watson. New York: Ace Books, 1983.

Watt-Evans, Lawrence. "I WAS a Bestselling Werewolf." In *Bruce Coville's Shapeshifters,* edited by Bruce Coville. New York: Avon Camelot, 1999.

Weaver, Michael D. *Wolf-Dreams.* New York: Avon, 1987.

———. *Nightreaver.* New York: Avon, 1988.

———. *Bloodfang.* New York: Avon, 1989.

Weighell, Ron. "The Shadow of the Wolf." In *The White Road and Other Stories.* London: The Ghost Story Press, 1997. Features Sherlock Holmes and Dr. Watson.

Weinberg, Robert. *The Devil's Auction.* King of Prussia, Penn.: Owlswick Press, 1988. New York: Leisure Books, 1990.

———. "Wolf Watch." In *The Ultimate Werewolf,* edited by Byron Preiss. New York: Dell, 1991.

Welch, Christopher. "The Werewolf of Ulthar." *Glyph* no. 4, 2001.

Wellen, Edward. "Waswolf." *The Magazine of Fantasy and Science Fiction,* September 1987.

Wellman, Manly Wade. "The Horror Undying." *Weird Tales,* May 1936. Reprinted in *The Rivals of Dracula,* edited by Michel Parry. London: Corgi, 1977.

———. "The Werewolf Snarls." *Weird Tales,* March 1937. Reprinted (as "Among Those Present") in *Worse Things Waiting.* Chapel Hill, N.C.: Carcosa, 1973.

———. "The Hairy Ones Shall Dance." Originally serialized in *Weird Tales,* January–March 1938, and credited to Gans T. Field. Reprinted under the author's real name in *The Mammoth Book of Werewolves,* edited by Stephen Jones. New York: Carroll and Graf, 1994; London: Robinson Books, 1994.

———. "The Last Grave of Lill Warran." *Weird Tales,* May 1951. Reprinted in *Vamps,* edited by Martin H. Greenberg and Charles G. Waugh. New York: DAW Books, 1987.

———. *The Hanging Stones.* Garden City, N.Y.: Doubleday, 1982. Werewolves make a cameo appearance.

West, Wallace. "Loup-Garou." *Weird Tales,* October 1927.

Wheeler, Wendy. "Little Red." In *Snow White, Blood Red,* edited by Ellen Datlow and Terri Windling. New York: Morrow AvoNova, 1993.

Whishaw, Fred. "The Were-Wolf." *Temple Bar,* November 1902.

White, T. H. "The Point of Thirty Miles." In *The Maharajah and Other Stories.* New York: Putnam's Sons, 1981. Reprinted in *Werewolf: Horror Stories of the Man-Beast,* edited by Peter Haining. London: Severn House, 1987.

Whitten, Leslie H. *Moon of the Wolf.* Garden City, N.Y.: Doubleday, 1967. New York: Ace Books, 1968.

Whittington, Don. *Werewolf Tonight.* New York: Morrow, 1995. For preteens.

Whittington, Mary K. "Wolfskin." In *Werewolves,* edited by Jane Yolen and Martin H. Greenberg. New York: Harper and Row, 1988.

Wieck, Stewart, ed. *When Will You Rage?*. Clarkston, Ga.: White Wolf, 1994.

Williams, Harper. *See* Williams, Margery.

Williams, Margery (a.k.a. Harper Williams). *The Thing in the Woods*. London: Duckworth, 1913. New York: McBride, 1924. The British edition was credited to Margery Williams and the American edition to Harper Williams. This has tended to confuse bibliographers, but recent research has established that the two books have identical texts.

Williams, Sidney. *When Darkness Falls*. New York: Pinnacle, 1992.

Williamson, J. N. "The Last Link between Life and Death." In *Werewolves*, edited by Martin H. Greenberg. New York: DAW Books, 1995.

Williamson, Jack. "Wolves of Darkness." *Strange Tales of Mystery and Terror*, January 1932. Reprinted in *Magazine of Horror*, November 1967. *Beware the Beasts*, edited by Roger Elwood and Vic Ghidalia. New York: MacFadden-Bartell, 1970.

———. *Darker Than You Think*. *Unknown*, December 1940. Book versions: Reading, Penn.: Fantasy Press, 1948. London: Sphere Books, 1976. New York: Tom Doherty, 1999.

———. *Demon Moon*. New York: Tor, 1995.

Wilson, David Niall. "A Taste of Blood and Roses." In *Werewolves*, edited by Martin H. Greenberg. New York: DAW Books, 1995.

Wilson, Eric. *The St. Andrews Werewolf*. New York: HarperCollins, 1993.

Wilson, Gabriel. "Master of the Werewolves." *Terror Tales*, July/August 1939.

Wind, D. M. *The Others*. New York: Leisure Books, 1993.

Windsor, Patricia. *The Blooding*. New York: Scholastic, 1996. Young adult novel.

Winninger, Ray. "The Bye-Bye Club." In *When Will You Rage?*, edited by Stewart Wieck. Clarkston, Ga.: White Wolf, 1994.

Winters, Mike. *Full Moon*. New York: Berkley Books, 1989.

Wintle, W. James. "The Voice in the Night." In *Ghost Gleams*. London: Heath, Cranton, 1921.

Wolfe, Gene. *Soldier of the Mist*. New York: Tor, 1986.

———. "The Hero as Werewolf." In *Tomorrow Bites*, edited by Greg Cox and T. K. F. Weisskopf. New York: Baen Books, 1995.

Woods, Jack. *Wolffile*. New York: Pageant Books, 1988.

Wurts, Janny. *The Master of Whitestorm*. London: Grafton, 1992.

Wynne-Tyson, Jon. "Mistral." *The Twilight Zone Magazine*, July/August 1983. Reprinted in *Horrorstory*. Vol. 4, edited by Karl Edward Wagner. Lancaster, Penn.: Underwood-Miller, 1990.

Yarbro, Chelsea Quinn. *The Godforsaken*. New York: Warner, 1983.

Yolen, Jane. "Green Messiah." In *Werewolves*, edited by Jane Yolen and Martin H. Greenberg. New York: Harper and Row, 1988.

Yolen, Jane, ed. *Shape Shifters*. New York: Seabury Press, 1978.

Yolen, Jane, and Martin H. Greenberg, eds. *Werewolves*. New York: Harper and Row, 1988.

Youngson, Jeanne. "The Lycanthrope." In *Count Dracula and the Unicorn*. Chicago: Adams, 1978.

Zelazny, Roger. "The White Beast." *Whispers* no. 13/14, October 1979.

———. *A Dark Traveling*. New York: Walker, 1987. Young adult novel.

Index

Index

A RAY AND PAT BROWNE BOOK

Series Editors
Ray B. Browne and Pat Browne

Baseball and Country Music
Don Cusic

The Essential Guide to Werewolf Literature
Brian J. Frost